God's Good News!

The Twenty-third Psalm

Lord is my shepherd; I shall not want.
He maketh me to lie down in green pastures;
He leadeth me beside the still waters.
He restoreth my soul;
He leadeth me in the paths of righteousness
for His name's sake.
Yea, though I walk through the valley
of the shadow of death, I will fear no evil:
for Thou art with me;
Thy rod and Thy staff they comfort me.
Thou preparest a table before me
in the presence of mine enemies;
Thou anointest my head with oil; My cup runneth over,
Surely goodness and mercy shall
follow me all the days of my life:
And I will dwell in the house of the Lord forever.

God's Good News!

Life-changing Beliefs that
Everybody Should Know

by Ira M. Lane, Jr.

also the author of *The Gospel*
and *Truths for Daily Living*

CEF

Christian Education Forum, Publisher
Nashville, Tennessee

God's Good News!

Christian Education Forum, Publisher
Nashville, Tennessee

Library of Congress Catalogue Card Number: 2004095365
ISBN Number: 0-9662647-2-X
Printed in the United States of America

You may wish to contact:
Christian Education Forum, Publisher
930 Downey Drive
Nashville, Tennessee 37205

Phone: (615) 352-0267

Dedication

*I dedicate this book to **Jesus Christ**, our Lord and Savior; the Son of God and the second person of the Trinity for dying on the cross to pay the penalty for our sins and being resurrected to conquer death, the devil, and sin.*

Acknowledgments

I express appreciation to my wife, Janice; our daughter, Carol; our son, Randy; and our two grandchildren, Chase and Thomas Ira, for their sacrifice of my time and their patience during the past two years I have spent in the research and writing this book.

My special appreciation is due to the late Dr. David Cooper, Sr., President of Bible Research Society, for the materials in his publications over a 30-year period which challenged my thinking and encouraged me to do further research. I also thank Evangelist Billy Graham, *Moody Monthly* magazine, the Bible Study Fellowship organization, and *Israel My Glory* for their publications over the years.

I extend deepest appreciation to my pastor of 33 years, Dr. Ronald Carrier, to my youthful pastor Rev. N. O. Nabors, and my Sunday School teachers. I also thank Jack Bouchard, executive leader of the Nashville Chapter of Bible Study Fellowship, for six years of teaching. My sincere appreciation is due to Joseph S. (Joe) Johnson, retired editor of Broadman & Holman Press, who has been my encourager, prayer warrior, and friend, and who has edited my three books.

And my special appreciation goes to the Board of Trustees of Christian Education Forum. The members of the Board have been my enablers, advisors, prayer warriors, helpers, and friends.

Yours in Christ
Ira M. Lane

Preface

God's Good News . . . presents basic truths that people should believe and understand if they are to have a balanced conception of the Bible's teachings. It covers the fundamentals of the Christian faith in a general way. Hopefully, this content will give insight into vital doctrines that will assist the thoughtful reader in gaining a comprehensive view of the truths presented in God's written Word, the Scriptures.

Introduction

This book has been made possible through the guidance, prompting, and teaching of the Holy Spirit and is written for believers to grow in Christ—and with a prayer that non-believers will have Christ revealed to them and will accept Him into their lives.

The life of the Christian is a journey and begins the moment one is "born again." It moves ahead with it ups and downs until we finally leave this earth. This journey is meant to be a preparation for eternity in heaven. The journey has profound implications for both this life and the life hereafter. The journey for new believers is only beginning, and they need a road map that will point them in the right direction and give them helpful resources for the long trip ahead.

Learning to live the abundant life in Christ is truly a magnificent experience. Let's face the fact that all of us will live eternally. The serious question is:

Where will we live—in heaven with God or in torment separated from God?

It is your choice. We can choose heaven by a few simple choices:

Confess and turn from our sins.

Believe through faith that Jesus died on the cross to pay the penalty for our sins, and that He was resurrected on the third day to assure our own resurrection and conquer the devil, sin, and death.

When we do that, the Holy Spirit, the abiding presence of God, enters our lives. When we have faith in Jesus Christ and accept Him as our Savior, we are baptized by the Holy Spirit and become a member of God's Kingdom. God grants us righteousness for our faith as a result of our faith and Christ's death and resurrection.

It is my conviction that God called me to write this book to help make the believer's journey as smooth as possible. For sure, Satan does not want this book to be published. I have gone through intense spiritual warfare since I started this project. God has been with me all the way, and I feel strongly he is doing the book through me. I am merely an instrument, and any glory goes to God. I will receive no compensation from the book. The pilgrimage to write and print this book has required two years and 1,500 hours of research, writing, and proofing, plus $10,000 of cost donated by my wife and me for the first printing.

Chapters 1—7 help us to know who God is, His power, love, righteousness, and His characteristics. Chapters 8—9 give what we must do to be "born again" and receive God's salvation. Chapters 10—12 cover the ups and downs of living a Christian life and seeking to be like Christ. Chapters 13—14 review necessary Christian beliefs and how we can put on the armor of God to fortify ourselves against the devil and his angels and false teachers. Chapters 15—17 tell us that the life we live on earth defines where we will spend eternity, which is our choice to make. Will we receive rewards in heaven or experience eternal regrets in hell?

It is my prayer that non-Christians, who are seeking the truth, will avail themselves of this book and allow Christ to enter their lives. They will discover that . . .

Christ is . . . the way, the truth, and the life (John 14: 6).

Ira M. Lane, Jr.

(615) 352-0267

Foreword

Working with Ira M. Lane is a blessing. His previous books, *The Gospel* and *Truths for Daily Living*, have enriched the lives of several thousand persons. Because of these books, under the influence of the Holy Spirit, a number of non-Christians have "passed from death unto life" and become believers; innumerable Christians have rededicated themselves and are walking closer to Christ because of their impact. Some have even remarked to me that, next to the Holy Bible, his books have benefited them the most because all of his content is based on that Bible.

Brother Lane is a retired businessman and lay church leader. He lives and breathes the glorious Gospel of the Lord Jesus Christ. This book, *God's Good News*, will help believers know the Lord intimately and to practice courageous Christianity that is desperately called for in these perilous times. As we better understand God's truth, holiness, and righteousness, we will better grasp and live out His plans and purposes for our lives.

Through these anointed pages, the vision of God will overcome confusion, and the reader can experience His truth. In this book the reader is challenged to apply profound truths about the nature and character of God to daily living. Throughout, Brother Lane pleads with the reader to choose Christ and live for Him now and in eternity. He points out vividly that it is our choice and how we live here will determine where we will spend eternity, either in heaven or hell.

This book is a must read.

Joseph (Joe) S. Johnson, Jr.

Author-Editor
Retired Editor of Inspirational/Trade Books
Broadman & Holman Press
LifeWay Christian Resources

Table of Contents

Acknowledgments vi

Preface vii

Introduction vii

Foreword ix

Chapters

1. The Revelation of God 1
2. God's Moral Government 14
3. The God of Creation 31
4. The Nature of Man 41
5. Christ our Savior, Redeemer, and Mediator 53
6. Christ's Life and Ministry 104
7. The Holy Spirit 119
8. God's Salvation Plan 142
9. What Does It Mean to Be "Born Again"? 158
10. Living a Christian Life 169
11. Seeking to Become Like Christ 191
12. God's Plan for Abundant Life 213
13. Basic Beliefs to Know 225
14. Putting on the Armor of God 238
15. Where Will You Spend Eternity—Heaven or Hell? 261
16. Highway to Heaven 270
17. Satan, Sin, and Hell 278
18. Epilogue 288

Chapter 1

The Revelation of God

The God who creates, rules, and sustains the universe is the caring Father who loves you as if you were the only one to love! God wants the best for you. Imagine it. The awesome God of glory wants to have intimate fellowship with you, to wipe the tears from your eyes, and to fill your life with incredible happiness. This sovereign God, as revealed in Jesus Christ, is supreme. He has a plan and purpose for everything and has done nothing accidentally. He "according to His purpose . . . works all things after the counsel of His will" (Eph. 1:11b). God is a unity. "Hear, 0 Israel: The LORD our God is one LORD" (Deut. 6:4, KJV).

The prophet asked the rhetorical question: "Has not one God created us?" (Mal. 2:10, KJV). God endowed each of His angels, and man who followed, with the power of free choice. He never bullies anyone's will but uses moral persuasion, always stopping short of coercion or forcing one's will. God could have created us as robots or puppets, but He wanted us to have a loving, personal relationship out of our free will.

The Existence of God

Man's makeup is such that he is capable of recognizing the existence of God. Man's innate powers enable him to behold by faith the existence of the Almighty by the things in the world, and around the world, he observes. In this connection we do well to notice the telling statement of the apostle Paul:

> *Because that which may be known of God is manifest in them, for God hath shewed it unto them. For the invisible things of him from the creation of the world are clearly seen, being understood by the things that are made, even his eternal power and Godhead; so that they are without excuse* (Rom. 1:19-20, KJV).

Pay attention to the psalmist King David who sang:

> *[1] The heavens declare the glory of God; and the firmament sheweth his handywork.[2] Day unto day uttereth speech, and night unto night sheweth knowledge. [3] There I's no speech nor language, where their voice is not heard. [4] Their line is gone out through all the earth, and their words to the end of the world. In them hath he set a tabernacle for the sun, [5] Which is as a bridegroom coming out of his chamber, and rejoiceth as a strong man to run a race. [6] His going forth is from the end of the heaven, and his circuit unto the ends of it, and there is nothing hid from the heat thereof* (Ps. 19:1-6, KJV).

We think of God as an Architect and a Master Builder who has created the Earth and the heavens according to a definite, specific plan. God was the Master Chemist who compounded all the elements from which He built the universe, including Earth.

The Revelation of God

Since God is pure spirit, as we learn from the Bible, God's written Word, man was created in the image and likeness of his Maker. "God is a Spirit: and they that worship Him must worship in spirit and truth" (John 4:24). He was made in the image of God in that he possesses intelligence, will, and a moral nature. Because of man's moral makeup, he should realize his dependence on his Maker.

God loves man, His creature. He wants him to be happy and blessed throughout his life and wants him to be saved eternally. God does not will that any should perish—that is, to die without Christ and spend eternity in hell—but that all should come to repentance (see 2

Pet. 3:9). "For God so loved the world, that he gave his only begotten Son, that whosoever believeth in him should not perish, but have everlasting life" (John 3:16, KJV).

The prophet Isaiah assumed that every honest seeker of the truth who desires facts can gaze into the heavens above and at things upon the Earth and can recognize that the One who created the universe is the One who is controlling the nations—and is working to carry out His plan.

Having seen that belief in God is virtually universal, we now wish to comprehend, if possible, whether this conviction is simply a matter of coincidence or whether it is absolute necessity. The knowledge of God is innate and intuitive. Man's inner feeling led man to believe there is a Supreme Being when he observes the creations of God.

The Positive Proof of God's Existence

In His wisdom and goodness, God has left certain chasms unabridged, which man by faith alone must cross. He must live by faith and serve His Creator in the spirit of Abraham, the spiritual father of all the faithful. The moral quality of man's service and dividend God would be obliterated if a margin has not been left for the exercise of his faith. From the very nature of his constitution and his relation to his Maker, he recognizes that the Almighty has revealed His wisdom and mercy . . . by withholding overwhelming proof that would force or coerce the will to a firm belief in His existence and man's total dependence on Him.

The Names and Attributes of God

God declared to Moses, "I AM WHO I AM"; and He said, "Thus you shall say to the sons of Israel, 'I AM has sent me to you'" (Exo. 3:14). God in the Bible has made Himself known through what is called "special revelation" regarding His nature, His attributes, and His name. God has revealed Himself through the Person of His only begotten ("one and only") Son, the Lord Jesus Christ. As we learn of Christ, we also learn of God, for He is a perfect blending of God and man (see John 1:1-3, 14).

The Names of God

"Jehovah" or "Yahweh" is the name revealing that God is eternal.

He has no beginning and no end. He is not subject to time. He is self-existent. He is the uncreated Creator—was not created. He has no origin. He is independent of everything but Himself. He is sufficient unto Himself. He is unchanging and is complete.

"Elohim" is the name of God that presents Him as the Almighty God who is sovereign over all things. He created everything out of nothing to begin with. Elohim is also the God of the covenant, who makes promises to His people. He has provided the means for the sustenance and redemption of the human race. The Bible reveals that God is infinite. He has no bounds or limits. He is everywhere and not limited by time or space.

The Word LORD in Joshua 3:11 is the Hebrew title "Adonai," one of the important names of God in the Old Testament. Thus, the various names of God are vital elements of His self-revelation to humankind. Adonai is used as a divine title for the first time in Genesis 15:2 and 8, where Abram (later Abraham) petitioned God using the compound title LORD (Adonai) God (Yahweh).

The doctrine of the spirituality of God implies personality. He is a person possessing all the marks and attributes of personality. These statements can mean only one thing—that God is self-existing, One who is absolutely independent of all else, whereas all are dependent upon Him. The perfections of God mean His moral attributes (traits, qualities, characteristics):

God Knows Everything (Omniscience)

He knows the number of the stars, for He created every one of them (Ps. 47:4). He knows every sparrow that falls to the ground (Matt. 10:29). He knows every thought of every person (Acts 15:8). He understands from afar off (Ps. 139:2). He realizes our needs (Matt. 6:8). He even counts the hairs of our heads (Matt. 10:30). As one comedian put it, "If we're bald, He counts our barren hair follicles!" There is nothing we can do or think that will escape the Almighty's eyes. Nothing is too small for His attention.

He knows the past and the future. Knowledge baffling to mankind is thoroughly known to God. His wisdom is unlimited, for by it He created all things (Rom. 11:33). He has all the power necessary to accomplish the objectives toward which He is working. He works all things after the counsel of His will (Eph. 1:11). Nothing is impossible with Him (Gen. 18:14; Luke 1:37). With Him all things are possible

(Matt. 19:6). We used to sing an old Gospel song: "Only believe, only believe, all things are possible, only believe" (Paul Rader). Numerous are the biblical passages showing God's ability to perform what He—in His infinite grace, love, mercy, and righteousness—purposes to accomplish. He has all power to do what is consistent with His will and holiness.

God Is All-powerful (Omnipotence)

The Lord declared, "I AM God." He upholds all things by the word of His power (Heb. 1:3). He does according to what He pleases after the counsel of His will (Eph. 1:11). I repeat: Nothing is impossible to Him (Matt. 19:26). At times He withholds His power, such as in giving rain to provide for crops (Amos 4:6). For good and sufficient reasons God put us on Earth to develop our character and to prepare us for heaven. When we are going in the wrong direction He has to get our attention. God gives us the necessities of life, including food, water, and the air we breathe. We are to cooperate in food production, but crops will not grow without water. Man plants the seed and cultivates the plants. God gathers elements from earth, air, and moisture—and then compounds them in proper proportion, subjecting them to certain processes. After a given period of time, He gives us ripened crops.

All the efforts people put forth cannot produce a grain of wheat or an ear of corn—or any seed that can germinate and perpetuate the species or any fruits or vegetables, which are essential for man's sustenance.

Sometimes God may not follow a routine method of supplying the food for man and gives us a miracle. A prime example was the Lord's feeding a company of 5,000 men, plus women and children (the crowd might have numbered 20,000 or more!). Jesus took five loaves and two fish and fed the whole multitude! (Matt. 14:13-21). And there were twelve baskets of food left over. Maybe one each for the apostles? This principle can be applied to all our needs and work out situations with God and man cooperating.

God Is Everywhere (Omnipresence)

God penetrates the entire universe He created and controls. Paul stated on Mars Hill in Athens: "that they would seek God, if perhaps they might grope for Him and find Him, though He is, not far from each one of us; for in Him we live and move and exist, as even some of your own poets have said, 'For we also are His children"' (Acts 17:27-28).

He is over His creation, but He is not part of it. Eastern religions, especially Hinduism, mistakenly teach that God is all, and all is God (pantheism). The true written revelation of God, the Bible, adheres to the fact that God is everywhere but that He is imminent (near) and yet also transcendent.

The Perfections of God

By perfections we mean His "moral nature."

God's Moral Nature: Truth

Pontius Pilate asked Jesus, "What is truth?" Truth is an inherent attribute of the Almighty. It is that characteristic in virtue of which His being and knowledge always conform one to the other. There is perfect concord and agreement between the nature of God and that which He knows. Keep in mind that God is the essence of truth. To know Him is truth. His nature is the very embodiment of truth. Jesus, the God-man, asserted, "I am the way, the truth, and the life: no man cometh unto the Father, but by me" (John 14:6, KJV). He further stated, "He that hath seen me hath seen the Father" (see John 14:9, KJV).

Jesus referred to the Holy Spirit—who inspired the men of God to write the Scriptures—as "the Spirit of truth (see John 15:26). The Word of God, the Bible, is called "the truth of God" (Rom. 1:25). God gave His written Word—His infallibly inspired and inerrant Word—to us for our salvation and profit. Bear in mind that the Scriptures are absolutely true and accurate and that God will fulfill every promise He has made in His Word. Also, He will carry out every threat of punishment to those who reject His love and mercy.

God instructed Adam and Eve that, if they would obey Him and carry out His will, they would live forever in paradise. He warned them that if they broke His commandment not to eat of the tree of the knowledge of good and evil, they would die spiritually and be separated from Him—and begin to die physically. The Scriptures inform us that God carried out His promise. God expelled Adam and Eve from the Garden of Eden, and they had to toil for a living (see Gen. chapter 3).

God's Love

Jesus gave us the supreme gift of love—His life." Greater love has no one than this, that one lay down his life for his friends" (John 15:13). Through Christ's living sacrifice on the Cross, God offers us full forgiveness of sins, and through the life power unleashed at His resurrection, He affords us the ability to live an abundant life pleasing to Him.

Acts of kindness have a ripple effect. We are to be kind and to be tolerant, giving generous service. They go out and affect other people—and eventually they come back to you. Before you can assimilate joy, you must suffer sorrow. We create our surroundings by the thoughts we think. We are sent here to live life fully, to find joy in our creations, to experience both failure and success, to use our free will to expand and magnify our lives.

Love Is Not optional

We are to love one another. We are to be kind and to be understanding of others, giving generous service. To love others as myself, I have to really love myself. If I want forgiveness, I must forgive. Jesus wants us to recognize that every person is of value and worth because he is a person created in God's image. The world looks at value and measures it by two criteria—appearance and performance. Where does this leave many of the uneducated, poor, disabled, and aged? Jesus' love does not depend on what we do for Him. Our value is inborn; we are valuable simply because God made us valuable.

A man once confided that as he grew up, he loved his mother and father. When he became grown, he loved a young lady and married her. Along came a beautiful baby, and he loved her. Later at a church service he accepted Christ and loved Him. Loving his family did not cause him to love anybody else, but when he loved Jesus, he loved everybody.

The Holy Spirit makes it possible for us to follow Jesus' instructions when He commanded, "But I say to you, love your enemies and pray for those who persecute you" (Matt. 5:44). God's love is an exercise of His goodness toward sinners whereby, having identified Himself with their welfare, He has sent His Son to be their Savior, and now helps them know and enjoy Him in a covenant relationship.

Goodness

Goodness in God is that perfection, through Christ, that prompts Him to live as a helpless baby and then, growing to manhood, to lay down His life for man's redemption. The idea, from a human standpoint, is absolutely unthinkable. It is recognized that the omnipotent God must be at the helm of the universe every moment directing it and keeping it under control.

> *For by Him [Christ] all things were created, both in the heavens and on earth, visible and invisible, whether thrones or dominions or rulers or authorities—all things have been created through Him and for Him. He is before all things, and in Him all things hold together*" (Col. 1:16-17).

The Son of God thus limited Himself temporarily by coming into the human realm to suffer for our salvation. While He was incarnate, the other personalities of the Godhead could and did run the universe.

Loving God

A man once stated that he often wondered why Christians are commanded to love, since feelings and emotions are not the sort of qualities that can be produced on demand. I replied that emotions are part of love—but only a part. Love also involves the mind and the will. The person who loves does what is best for another person, but how can we ascertain what is best for God? We reveal our love for God by living in light of His revealed will, by putting His commands into practice.

The Apostle Matthew records that Jesus was once asked to name the most important commandment in Old Testament Law. Jesus answered by citing the command:

> *And He said to him, "You shall love the Lord your God with all your heart, and with all your soul, and with all your mind." This is the great and foremost commandment. The second is like it, "You shall love your neighbor as yourself." On these two commandments depend the whole Law and the Prophets* (Matt. 22:37-40).

In the Sermon on the Mount He explained:

> *You have heard that it was said, "You shall love your neighbor and hate your enemy." But I say to you, love your enemies and pray for those who persecute you* (Matt. 5:43-44).

Holiness

The dominant characteristic of the Almighty's nature is His holiness. "Ye shall be holy; for I Jehovah your God am holy" (Lev. 19:2, KJV). God's holiness is positively and aggressively set and fixed upon purity. His holiness will not countenance evil in the least.

> *Are You not from everlasting, 0 Lord, my God, my Holy One? We will not die. You, 0 Lord, have appointed them to judge; And You, 0 Rock, have established them to correct. Your eyes are too pure to approve evil, And You can not look on wickedness with favor. Why do You look with favor on those who deal treacherously? Why are You silent when the wicked swallow up those more righteous than they?* (Hab. 1:12-13).

If holiness were God's only characteristic, His wrath would be stirred, and He would always deal drastically with the sinner, but His love is a check upon His holiness. We praise God for the fact that He is what He is. God has dealt with sin since His highest angel rebelled against the Almighty and became Satan.

Before God created angels and man, He knew that the "anointed cherub," Lucifer, and man, Adam, would fall. Because God can see into the future, He gave angels and man the right of "free choice." He wanted angels and man to love Him out of their "free will" and not as robots or puppets. He foresaw that Lucifer would lead other angels to rebel against His authority. God also was aware that when He would create man (Gen. 1:26) the latter would likewise rebel against His will and would fall, bringing untold misery, sin, and suffering upon Adam's descendants. (Chapter 2, "God's Moral Government," will provide more insight into this matter.)

Mercy and Goodness

> *"But when the kindness of God our Savior and His love for mankind appeared He saved us, not on the basis of deeds which we have done in righteousness, but according to His mercy, by the*

> *washing of regeneration and renewing by the Holy Spirit*" (Titus 3:4-5).
>
> "*But God demonstrates His own love toward us, in that while we were yet sinners, Christ died for us*" (Rom. 5:8).
>
> "*For God so loved the world, that He gave His only begotten Son, that whoever believes in Him shall not perish, but have eternal life*" (John 3:16).

Through His mercy and goodness, God has granted us opportunity to re-establish fellowship with Him.

Justice and Righteousness

God loved the world (every individual in it) that He gave His only begotten, one-and-only Son to die that we might have His righteousness. God provided the mechanism for righteousness, but man must reach out and receive it by confession/belief/faith in Jesus' death and resurrection. When we accept Christ, God's Holy Spirit not only has convicted and converted us, but He indwells us.

God permits various experiences to enter individuals' lives, as well as nations, in order to prove and test them. In doing so He punishes those who reject Him and purges sin from the lives of those who are obedient to Him.

God Is Immutable—He Does Not Change

The Spirituality of God

By the term "spirituality" I mean to connote the idea that God is a Spirit. That this is true is clear from such statements as Isaiah 31:3: "Now the Egyptians are men and not God, And their horses are flesh and not spirit; So the Lord will stretch out His hand, And he who helps will stumble And he who is helped will fall, And all of them will come to an end together." In this statement the Egyptians, who were men, are contrasted with God; in the parallel clause, horses, that were flesh, are contrasted with spirit. In this parallel we have an affirmation that God is pure Spirit without physical, bodily parts.

This idea is affirmed in John 4:23-24, where the Lord Jesus declared: "But an hour is coming, and now is, when the true worshipers will worship the Father in spirit and truth; for such people the Father seeks to be His worshipers. God is spirit, and those who worship Him must worship in spirit and truth." Again the spiritual character of God is emphasized in Romans 1:18-20:

For the wrath of God is revealed from heaven against all ungodliness and unrighteousness of men who suppress the truth in unrighteousness, because that which is known about God is evident within them; for God made it evident to them. For since the creation of the world His invisible attributes, His eternal power and divine nature, have been clearly seen, being understood through what has been made, so that they are without excuse.

Here the Apostle Paul spoke of the invisible things of God, even "His eternal power and divine nature," that are manifested by those things He has created. Thus, the material world constitutes a screen, as it were, behind which the spirituality of God is veiled. Once again, the Apostle in 1 Timothy 1:17 spoke of God as being "eternal, immortal, invisible" (KJV). These adjectives connote the spirituality of the Eternal One. In the Colossian letter the Apostle Paul spoke of Christ who is the image of the "invisible God" (1:15, KJV). From these and many other passages, we recognize that God is a Spirit.

Being a Spirit, God has life within Himself. As Jeremiah the prophet denounced idols and presented Jehovah, the God of Israel, as the one and only Supreme Being, he declared: "But the Lord is the true God; He is the living God and the everlasting King. At His wrath the earth quakes, And the nations cannot endure His indignation."

In writing to the Thessalonian brethren, Paul, speaking of their conversion, stated that they had turned from idols to serve the "true and living God." In referring to God the Father, Jesus taught: "For just as the Father has life in Himself, even so He gave to the Son also to have life in Himself' (John 5:26). These and numerous other passages either state or imply that the Eternal God is the source of all life.

The doctrine of the spirituality of God implies *personality*. The Lord appeared to Moses in the burning bush, giving him a commission to go and deliver the Hebrews from Egyptian bondage. Israel's great leader asked the Almighty who he should say sent him when he would be asked about his authority. God commanded him to reply: "I AM THAT I AM [Yahweh or Jehovah] ... hath sent me unto you." That name of God means "He is and was and ever shall be"—the Eternal God who has neither beginning nor ending. He always was and ever shall be!

God Is Triune

The terms "triune," "triunity," and "trinity" do not appear in the Bible, but the concept of the triunity of God is found there. The basis of that principle is threefold. First, the Bible calls three persons God. Second, the Bible presents those three persons as separate, or distinct, from one another. Third, the Bible declares that there is only one God. The human mind cannot fathom this truth. Many accuse Christians of being polytheistic—that is, believing in multiple gods, which is not the case.

It is awesome to learn that our magnificent and merciful God has revealed to mankind that He exists in three distinct persons.

God the Father

The Creator God is one in essence but at the same time is three different persons. It is exciting to realize that before time was, God existed in perfect fellowship and blessed communion within the Godhead. All three are equal in power, majesty, glory, and sovereignty. Each is equal within divine attributes. Although we may not understand the Holy Trinity, we must accept it as it is, God in three persons.

The Bible shows us that God the Father was involved in creation, designed the plan for our salvation, and is Ruler of all things. He is the Author of the plan of redemption, free choice, and election. He is the Founder of the master plan that involves each and every one of us.

God the Son

Jesus the Christ submitted to the incarnation by becoming a man so He could secure our redemption by bearing our sins at His crucifixion and assured us of being resurrected by His resurrection and defeating Satan, sin, and death.

God the Holy Spirit

The Holy Spirit convicts us of sin, calls us to redemption, and guides, leads, and teaches us about Christ and the avenue of holy living. We observe the three divine personalities in John 16:1-15. Jesus called the Holy Spirit "the Comforter" (*parakletos*, one who goes alongside to guide and counsel) in verse 7 and "the Spirit of truth" in verse 13. Jesus taught His disciples throughout this passage. The three divine personalities of the Trinity appear in 2 Corinthians 13:14: "The grace of the

Lord Jesus Christ, and the love of God, and the fellowship of the Holy Spirit, be with you all."

Chapter 2

God's Moral Government

God's government of the universe is of a moral character. God Almighty is free in every particular, being bound only by His own holy and divine nature. He is the very embodiment of righteousness, truth, justice, and love.

Angels—Freedom of Choice

God created the celestial beings with freedom of choice. They could worship and serve God or rebel against and reject Him. They were allowed to exercise their liberty in being submissive to Him or in rising in rebellion against Him. He created the cherubim, seraphim, angels, and man, giving them the power of freedom of choice. Being thus constituted, God Almighty deals with them, respecting the exercise of their wills. With our finite minds, we will never be able to understand why He allowed us to have so much volition-in His own wisdom He simply did.

To pass over the threshold of His creatures' individuality would destroy their free agency. Though man has sinned and plunged himself into the deep abyss of wickedness, God still respects man's freedom of choice—but uses all moral persuasion, short of forcing man's will, to lead mankind to repentance and faith. God's moral government, therefore, requires that He deal with His creatures on a moral and spiritual basis.

The Angels' Rebellion

One third of these creatures chose to pit their wills against Him.

Under the leadership of Lucifer, later called Satan, they revolted and fell from their high estate. They are usually referred to as devils or demons. They are spoken of as spiritual beings (Matt. 8:16; 10:1; 12:43–45) at enmity with God, and as having a certain power over man (Jas. 2:19; Rev. 16:14). They recognize our Lord as the Son of God (Matt. 8:20; Luke 4:41). They belong to the number of those angels that "kept not their first estate," "unclean spirits," "fallen angels," the angels of the devil (Matt. 25:41; Rev. 12:7–9). They are the "principalities and powers" against which we must "wrestle" (Eph. 6:12, KJV). Thankfully, the other two-thirds of these celestial beings were satisfied to sit in with God's program and advance His plans and purposes.

Man's Free Moral Agency

God also made man a free-moral agent. Being endowed with the power of choice, he has the ability to accept by faith the will of God and to bask in the sunlight of His love. On the contrary, he can set his own will in opposition to that of His Maker, as the majority of the human family seems to have done-and continues to do so.

God is holy and cannot put up with sin in any form. Yet, as pointed out, He is also a God of love.

> *The one who does not love does not know God, for God is love. By this the love of God was manifested in us, that God has sent His only begotten Son into the world so that we might live through Him. In this is love, not that we loved God, but that He loved us and sent His Son to be the propitiation for our sins* (1 John 4:8-10).

What His holiness demands, His love provides. God demanded, by virtue of His righteousness, a penalty for man's sins. Because of His love, He gave His own Son as a sacrifice to pay the penalty on behalf of man. The Word of God plainly teaches the freedom of man. For instance, focus on John 3:16-17: "For God so loved the world, that He gave His only begotten Son, that whoever believes in Him shall not perish, but have eternal life. For God did not send the Son into the world to judge the world, but that the world might be saved through Him."

God gave His only begotten Son in order that the one *believing* in

Him might have everlasting life. God had only one purpose in sending His Son into this sin-cursed world—that every person might have life. "The Lord is not slow about His promise, as some count slowness, but is patient toward you, not wishing for any to perish but for all to come to repentance" (2 Pet. 3:9). It is not the will of God that even one soul should perish (die spiritually and spend eternity in hell), but that all might come to the knowledge of His truth. Jesus, of course, is the embodiment of truth (John 14:6). These facts demonstrate plainly that man is free to make his own decisions—even when his choices involve his eternal destiny.

This freedom of choice is seen in John 5:24: "Truly, truly, I say to you, he who hears My word, and believes Him who sent Me, has eternal life, and does not come into judgment, but has passed out of death into life." So, the person who wills to hear, accepts the message, and believes God for his salvation . . . has eternal life right now, will not be condemned for his sins, and has passed from death into life. Also notice this truth in John 5:40: "and you are unwilling to come to Me so that you may have life."

It is clear that the people to whom Jesus spoke could have come to Him if they had wished, and with their coming to Him could have had eternal life. But He would not force them to accept Him, although He wanted them to do so. Billy Graham has often expressed the truth that Jesus is a "gentleman" and has never forced Himself on anyone—and that He knocks on the door but never kicks it down and pushes His way in.

The matter was left to them, and it is left to you!

The genuine Christians, real believers in Christ, are those who accept God's plan of redemption and who yield their lives to Him—and develop certain character traits that will fit and prepare them for positions of honor, glory, trust, and power to enjoy the blessedness of eternity. They are empowered by the Holy Spirit who dwells within their lives. "But grow in the grace and knowledge of our Lord and Savior Jesus Christ. To Him be the glory, both now and to the day of eternity. Amen" (2 Pet. 3:18). This will depend on spiritual growth and development to which we attain in this life. God wants believers in Christ to grow on earth, and we shall also continually grow and increase in capacity throughout eternity.

What is the meaning of the foreknowledge of God? Simply that God has set up His government rules, regulations, and policies on how to achieve His master plan. God's knowledge and power enable Him to look into the future as to the type of life each of us will live. He knows facts and people before the event occurs or the person is born.

God's Sovereignty

Webster's New International Dictionary defines the adjective "sovereign" as: "Supreme or highest in power, superior in position to all others, unlimited by any other; possessing or entitled to original and independent authority or jurisdiction. "You are My witnesses," declares the Lord, "And My servant whom I have chosen, So that you may know and believe Me And understand that I am He. Before Me there was no God formed, And there will be none after Me." . . . "Thus says the Lord, the King of Israel and his Redeemer, the Lord of hosts: 'I am the first and I am the last, And there is no God besides Me'" (Isa. 44:6, 10).

In God's providence, His throne stands forever. He is overruling all things. He observes the actions of men and fathoms their purpose, even their minutest, inmost thoughts.

God's Discipline

He causes the righteous to pass through experiences that will refine them as silver and gold are purified in the furnace, but the unsaved are insufferably worse off, for they will undergo eternal punishment. God is indeed the absolute Sovereign of the universe.

To the thinking observer who studies the movements of the heavenly bodies in connection with the Earth, it becomes unquestionable that the Supreme Being has everything under His control. Each of the material bodies, as it moves in outer space, is being directed by our Omnipotent God. It is seen that each lends its part to the purpose and movement of the entire universe. Astronomers assert that various nebulae are moving in certain directions. That would seem to indicate an ultimate objective. Each of these bodies—and they are innumerable—contributes its part to the whole in carrying out God's purpose. All of this demonstrates that God is sovereign over the material universe. "The heavens are telling of the glory of God; And their expanse is declaring the work of His hands" (Ps. 19:1).

An analysis of any physical phenomenon shows that each separate element displays certain characteristics. Each acts and reacts in a specific way when coming into contact with other elements. Who gave the elements their traits? There is only one satisfactory answer. "Who has measured the waters in the hollow of His hand, And marked off the heavens by the span, And calculated the dust of the earth by the measure, And weighed the mountains in a balance And the hills in a pair of scales?" (Isa. 40:12)

God is the Chemist who first made all of the elements, who blended them into specific measures, and who lent them their inborn qualities. In performing all of that, He was not pushed by any other force or power. He alone is sovereign. Everything He has done is out of His desire and good pleasure.

Throughout eternity in the past, during time in the present, and throughout the ages in the eternity of the future, our sovereign God has directed and is directing everything that contributes to His own glory and revelation and to the benefit of His creatures.

Angels Again

God's meaningful relationships with the angels bespeak His sovereignty over them. God created *the angels, showing that He is their sovereign Ruler.* In eternity past, God decided to have a kingdom He would rule as King. And He made two major kinds of personal subjects for that kingdom. First, He created an immense company of angels to serve Him, mainly in the heavenly sphere of His universal Kingdom. The Apostle John beheld hundreds of millions of angels around the throne of God in Heaven. "Then I looked, and I heard the voice of many angels around the throne and the living creatures and the elders; and the number of them was myriads of myriads, and thousands of thousands" (Rev. 5:11). The Prophet Daniel also viewed a similar spectacle.

> *I kept looking until thrones were set up, And the Ancient of Days took His seat; His vesture was like white snow And the hair of His head like pure wool. His throne was ablaze with flames, Its wheels were a burning fire. A river of fire was flowing And coming out from before Him; Thousands upon thousands were attending Him, And myriads upon myriads were standing before Him; The court sat, And the books were opened* (Dan. 7:9-10).

Since the angels were created by God, certainly they owe their being to Him. In Psalm 148:2-5, all of His angels are commanded to praise Him: "Praise Him, all His angels; Praise Him, all His hosts! Praise Him, sun and moon; Praise Him, all stars of light! Praise Him, highest heavens, And the waters that are above the heavens! Let them praise the name of the Lord, For He commanded and they were created." The Apostle Paul declared that angels were created (Colossians 1:16).

God Has Authority Over the Angels, Thus Signifying His Sovereignty

God created angels with varying degrees of intelligence and power. He established them in ranks on the basis of these variations; He then organized them similarly to military forces, so God is referred to as "LORD of hosts" in the Old Testament (Ps. 24:10). The Hebrew word translated "hosts" means "armies." Thus, God is "LORD of armies."

The angels comprise a powerful, heavenly army that is divided into legions (Matt. 26:53), is under the command of other angels; and wages angelic warfare (Rev. 12:7). So, God's title "LORD of armies" connotes that He is the Commander-in-Chief of the angelic armies of Heaven.

Further, Angels Obey God's Commands, Revealing that God Is Sovereign over Them

King David sang: "Bless the Lord, you His angels, Mighty in strength, who perform His word, Obeying the voice of His word! Bless the Lord, all you His hosts, You who serve Him, doing His will" (Ps. 103:20-21).

Angels Worship and Adore God, Signifying that He is Sovereign over Them

The Apostle John viewed the four beasts, 24 elders, and all the holy angels worship God in heaven (Rev. 4:8-11; 5:13-14; 7:11-12). God's angels are charged to praise Him. "Praise Him, all His angels; Praise Him, all His hosts!" (Ps. 148:2). The multitude of angels who appeared to the shepherds at Bethlehem praised God and attributed glory to Him. "And suddenly there appeared with the angel a multitude of the heavenly host praising God and saying, 'Glory to God in the highest, And on earth peace among men with whom He is pleased'" (Luke 2:13-14).

God Has Authority to Judge the Fallen, Evil Angels, Indicating that He Is Sovereign over Them

God has already carried out some forms of judgment on these angels, I. e., the wise "anointed cherub that covereth" (Ezek. 28:14, KJV) was thrown from God's heaven . . . to the first heaven above the Earth. Why? Because that exalted angel became eaten up with pride and became God's awful enemy, Satan (Ezek. 28:11-17; Eph. 2:2; 1 Tim. 3:6). God cast other angels from His heaven when they followed Satan in their defiance. These angels are aligned with Satan and under his command (Eph. 2:2; 6:12; Rev. 12:7-9). Because some fallen angels carried out another serious sin later, God imprisoned them in *tartaras* (Greek for the abyss or bottomless pit) until the great day of judgment (2 Pet. 2:4; Jude 6-7).

God will carry out other forms of judgment in the future. In the middle of the seven-year tribulation, Satan and his fallen, free angels will be cast from the first heaven to the Earth, and will be confined here for three-and-one-half years (Rev. 12:7-17). Satan and these angels will be removed from the Earth and imprisoned in the bottomless pit in conjunction with Christ's second coming after the tribulation (Isa. 24:21-23; Rev. 20:1-3). They will remain there throughout the thousand-year millennial reign of Christ and His saints on Earth (Rev. 20:2-6).

Lucifer—the Anointed Cherub

"You were the anointed cherub who covers, And I placed you there. You were on the holy mountain of God; You walked in the midst of the stones of fire" (Ezek. 28:14). The reference to his being "on the holy mountain of God" is probably a parallel of Isaiah 14:12-14: "How you have fallen from heaven, 0 star of the morning, son of the dawn! You have been cut down to the earth, You who have weakened the nations! But you said in your heart, 'I will ascend to heaven; I will raise my throne above the stars of God, And I will sit on the mount of assembly In the recesses of the north.'I will ascend above the heights of the clouds; I will make myself like the Most High.'"

Ezekiel beheld coming out of the north (i. e., the area of the polar star) "a great cloud, with a fire unfolding itself, and a brightness round about it, and out of the midst thereof as it were glowing metal, out of the midst of the fire" (Ezek. 1:4, KJV). Out of this fire there emerged four living creatures, each having four faces and four wings. Beside each of them were wheels within a wheel. As the anointed cherub (angelic being) he was in the mount of God amid stones of fire (Ezek. 28:16).

"The anointed cherub who covers" no doubt refers to Lucifer's position of being the chief of the other cherubs in the vision. Above the firmament over the heads and wings of the cherubim was a glorious throne. Seated on the throne was the Almighty, the supreme ruler and potentate of the universe. From Ezekiel chapters 1 and 28, we gather that the covering cherub was the commander-in-chief of a mighty army. The cherubim (Ezek. 1) are the celestial beings who support the firmament on which the throne of God rests. But Lucifer was supreme over all the other cherubim, and there is ample reason to believe, over all the hosts of heaven. It appears there was no creature beneath Deity who was his equal.

As chief he was nearest the throne of God and was on the holy mountain of God. Those verses from Ezekiel refer to Satan's original position of authority and power before the creation of the universe.

First Man and Woman

After God created an immense host of angels to serve Him, mainly in the realm of His universal Kingdom, He created the Earth, and then made man, the second type of personal subject. God gave man dominion over all the Earth (Gen. 1:26-29). That act of God discloses the original form of government He ordained for the Earth—a theocracy. In a theocracy, God's rule is carried out by a representative. God appointed the first man, Adam, to be his representative.

After God finished the creation of His kingdom, He graded everything as "very good" (Gen. 1:31). No aspect of His Kingdom had yet sided against Him. Later Lucifer, puffed with pride, began a revolt to make himself like God, the Most High God Isa. 14:12-14). Satan wanted to supplant God on the throne and to become the sovereign of the universe, the ruler and king in lieu of God Almighty. Since Satan was only a creature and not the Creator, he lacked the power to create angels and humans. The maximum he could wish for was to convince God's angels and humans to assist him in a revolt against God.

Satan was able to convince a sizable number of angels to join him. So, the Bible refers to "the devil and his angels" (Matt. 24:41; Rev. 12:7-9). He also succeeded into luring Adam and Eve, the first humans, to follow suit (Gen. 3:1-6). Thus, the theocracy was lost from the Earth. Satan was able to usurp the rule of the world system away from God. He and his forces have dominated the world system ever since. Satan indicated that he has authority to give the rule of the world to whomever he wishes because it had been handed over to him (Luke 4:5-6). Jesus called Satan the ruler of this world (John 14:30).

Paul referred to him as "the god of this age" (2 Cor. 4:4). At the beginning of the great tribulation, Satan's right of access to God as accuser will be abrogated (Rev. 12:7-12). At Christ's return in glory, Satan will be bound for 1,000 years (Rev. 20:1). Then he will be "loosed for a little season," (Rev. 20:3, 7, 8, KJV); he will become the leader of a final effort to overthrow God's kingdom. He will be utterly defeated and then be cast into the lake of fire, *gehenna*, his ultimate doom.

Areas of God's Sovereignty

God's Word discloses several areas that God is sovereign over.

The Universe

The fact that God created the universe, of course, indicates that He is sovereign over it. The Bible over and over again declares that Jehovah is the source of the entire universe. Moses said, "For in six days the LORD made heaven and earth, the sea, and all that in them is" (Ex. 20:1, KJV; cf. Rev. 10:6). In His conversation with Job, Jehovah stressed His distinctive wisdom and omnipotence, through which He created the heavens and Earth with their features, life forms, and the mandates by which they run. In Isaiah 40, God emphasizes that He and He only has the know-how and strength to create the Earth with exact measurements, the vast expanse of the heavens with a specific number of heavenly bodies, and to call all those bodies by name (vv. 12-14, 22, 26). According to astronomers, there is no end to the universe, and new galaxies with innumerable constellations are coming into existence every moment. The sovereign God keeps on creating!

God stated that no one can be compared to or equal with Him, "the everlasting God, the LORD. The Creator" (Isa. 40:28; 42:5; 12,

18; Jer. 10:12). God announces, "I am a great King" (Mal. 1:14) and points out the sphere of His reign: "Thus says the Lord, 'Heaven is My throne and the earth is My footstool. Where then is a house you could build for Me? And where is a place that I may rest?'" (Isa. 66:1). God is King of all and rules over all, and all creation is subject to Him. He has that rule because He has created everything—everything but evil.

David sang, "The Lord has established His throne in the heavens, And His sovereignty rules over all" (Ps.103:19). King Nebuchadnezzar of Babylon honored God: "Now I, Nebuchadnezzar, praise, exalt and honor the King of heaven, for all His works are true and His ways just, and He is able to humble those who walk in pride" (Dan. 4:37). Psalm 47:2 exults, "For the Lord Most High is to be feared, A great King over all the earth."

According to the 24 elders in heaven, God "created all things, and because of Your will they existed, and were created" (Rev. 4:11). The Apostle Paul realized that God, as its Creator, is sovereign over the universe. "The God who made the world and all things in it, since He is Lord of heaven and earth, does not dwell in temples made with hands" (Acts 17:24).

Psalm 93 revels, "The Lord reigneth," affirming that God is sovereign. Verse 2 goes on to declare: "Thy throne is established of old; thou art from everlasting" (KJV). God has always existed. No one need prove His existence. He is eternal, everlasting. A mystery yes, but it is true. He is eternal, but His throne, or sovereign rule, was not established until creation. In eternity past God determined to have a kingdom to rule over. He created the universe and all in it to be His Kingdom. David further declared that "the Lord abides forever; He has established His throne for judgment, And He will judge the world in righteousness; He will execute judgment for the peoples with equity" (Ps. 9:7-8).

God Himself announced, "Once more in a little while, I am going to shake the heavens and the earth, the sea also and the dry land . . . .Speak to Zerubbabel governor of Judah, saying, 'I am going to shake the heavens and the earth'" (Hag. 2:6, 21). God will cause disturbances in the heavens and upheavals on the Earth during the seven-year tribulation and Christ's second coming (Rev. 6—19; Matt. 24:29). He will destroy the present heavens and Earth after the millennium (2 Pet. 3:10-12; Rev. 20:11; 21:1).

Christ Has Supremacy

In Colossians 1, the Apostle Paul affirmed that Jesus Christ, the Son of God, is the Person of the triune Godhead who not only created the universe but also sustains it—keeps it together and maintains its operation.

> *He is the image of the invisible God, the firstborn of all creation. For by Him all things were created, both in the heavens and on earth, visible and invisible, whether thrones or dominions or rulers or authorities—all things have been created through Him and for Him. He is before all things, and in Him all things hold together* (vv. 15-17).

To sustain the universe, Christ must have rulership and supremacy over all of creation. Paul's identification of Christ as "the firstborn of all creation" (v. 15) underlines that He has the supremacy. David wrote that God is sovereign over the universe, He has created and owns the universe:

> *Yours, 0 Lord, is the greatness and the power and the glory and the victory and the majesty, indeed everything that is in the heavens and the earth; Yours is the dominion, 0 Lord, and You exalt Yourself as head over all. Both riches and honor came from You, and You rule over all, and in Your hand is power and might; and it lies in Your hand to make great and to strengthen everyone* (1 Chr. 29:11-12).

Two Spiritual Kingdoms

It is apparent to students of God's Word that there are two spiritual kingdoms in the universe—God's kingdom and Satan's. God was already the Ruler of the universe, but Satan tried to overthrow Him and His position by waging war against God and His Kingdom. Satan is so pitifully weak in comparison to the KING OF KINGS and LORD OF LORDS. He should have known better but did not, and that war has continued throughout history.

Satan's purpose for history is to make himself the sovereign ruler of the universe, but that will never happen. God's ultimate purpose for history is to glorify Himself by revealing that He only is the universe's sovereign ruler. To fulfill that purpose, God will crush Satan by ridding the world of him and his rule, thus restoring His theocracy to the Earth. In God's economy, the millennium is necessary for Him to fulfill His purpose for history.

Then, for God to restore His rule, He must have a human representative, an "Adam," who will implement His reign over all the Earth. That "Adam" is "the last Adam" (1 Cor. 15: 45). The theocracy was lost from the Earth because the first Adam rebelled against God. Christ will return to the Earth in His second coming as the last Adam, reinstating the theocracy and carrying out God's rule over the Earth. Jesus' incarnation was absolutely essential for this to eventuate.

How, then, will God crush Satan, ridding the Earth of him and his temporary rule? He will employ both the tribulation and the second coming. Throughout the tribulation, God will devastate Satan's kingdom by turning loose three series of judgments on him and his earthly domain. The last series will climax with the second coming, the end of Satan's rule, and the restoration of the theocracy. The last series will be unfurled with the sounding of the seventh trumpet, and mighty voices in heaven will proclaim, "The kingdom of the world has become the kingdom of our Lord and of His Christ; and He will reign forever and ever" (Rev. 11:15). He will reign for a thousand years on this Earth and then throughout eternity.

After the Tribulation, Christ will descend from heaven as God's warrior to finish crushing Satan and his domain (Rev. 19:11). He will rid the Earth of the Antichrist, the false prophet, and all the political rulers and armed forces of Satan's kingdom.

> *And I saw the beast and the kings of the earth and their armies assembled to make war against Him who sat on the horse and against His army. And the beast was seized, and with him the false prophet who performed the signs in his presence, by which he deceived those who had received the mark of the beast and those who worshiped his image; these two were thrown alive into the lake of fire which burns with brimstone. And the rest were killed with the sword which came from the mouth of Him who sat on the horse, and all the birds were filled with their flesh* (Rev. 19:19-21).

He will further dispose of all unsaved survivors of the tribulation

(Matt. 13:40-42, 47-50; 24:37-41), Satan (Rev. 20:1-3), and all evil angels (Isa. 24:21-23). Then Christ will restore the theocracy to Earth. As the last Adam, He will conduct God's rule over this earthly province of God's universal Kingdom for the last thousand years of its history (Rev. 20:4-7). "And the Lord will be king over all the earth; in that day the Lord will be the only one, and His name the only one" (Zech. 14:9). Hallelujah, which means "Praise the Lord God Jehovah!"

Recap: The Origin of Evil

Though Satan was deposed from his high position—which he occupied before his rebellion—he has not yet been divested of his power. The teaching of the Scriptures causes us to believe that he still has tremendous sway in the Earth, though his influence is not equal to what he had before his rebellion.

The Powers of Evil: Liberties and Limitations

Satan by no means enjoys the liberty he possessed before his "coup d'etat. " Yet, he does have a certain freedom of action, as seen from Job chapters 1 and 2. After going all over the Earth to size up the situation, he appeared before God. However, from these two chapters, we ascertain that he is limited in his activity, particularly toward the children of God. Before he could touch Job, he had to receive God's permission! When this permission was granted, he worked his hardest to purloin Job's possessions. He used the elements to wipe out the patriarch's property. Then, he once again came into God's presence, that time to gain permission for touching Job's body. He then put Job flat on his back, but he was not allowed to snuff out Job. Nail this down: he could go only so far as God would let him!

We notice this same freedom and limitation in the Gospels (Matthew, Mark, Luke, and John). In Luke 22:3-34 Jesus told Simon Peter that Satan had appeared before God, requesting permission to sift him (Peter) as wheat. Jesus was onto Satan's behind-the-scenes activity and thus constantly prayed to the Father that the Apostles' faith would remain strong. In Peter's case, it didn't, for he denied his Lord three times; later, repentant Peter stood up powerfully.

In New Testament times, Satan still had liberty to travel the Earth and also to stand before the Almighty—and he still avails himself of that liberty today (Rev. 12:7-12). The same limitations and liberties are seen in 1 Corinthians 10:13: "No temptation has overtaken you but such as is common to man; and God is faithful, who will not allow you to be tempted beyond what you are able, but with the temptation will provide the way of escape also, so that you will be able to endure it." It is clear that Paul had Satan and his wiles in mind. In particular situations God gives Satan permission to tempt or try His children, but He always limits the devil's activity. God never allows him to put an overpowering temptation on a Christian. Also, when the Lord allows a demon to tempt one of His children, He always affords a window of escape. As H.R. Palmer wrote:

Yield not to temptation, for yielding is sin
Each victory will help you
Some other to win.
Fight manfully onward, dark passions subdue.
Look ever to Jesus,
He'll carry you through.

An account of Jesus' visit to Gadara, near the Sea of Galilee, is found in Matthew 8:28-34 (similar accounts in Mark 2:3-12 and Luke 5:18-26). Our Lord encountered two men possessed by demons. It seems demons always recognize Jesus' identity. From within the men, the demons hollered, "What have we to do with thee, thou Son of God? Art thou come hither to torment us before the time?" (v. 29, KJV, meaning the time for their final judgment and being cast into the lake of fire). The demons then begged Jesus to cast them out into a herd of hogs feeding nearby. Our Lord granted their request. Yes, those demons acknowledged Jesus as the Son of God.

Throughout their existence they have shaken and trembled in His presence. James in his Epistle noted, "You believe that God is one. You do well; the demons also believe, and shudder" ["tremble," KJV] (James 2:19). Demons are well aware that they are placed under limitations and that their ultimate doom is a place of eternal torment. Yes, and they had to get permission from Him before they would even dare to enter the swine. Praise God! The powers of evil under Satan's leadership are given certain liberties—but are confined within particular boundaries. They are restricted particularly in their approach and activity toward the saints of God. If you are born again, you are one of those saints, those set-apart ones under the blood of Jesus!

In these "last days," we should constantly thank God that Satan's access to God's people is hampered. Those of us who have Christ as Lord and Savior should, in one sense, flee from the devil (James 4:7)—in another, resist him in the power of the Holy Spirit and the Word of God. Do not underestimate Satan. Also, do not overestimate him. He is a conquered foe. He cannot have success against the puniest child of God if that child will stand on the promises of God for strength.

Focus on these precious promises;

> *But in all these things we overwhelmingly conquer through Him who loved us. For I am convinced that neither death, nor life, nor angels, nor principalities, nor things present, nor things to come, nor powers, nor height, nor depth, nor any other created thing, will be able to separate us from the love of God, which is in Christ Jesus our Lord (Rom. 8:37-39).*

> *But thanks be to God, who gives us the victory through our Lord Jesus Christ. Therefore, my beloved brethren, be steadfast, immovable, always abounding in the work of the Lord, knowing that your toil is not in vain in the Lord (1 Cor. 15:57-58).*

> *For whatever is born of God overcomes the world; and this is the victory that has overcome the world—our faith. Who is the one who overcomes the world, but he who believes that Jesus is the Son of God?* (1 John 5:4-5).

God Permits Evil to Run Its Course

We are often at a loss to fathom why God could or would possibly allow sin and wrong to exist. For centuries people have asked, "Why?" Why does God permit evil since He is all-powerful and can abolish wickedness from the Earth in the twinkling of an eye? Why? Because of His moral government. He permits sin to run its dreadful course. Since His rule is moral, forcing His will is not in His character. Let us also remember that Satan and his cohorts are given the power of free choice, yet within limitations already explored previously. Thus, God respects the granting of this freedom. Understand it fully we cannot; accept it we must.

Noah's generation was a prime example of this principle. Genesis 6:1-6 depicts how the human family had plunged into the depths of depravity. "Then the Lord saw that the wickedness of man was great on the earth, and that every intent of the thoughts of his heart was only evil continually. The Lord was sorry that He had made man on the earth, and He was grieved in His heart" (Gen. 6:5-6). When mankind had descended to that low point, evil had run its course, and the world was ready for judgment. To permit such a low-life stock to perpetuate its species might have been considered unkind toward unborn generations. So, God sent the Flood that destroyed all but Noah, his wife, and his three sons—Shem, Ham, and Japheth—and their wives. The Lord's extermination of that twisted generation was indeed an act of mercy. One can only wonder how God has spared this perverse world since the Flood!

Another example was the case of the Canaanites. When God entered into a covenant with Abraham, He promised that his descendants would be wayfarers in a country not their own, that they would be oppressed for 400 years, and that at the conclusion of that period, they would return from Egypt to their own land. The reason for their having to wait until that time is succinctly expressed in these words: "Then in the fourth generation they will return here, for the iniquity of the Amorite is not yet complete" (Gen. 15:16). The Lord, in His foreknowledge and wisdom, realized that the Amorites (and the Canaanite people in general) were on a "slippery slope." They were careening helter skelter toward the depths of sin, but they would not reach the pits until the expiration of the foretold period. In other words, God announced that He would allow evil to follow its contemptible course—He would not snuff out those miscreants until they had drunk the dregs of sin's cup.

So, when men or nations plunge toward the abyss of sin, the Lord allows them to keep on until sin has run its degrading gamut. When they reach the end, the axe of judgment falls. Perhaps this principle may help us understand why God allows evil and why evil nations, as well as individuals, may continue in a seeming state of prosperity and peace. We must bear in mind that viable precept, which is ever functional in God's moral government.

God Uses Nations in Keeping Peace and Punishing Aggressors

Right after the Flood, God mandated the establishment of civil government to punish the transgressors and to maintain law and order. This is set forth in Genesis 9:5-6: "Surely I will require your lifeblood; from every beast I will require it. And from every man, from every man's brother I will require the life of man. Whoever sheds man's blood, By man his blood shall be shed, For in the image of God He made man."

In His moral government, God respects the freedom of choice He has given to human beings. He allows evil to continue and at times seemingly to prevail over the righteous. An old adage expressed it: "The wheels of God's judgment mill grind slowly, but they grind exceedingly fine." So be it!

The Final Expulsion of Sin from the World

According to Isaiah 24:21-23 the Lord will, at the end of the Tribulation, imprison the hosts of "the high ones on high" (KJV)—Satan and his evil associates—together with the rulers of the Earth, consigning them to the pit of the abyss where they will remain for "many days"—the one thousand years of the millennium. During that period the inhabitants of the world will suffer no attacks from them. The reign of righteousness will set in. No disorders in the realm of nature. All disputers between individuals will be settled by Yahweh and his saints, who will reign with Him over the Earth.

At the end of the millennium, Satan will be turned loose for a short season and will attempt to deceive the nations. After that period the judgment of the great white throne will occur. Satan and all of the wicked will be delegated to their eternal abode, the lake of fire, which is the second death (Rev. 20:10-15). At that time the present material universe will pass out of existence (Rev. 20:11).

After that God will create the eternal order. All things will be new. Nothing from the present besmirched universe will enter into the construction of the new and everlasting creation. God will have solved the problem of evil forever! Throughout the innumerable ages of the future, His plans will be continually unfurled, all of which will prove a never-ending blessing to saved humanity. God's holiness, righteousness, love, and mercy will shine throughout eternity.

Chapter 3
The God of Creation

The first two chapters of Genesis record the creation of man, demonstrating his intended purpose to honor God and his value that he is a special creation of the Almighty (Gen. 1:27). God created Adam and Eve, the first man and woman, in perfect fellowship and harmony with Him, but they sinned against Him in the Garden of Eden. All the pain, all the evil, and all the chaos in the world is traceable to that original act of rebellion, often called the "fall of man." Human beings have a spiritual, as well as a physical, dimension. The precise moment a baby is born, the process is set in motion for him to die physically. His spirit, however, lives forever.

As seen in Genesis chapters I and 2, man was created in the image of God and was given dominion, authority, and power over the Earth. He was situated in the most salutary surroundings. Had he not sinned, he could have lived there indefinitely. The animals were completely submissive to him. The situation was ideal. To use a contemporary term, Adam and Eve "had it made." Adam was the master of all he surveyed. It is likely that, if he had remained in fellowship with his Maker and had not violated God's will, he would have developed his physical nature—and his natural body would have become transformed into its glorified state.

The story of creation proceeds along a logical path. The Bible suggests that mankind was God's greatest achievement. As a sculptor begins with rough forms before devoting himself to finer details, God began the work of creation by separating and shaping. The farther along God moved, the more defined His creation became. Consider the sequence of creation's days:

Day I (Gen. 1:3-5)

Light is created and is separated from darkness to designate day and night.

Day 2 (Gen. 1:6-8)

God structures an expanse called "sky" to separate the water on Earth from the water above.

Day 3 (Gen. 1:9-13)

The water on Earth is gathered to form seas distinct from land. Vegetation is created with the capability of reproducing from seeds.

Day 4 (Gen. 1:14-19)

Heavenly bodies (sun, moon, and stars) are created to provide light and mark seasons.

Day 5 (Gen. 1:20-23)

Birds and sea creatures are formed with the capability of reproducing "according to their kinds."

Day 6 (Gen. 1:24—2:1)

God turns His attention to land creatures, completing His work with the creation of humankind—both male and female.

Day 7 (Gen. 2:2-3)

God rests—the Sabbath Day.

The Genesis account of creation describes God as speaking each day's work into existence. We are recurrently reminded: God saw that His work was "good." When it was over, and He evaluated all of His creation, He exclaimed that it was "very good" (Gen. 1:31).

When God was ready to create man, He suggested: "'Let Us

make man in Our image, according to Our likeness; and let them rule over the fish of the sea and over the birds of the sky and over the cattle and over all the earth, and over every creeping thing that creeps on the earth.' God created man in His own image, in the image of God He created him; male and female. He created them. God blessed them; and God said to them, 'Be fruitful and multiply, and fill the earth, and subdue it; and rule over the fish of the sea and over the birds of the sky and over every living thing that moves on the earth'" (Gen. 1:26-28). What was meant by "Let Us . . ."? It speaks of the Holy Trinity. The Father, Son, and Holy Spirit were in consultation. Through the centuries Jewish rabbis have scratched their heads over this plural pronoun of Deity.

Man: A Child of God by Direct Creation

"God created man in His own image, in the image of God He created him; male and female He created them. . . . Then the Lord God formed man of dust from the ground, and breathed into his nostrils the breath of life; and man became a living being" ["soul," KJV] (Gen. 1:27, 2:7). In the first of these quotations we are told that God created man in His image, after His likeness. God formed dirt into the shape of a man and then breathed life into him.

When God named Adam, He then placed Him in a verdant paradise, the Garden of Eden. It was filled with trees, rivers, and food. At the center of the Garden were two significant trees: the Tree of Life and the Tree of the Knowledge of Good and Evil. God granted Adam almost unlimited freedom—with one restriction, that he and Eve had to avoid eating from the Tree of the Knowledge of Good and Evil

God felt that Adam should have a helpmate.

> *"Then the Lord God said, 'It is not good for the man to be alone; I will make him a helper suitable for him.' Out of the ground the Lord God formed every beast of the field and every bird of the sky, and brought them to the man to see what he would call them; and whatever the man called a living creature, that was its name. The man gave names to all the cattle, and to the birds of the sky, and to every beast of the field, but for Adam there was not found a helper suitable for him. So the Lord God caused a deep sleep to fall upon the man, and he slept; then He took one of his ribs and closed up the flesh at*

> *that place. The Lord God fashioned into a woman the rib which He had taken from the man, and brought her to the man. The man said, 'This is now bone of my bones, And flesh of my flesh; She shall be called Woman, Because she was taken out of man'"* (Gen. 2:18-23).

Instead, the slick being he is, he asked Eve a seemingly innocuous question that caused her to doubt the instructions God had given. Before she had time to think plainly, he came through with an insidious innuendo that maybe God had a hidden agenda. "For God knows that in the day you eat from it your eyes will be opened, and you will be like God, knowing good and evil" (Gen. 3:5). The Satan-serpent was successful in pulling Eve's focus away from the abundance of paradise to a single, taboo tree and the fruit hanging there. Isn't that the nature of sin then and now—the appeal to the very thing that is forbidden? John wrote untold centuries later:

> *Do not love the world nor the things in the world. If anyone loves the world, the love of the Father is not in him. For all that is in the world, the lust of the flesh and the lust of the eyes and the boastful pride of life, is not from the Father, but is from the world. The world is passing away, and also its lusts; but the one who does the will of God lives forever* (I John 2:15-17, author's italics).

And James observed: "Then when lust hath conceived, it bringeth forth sin: and sin, when it is finished, bringeth forth death" (James 1:15, KJV).

The fruit, whatever it was, appealed to "the lust of the eyes." Eve grabbed a piece and ate it. Yum. Yum. She handed it to Adam so he could also enjoy the forbidden fruit. Hadn't Satan promised, "Eat this fruit, and you will be like God"? The fruit didn't make them smarter. Only "dumb and dumber"! After being naked and unashamed, they suddenly decided to hide from God. When they finally came out, they were wearing clothes of fig leaves. You can't hide from God. Even if you are fully clothed, He views you in nakedness of soul—and also of body. He cried out, "Who told you that you were naked? Have you eaten from the tree of which I commanded you not to eat?" (Gen. 3:11). He already knew, of course. Were it not for sin, all of us would be walking around naked and unashamed.

For if by the transgression of the one, death reigned through the one, much more those who receive the abundance of grace and of the gift of righteousness will reign in life through the One, Jesus Christ. So then as through one transgression there resulted condemnation to all men, even so through one act of righteousness there resulted justification of life to all men. For as through the one man's disobedience the many were made sinners, even so through the obedience of the One the many will be made righteous. The Law came in so that the transgression would increase; but where sin increased, grace abounded all the more (Rom. 5:12-20).

The Creation Account

God explained the Creation in the Book of Genesis (meaning "Beginning") in a manner that makes complete and logical sense. God had created a perfect and orderly Earth where everything reproduced "after its own kind." That is why, to this day, cherry trees always reproduce cherry trees; dogs give birth to dogs; cats to cats; monkeys to monkeys; and human beings always reproduce other human beings. So much for evolution, one of Satan's ruses foisted on mankind. For sure, monkeys haven't yet turned into humans, even though humans act like monkeys—and far worse.

Adam and Eve were particularly distinct from the rest of God's creation. They alone were created "in the image of God."

Then God said, "Let Us make man in Our image, according to Our likeness; and let them rule over the fish of the sea and over the birds of the sky and over the cattle and over all the earth, and over every creeping thing that creeps on the earth." God created man in His own image, in the image of God He created him; male and female He created them (Gen. 1:26-27).

They possessed the abilities to think and reason logically and to discipline themselves to live on a higher level than animalistic instinct. They had the free will to make conscious decisions about the directions their lives would follow. Sadly, early on they made a disastrous wrong decision. Eve yielded to temptation and sinned by disobeying God. Then she caused Adam to follow suit. But Adam sinned with his eyes wide open. He understood precisely what he was doing. He did it willingly and in total insubordination toward his Creator and Heavenly Father. Billy Graham has often noted, "Adam was the Federal head of the human race." The first man became a sinner. He went his own obstinate way instead of God's way. "All we like sheep have gone astray; we have turned every one to his own way, and the Lord hath laid on Him the iniquity of us all" (Isa. 53:6, KJV), Since the father carries the seed, he conveys the sin nature. So, Adam laid on all subsequent generations the inclination to sin. David cried out, "Behold, I was brought forth in iniquity and in sin my mother conceived me" (Ps. 51:5).

By the transgression of one sole commandment concerning the Tree of the Knowledge of Good and Evil, man plunged headlong into sin—from his sinless condition into a state of depravity and rebellion. The consequences were ghastly. Because of their disobedience, Adam and Eve were expelled from the Garden of Eden and lost fellowship with their Creator. God is loving, merciful, and longsuffering. By His wisdom He realized the grave repercussions that would ensue if man ate of the forbidden fruit. God established righteous laws and powers and then warned His creatures what would result if they disobeyed. He recognized that, if man disobeyed this command, the death process would begin to prey on man's body, and the force of sin would enter man's soul, corrupting his moral being.

God further knew that if man were to eat of the forbidden fruit, Satan would be allowed to take the rulership over the Earth from man, and from that day he would be buffeted by Satan. The one who brought this awful change into the world is Satan whom Paul called "the god of this world" (2 Cor. 4:4). He used the serpent as his pawn. He is also called "the prince of this world" (John 12:31). He was created the highest being possible. He was full of wisdom and was perfect in beauty. He was the highest and most powerful being that God ever created. God gave him immense power in the organization of divine government.

Though he fell, he still retained his power with certain limitations. When man sinned and forfeited his rulership over the Earth to Satan, the latter ravenously grabbed it. For centuries he tenaciously held everything on Earth in his clutches. No created being even dared to challenge him. Only God could do that. Michael the archangel would not spar with him but rather turned the situation over to the Lord. "But Michael the archangel, when he disputed with the devil and argued about the body of Moses, did not dare pronounce against him a railing judgment, but said, 'The Lord rebuke you!'" (Jude 1:9).

From a human standpoint, the problem that confronted God was to wrest the Earth, especially man, from the clutches of Satan. How could He do that? If the situation had involved power only, God certainly had that, since He is all-powerful. But other matters were involved, as we gather from God's Word. In God's prophecy to the serpent there is what scholars call the "Protoevangeliurn"—the first mention of redemption in the Bible. "And, I will put enmity between you and the woman, And between your seed and her seed; He shall bruise you on the head, And you shall bruise him on the heel" (Gen. 3:15). The seed of the woman will gloriously triumph over Satan and his number-one crony, the Antichrist, and their forces.

Man, being the highest of the Almighty's earthly creatures, received from God authority and rulership of the fowls of the air, the beasts of the field, and the fish of the sea. Man was in a position to have charge of the lower animals. This authority he lost. This same authority will be returned to him in the millennium. Since he was created in the image of God, man had blessed fellowship with the Lord, who often visited with Adam and Eve and even carried on conversations with them. However, when Adam chose to disobey God, sin entered into Adam and into the entire human race. Fellowship with God was destroyed, and a curse was placed on Adam and Eve, the Earth itself, and on Satan. Death entered the world. Satan was, as already pointed out, allowed a limited amount of influence, sin flourished, and all creation needed to be reclaimed from final destruction.

Three Miraculous Events

The Lord Jesus Christ designed a plan to effect three miraculous events that would provide the avenue to victory over sin. What are those miracles?

1. **Christ would come to Earth and become the God-man, born of a virgin.**
2. **Christ would die on the cross to pay the penalty for sin; if human beings would have faith In what He did for them, God would justify them and grant them righteousness.**
3. **Christ would rise from the grave. Christ's resurrection assures us that, if we trust Him, we too will rise from the dead and have a home in heaven eternally with Him.**

Paul exclaimed in Romans 5:17-20:

> *For if by the transgression of the one, death reigned through the one, much more those who receive the abundance of grace and of the gift of righteousness will reign in life through the One, Jesus Christ. So then as through one transgression there resulted condemnation to all men, even so through one act of righteousness there resulted justification of life to all men. For as through the one man's disobedience the many were made sinners, even so through the obedience of the One the many will be made righteous. The Law came in so that the transgression would increase; but where sin increased, grace abounded all the more.*

God created man as the highest type of being possible. If He had created either you or me, and placed us in Eden instead of Adam and Eve, we would have done exactly as Adam did. When Adam was on trial, you and I were on trial. You and I possess the same humanity as the first couple. All men were condemned to death by Adam's one act of disobedience. In reverse, by the one act of Jesus' righteousness giving His life on the cross, the free gift came unto all who believe in Christ, thus inviting Him into their lives.

This remarkable Pauline passage does not mean that all people will be saved but rather that all sin is atoned for by Christ's sacrifice, but only for those who accept it and believe on the Lord Jesus Christ. "Sirs, what must I do to be saved? They said, 'Believe in the Lord Jesus, and you will be saved, you and your household'" (Acts 16:30-31). Jesus Christ tasted death for every person, making it possible that all might be saved. Those who reach the "age of accountability" (a varying age when a person can make moral judgments) and yet do not accept the provision for their salvation, of course will not be made righteousness.

Sin Is Imbedded

Sin is a force or power in mankind that causes humans to do wrong and prevents them from doing what they recognize as being right. Sin is properly used to denote the moral corruption of man and nature inherited by all mankind from Adam. This inherited moral corruption consists in the loss of original righteousness and the presence of a continual inclination to evil, the root and origin of all actual sin.

It is called sin (Rom. 6:12,14,17; 7:5,17), the flesh (Gal. 5:17, 24), lust (James 1:14, 15), the body of sin (Rom. 6:6), ignorance, blindness of heart, and alienation from the life of God (Eph. 4:18,19). It influences and depraves the whole man, and its tendency is downward to worse and worse degeneration. It is a total depravity and is also universally inherited by all the descendants of Adam (Rom. 3:10-23; 5:12-21; 8:7). In his natural state, man is spiritually dead, "dead in trespasses and sins" (see Eph. 2:1; 1 John 3:14).

From the fact of the universal sinfulness of men, there is no person who does not sin (1 Kings 8:46; Isa. 53:6; Ps. 130:3; Rom. 3:19, 22, 23; Gal. 3:22). From the total depravity of man, all persons are pronounced devoid of any principle of spiritual life. Mankind's infidelity toward God is total and complete (Job 15:14-16; Gen. 6:5, 6). From early on, it is manifested (Ps. 58:3; Prov. 22:15).

All kinds of sin are mentioned in God's Word: 1. presumptuous sins, or as literally rendered, "sins with an uplifted hand," i.e., defiant acts of sin, in contrast with errors or inadvertencies (Ps. 19:13); 2. secret, i.e., hidden sins (19:12), sins that escape the notice of the soul; 3. sins against the Holy Ghost ("the unpardonable sin") or a "sin unto death" (Matt. 12:31, 32; 1 John 5:16), which many think a believer can commit.

The Remedy: Being "Born Again"

Mankind is hopelessly lost and unsaved because of its sin-mired condition. The prophet Isaiah cried out:

> *1 Behold, the Lord's hand is not so short That it cannot save;*
> *Nor is His ear so dull That it cannot hear.*
> *2 But your iniquities have made a separation between you and your God And your sins have hidden His face from you so that He does not hear.*
> *3 For your hands are defiled with blood And your fingers with iniquity;*
> *Your lips have spoken falsehood,*
> *Your tongue mutters wickedness.*
> *4 No one sees righteously and no one pleads honestly.*
> *They trust in confusion and speak lies;*
> *They conceive mischief and bring forth iniquity.*
> *5 They hatch adders' eggs and weave the spider's web;*

> *He who eats of their eggs dies,*
> *And from that which is crushed a snake breaks forth* (Isa. 59:1-5).
> *6 But we are all as an unclean thing, and all our righteousnesses are as filthy rags; and we all do fade as a leaf; and our iniquities, like the wind, have taken us a way.*
> *7 And there is none that calleth upon thy name, that stirreth up himself to take hold of thee: for thou hast hid thy face from us, and hast consumed us, because of our iniquities* (Isa. 64:6-7, KJV).

So, God had to intervene. The only route of deliverance comes through Jesus Christ. He came and made reconciliation for us. "And all things are of God, who hath reconciled us to himself by Jesus Christ, and hath given to us the ministry of reconciliation; To wit, that God was in Christ, reconciling the world unto himself, not imputing their trespasses unto them, and hath committed unto us the word of reconciliation" (2 Cor. 5:18-19, KJV).

CHAPTER 4
The Nature of Humans

God created man from the dust of the earth and "breathed into his nostrils the breath of life; and man became a living soul" (Gen. 2:7, KJV). The word "soul" from the Hebrew, *nephesh*, meaning "breathing one," was also often used in reference to animals. God created them and gave them a life or a soul. However, when He created man, it was different. Man is *a living soul.* The animals have a soul or life, but they have a limited intellect and certainly cannot make moral or ethical decisions. God endowed man with an intellectual and spiritual nature that is capable of considerable development and achievement.

What is meant, then, by the "soul" of man? According to Numbers 16:22 God is "the God of the spirits of all flesh" (KJV). Zechariah 12:1 states that Jehovah God formed "the spirit of man within him" (KJV). The Apostle Paul wrote: But God hath revealed them unto us by His Spirit: for the Spirit searcheth all things, yea, the deep things of God. For what man knoweth the things of a man, save the spirit of man which is in him? even so the things of God knoweth no man, but the Spirit of God" (2 Cor. 2:10-11, KJV).

From these references it is lucid that man has a spirit and that it is different from the Spirit of God. "It came about as her [Rachel's] soul was departing (for she died), that she named him Ben-oni; but his father called him Benjamin" (Gen. 35:18). Rachel's soul departed from her body. In 1 Kings 17:21 Elijah prayed that the soul of the widow's son might return to his body: "Then he stretched himself upon the child three times, and called to the Lord and said, 'O Lord my God, I pray You, let this child's life return to him." And the child's life (soul) did return! In speaking of a person, James wrote: "For just as the body without the spirit is dead, so also faith without works is dead" (Jas. 2:26). The first of these cited passages makes a difference between the spirit of a person and God's Holy Spirit. These other citations stress the spiritual nature of the soul and differentiate it from the physical body.

The terms "soul" and "spirit" are used interchangeably in God's Word. Genesis notes that Pharaoh's "*spirit was troubled*; and he sent and called for all the magicians of Egypt, and all the wise men thereof: and Pharaoh told them his dream; but there was none that could interpret them unto Pharaoh" (Gen. 41:8, KJV, author's italics). The psalmist cried, "O my God, my soul is cast down within me: therefore will I remember thee from the land of Jordan, and of the Hermonites, from the hill Mizar" (Ps. 42:6, KJV, author's italics). In Genesis 41:8 Pharaoh's spirit is spoken of as being troubled; the psalmist wrote that his soul was cast down. To what did the psalmist refer? No doubt he was speaking of his spirit, yet he called it his soul.

Our Lord Jesus referred to being troubled in His soul and spirit. John 11:33: "When Jesus therefore saw her weeping, and the Jews who came with her also weeping, He was deeply *moved in spirit* and was troubled" (author's italics). John 13:21 notes that, ". . . he was troubled in the spirit" (KJV). "And He [Jesus] said to them, 'My soul is deeply grieved to the point of death; remain here and keep watch'" (Mark 14:34). He was deeply grieved or deeply moved ("troubled" in the KJV) in those instances. In one case His spiritual nature was called His soul—in the other, His spirit.

According to Matthew 20:28 Jesus came to "give his life a ransom for many." The term translated life is the word soul. The emphasis is placed on the spiritual sacrifice the Lord Jesus made in offering redemption to mankind. In referring to the Lord's death, Matthew wrote that He "yielded up his spirit" (Matt. 27:50, KJV). From those and numerous other passages, it is plain that soul and spirit are employed as synonyms in reference to the spiritual nature of man.

More proof of this truth is revealed in the phrase, "spirits of just men made perfect" (Heb. 12:23, KJV). The NASB renders it "spirits of the righteous made perfect." From the surrounding text it is clear that the author was thinking of saved people who will have gotten their spiritual bodies at the future time seen in that vision. So, he called them "spirits." John the Revelator wrote: "When the Lamb broke the fifth seal, I saw underneath the altar the *souls* of those who had been slain because of the word of God, and because of the testimony which they had maintained" (Rev. 6:9, author's italics). Soul here means spirit. Soul and spirit are interchangeable.

Further understanding about man's makeup comes from such expressions as Matthew 10:28. "Do not fear those who kill the body but are unable to kill the soul; but rather fear Him who is able to destroy both soul and body in hell" (see also Luke 12:4-5). In these instances Jesus spoke of man as being composed of body and spirit. The Apostle Paul wrote of himself as having a body and a spirit: "For I, on my part, though absent in body but present in spirit, have already judged him who has so committed this, as though I were present" (1 Cor. 5:3).

More proof that the soul and the spirit are the same is in Amos 6:8 where the prophet affirmed, "The Lord God has sworn by Himself, the Lord God of hosts has declared: 'I loathe the arrogance of Jacob, And detest his citadels; Therefore I will deliver up the city and all it contains.'" In Hebrew the word translated Himself is soul. Isaiah, standing in for Jehovah, declared: "Behold, my servant, whom I uphold; my chosen, in whom my soul delighteth: I have put my Spirit upon him; he will bring forth justice to the Gentiles" (Isa. 42 :1, KJV). Here the Lord speaks of His soul's taking delight in His Servant, the Messiah. Through Jeremiah, God asked, "'Shall I not punish them for these things?' declares the Lord. 'On a nation such as this Shall I not avenge Myself?'" (Jer. 9:9). In Hebrews 10:38, God announced, "But My righteous one shall live by faith; And if he shrinks back, My soul has no pleasure in him." It is plain from these and other references that God refers to His spirit as His soul.

Jesus, teaching about man's spiritual nature, called it his soul. In Mark 12:29-30, "Jesus answered, 'The foremost is, Hear, O Israel! The Lord our God is one Lord; and you shall love the Lord your God with all your heart, and with all your soul, and with all your mind, and with all your strength. The first [commandment] is, Hear, O Israel; The Lord our God, the Lord is one: and thou shalt love the Lord thy God with all thy heart, and with all thy soul, and with all thy mind, and with all thy strength" (KJV). The loftiest workings of the human spirit are here viewed as being carried out by the soul.

Jesus' mother, Mary, in her joy praised God and exulted, "My soul doth magnify the Lord, And my spirit hath rejoiced in God my Savior" (Luke 2:46-47, KJV). According to Hebrew usage, soul in the first line corresponds to spirit in the second and shows that they are one and the same. That is fortified by the truth that this points to worship, which is rendered by the soul. Let's notice, then, Mark 8:36- 37 : "For what doth it profit a man, to gain the whole world, and forfeit his life? For what should a man give in exchange for his life [Greek: soul] ?" What does this reveal? It is apparent that soul in this instance means man's spiritual nature. If he loses that, he forfeits everything.

People often single out passages like I Thessalonians 5:23: "Now may the God of peace Himself sanctify you entirely; and may your spirit and soul and body be preserved complete, without blame at the coming of our Lord Jesus Christ." From that verse it is often believed that man is a threefold being, consisting of body, soul, and spirit. We have to interpret this, bearing in mind other things about man's spiritual and corporeal nature. Man consists of soul and body or spirit and body, as borne out in these scriptures. Spirit and soul are used as synonyms in the passages I have pointed out and in numerous others.

The Lord Jesus indicated that Israel was commanded: "Thou shalt love the Lord thy God with all thy heart, and with all thy soul, and with all thy mind. This is the first and great commandment. And the second is like unto it, Thou shalt love thy neighbor as thyself. On these two commandments hang all the law and the prophets" (Matt. 22:37-40, KJV). Here Jesus uses four nouns: heart, soul, mind, and strength. Would this lead us to believe that man is a fivefold being? No way. The passages in which these words appear indicate that the first three of them are used interchangeably. In this passage, though, strength is used as a synonym of the first three. Likewise, we are not to decide that man has a threefold nature from Paul's use of spirit, body, and soul in I Thessalonians 5 :23.

Then you may ask about Hebrews 4:12: "For the word of God is living and active and sharper than any two-edged sword, and piercing as far as the division of soul and spirit, of both joints and marrow, and able to judge the thoughts and intentions of the heart." From the surrounding verses, we recognize that the writer of this verse was referring to Christ, the living Word, who is "sharper than any two-edged sword, and piercing as far as the division of soul and spirit, of both joints and marrow, and able to judge the thoughts and intentions of the heart."

Understanding this most important subject enables one to avoid many serious and grave errors and heresies which grow out of a forced interpretation of I Thessalonians 5 :23-25 and Hebrews 5:12.

Noah and His Ark

People in Noah's generation became increasingly wicked. God was ready to wipe them off of the Earth. Yet, one man and his family were saved—Noah, his wife, their three sons, and their wives. God confided in Noah about the upcoming Deluge and instructed him to build an ark. It had never rained at that time, and Noah was far removed from an ocean. Yet, Noah through faith began to build the ark. What a project! It took him and his sons 120 years to finish the project!

The ark was 450 feet long, 75 feet wide, and 45 feet high. Each of the three decks was the size of one-and-a-half football fields. God instructed Noah to gather two of each kind of living creatures, one male and one female. In the case of "clean" animals (those all right for offerings and for food), Noah was to select seven of each. He also carried seven of each kind of fowl, so sending out the dove later was not a risk. When the ark was completed, the animals came to Noah in pairs (Gen. 7:8-9,15). Noah and his folks also boarded. Once inside the Lord shut them in (7:16).

It began to rain. George Beverly Shea used to sing, "My, didn't it rain? My, didn't it rain? It rained for 40 days and nights. My, didn't it rain!" But another catastrophe occurred—"In the six hundredth year of Noah's life, in the second month, on the seventeenth day of the month, on the same day all the fountains of the great deep burst open, and the floodgates of the sky were opened" (v. 11). Coleridge wrote about "water, water everywhere." That was the case. Water from above and below. It was a worldwide cataclysm. Even the highest mountains were covered. When the water receded, the ark ended up on Mount Ararat (which is in modern-day Turkey). Noah, his family, and the animals departed the ark. Then Noah sacrificed to God using some of the clean animals.

Abraham's Faith

When we first encounter Abraham, he is 75 years old. Life expectancies had decreased, but he still lived to be 175. (Noah was 500 while building the ark.) Abraham's name had been Abram, but God changed it. "For the eyes of the Lord move to and fro throughout the earth that

He may strongly support those whose heart is completely His. . . . " (2 Chron. 16:9a). In Abram the Lord found that kind of man in the days of Hammurabi of the Chaldeans. Abram lived in Ur amid idolatry and corruption. The people worshiped the moon goddess, among other idols. The Lord called him to leave his people and his homeland for "a country" He would reveal to him—Canaan, the Promised Land.

Abram (Abraham) obeyed without questioning. He had no idea where he was going, but he went regardless. Finally he reached Canaan and lived there. He lived in tents as a nomad in a "strange" land, though God had promised it to him and his descendants. When Abraham was 99 years old, and his wife Sarah, 89, God performed a miracle in their lives with the birth of the son of promise, Isaac. That birth fulfilled God's promise, and through him and succeeding generations, God would bless the entire world.

"Abraham believed God, and He credited it to him for righteousness" (Gen. 15:6). Sarah was unable to conceive in a culture where childbearing was a primary source of a woman's fulfillment and self-esteem. God had entered into a covenant (a mutual promise) with Abraham that he would be the leader of a great nation and "nations" whose numbers would be innumerable as the stars in the sky and sands on the beach. The new covenant defined the boundaries to the land promised to Abraham.

When God called Abraham, He informed him that he and his descendants would be the repositories of His truth. He assured Abraham that in him and his "seed" would all the families of the earth be blessed.

> *Now the LORD had said unto Abram, Get thee out of thy country, and from thy kindred, and from thy father's house, unto a land that I will shew thee: And I will make of thee a great nation, and I will bless thee, and make thy name great; and thou shalt be a blessing: And I will bless them that bless thee, and curse him that curseth thee: and in thee shall all families of the earth be blessed* (Gen. 12:1-2, KJV; see also Gen. 15; 17:1–22; Mic. 7:20; Luke 1:73; Rom. 4:13; 15:8; Heb. 6:13-14; Gal. 3:6–18,29; 4:22–31).

As seen by a careful study of both the Old and New testaments, God's message was committed to Israel, whom Abraham "fathered," as the chosen nation to deliver the truth to the entire world. They would present God as the Creator of all things, the Preserver and Controller of the universe, and the One in whom ". . . we live, and move, and have our being . . ." (see Acts 17:28, KJV), and the One who provides all mankind's necessities.

Think about it. Abraham went out, and he didn't know his destination—except that Yahweh God had promised to be with him and to lead him. Add to that the complications of moving servants and cattle and the need to find a nightly supply of water. The patriarch could have answered no and refused to obey God . . . but

> *By faith Abraham, when he was called to go out into a place which he should after receive for an inheritance, obeyed; and he went out, not knowing whither he went. By faith he sojourned in the land of promise, as in a strange country, dwelling in tabernacles with Isaac and Jacob, the heirs with him of the same promise: For he looked for a city which hath foundations, whose builder and maker is God. Through faith also Sara herself received strength to conceive seed, and was delivered of a child when she was past age, because she judged him faithful who had promised. Therefore sprang there even of one, and him as good as dead, so many as the stars of the sky in multitude, and as the sand which is by the sea shore innumerable* (Acts 11:8-12, KJV).

What would cause a person to respond as Abraham did? He had no idea where he was going; he was not secure about conditions in alien territory; and his water and food could eventually run out. In today's terms, it was "scary." But it was enough that God had called him. His father, Terah, started the process and set out from Ur to enter the land of Canaan. They stopped at Haran and sojourned there (Gen. 11:31). At the age of 250 Terah died there (v. 32). Then Abraham traveled on with his family, including his nephew Lot, his servants, and livestock. So, "he went out, not knowing whither he went."

Abraham and Sarah were childless, though God had promised them a son. Sarah offered a faithless solution—Abraham would have a child by his Egyptian handmaid, Hagar. Abraham complied, and Ishmael was born (Gen. 16:3,15). Ishmael's descendants, the Arabs, have plagued Abraham's "seed," the Hebrews (later called Israelites and then Jews) through the centuries. That is borne out every day, not only in the Holy Land but around the world. It seems that Abraham would have settled for Ishmael as his heir, but God had His own plans. Abram's name was changed to Abraham (Gen. 17:5; Neh. 9:7). God proclaimed that the son born to him and Sarah would be called Isaac, and God established circumcision as a sign by which Hebrew males would be identified (Gen. 17:10-14, 23-27).

After his circumcision, Abraham has three amazing visitors. Two of them were definitely angels; the third more than likely was Yahweh Himself. All three appeared in human form. Although he did not recognize them as being divine, Abraham afforded them full hospitality, bowing before them, washing their feet, preparing food, and other Middle-Eastern amenities. The visitors inquired about Sarah, promising that she would have a son within a year. Then Abraham may have realized the origin of those he was entertaining. Sarah heard them talking and laughed. After all, it was ridiculous to think she would bear a child. She was 89 years old! One year later they were blessed with Isaac.

The two angels departed, but God remained to converse more with Abraham. Because of God's respect for Abraham and their covenant, He decided to share with the patriarch a glimpse of His plans. God was observing the perverse cities of Sodom and Gomorrah. He wanted Abraham and later his nephew, Lot, to understand that His judgments were well thought out and not hasty. Before God could speak a word about judgment, Abraham was pleading for the dwellers of Sodom because Lot lived there. "Abraham came near and said, 'Will You indeed sweep away the righteous with the wicked? Suppose there are fifty righteous within the city; will You indeed sweep it away and not spare the place for the sake of the fifty righteous who are in it?'" (Gen. 18:23-24). God promised to spare the city if 50 righteous people were there. As it happened, not even 10 were found! One would think that, counting Lot and his folks, there would have been at least that few. But no.

It is no wonder that a twisted sexual sin is named from Sodom. Homosexuality was prevalent in that city of the plain. When the angels entered town (Gen. 19) Lot insisted that they stay with him. As a resident, he was aware of the city's immorality. Shortly after supper the men of Sodom surrounded his home and yelled, "Where are the men who came to you tonight? Bring them out to us that we may have relations [some translations render that sex] with them" (Gen.

19:5). The nature of raging homosexuality has not changed in four millennia!

Lot was called "a righteous man" in 2 Peter 2:7, but he had certainly backslidden. However, he wanted to protect those who visited him (Gen. 19:8). The angels took charge. They pulled Lot back inside to safety—then they blinded the crowd. Next, they instructed Lot to gather his household and "get out of Dodge"—er—Sodom, for that wicked city would be destroyed. In agreement with the Lord, Lot escaped to the town of Zoar and later fled to a mountain (vv. 20-23). "Then the Lord rained on Sodom and Gomorrah brimstone and fire from the Lord out of heaven, and He overthrew those cities, and all the valley, and all the inhabitants of the cities, and what grew on the ground. But his wife, from behind him, looked back, and she became a pillar of salt" (vv. 24-26). From a distance Abraham beheld the destruction of Sodom and Gomorrah (vv. 27-28).

At long last the child of promise, Isaac, was born. Of course, this intensified the conflict between Sarah and Hagar. To Abraham's distress, Sarah demanded that Hagar and Ishmael be cast out (Gen. 21:2-3; see also Gal. 4:22-30). Though Ishmael was not the promised child, God still cared for him and Hagar (Gen. 21:20).

In the meantime, Abraham was coping with life (Gen. 21:22-34). With joy he was watching Isaac grow up. Then, all of a sudden, God asked the incredible of Abraham. "Take now your son, your only son, whom you love, Isaac, and go to the land of Moriah, and offer him there as a burnt offering on one of the mountains of which I will tell you." The Word of God declares that God did this to test his faith. God referred to Isaac as "your son, your only son." Why "only"? It was not merely because Hagar and Ishmael could no longer be part of Abraham's life. Isaac was the promised one, the heir through whom God's other promises would be fulfilled. What a picture of God's offering His only Son, the Lord Jesus Christ, as the offering for mankind's sins!

What Has Happened to Abraham's Seed?

Why has Israel, the descendants of Abraham, suffered as she has? Her history is written in blood. Why must she have endured the persecutions heaped on her through the centuries? And why does a loving, yet righteous, God permit the anti-Semites to win over His chosen, beloved people? The answer is found in Isaiah 30:18-19:

Therefore the Lord longs to be gracious to you, And therefore He waits on high to have compassion on you. For the Lord is a God of justice; How blessed are all those who long for Him. O people in Zion, inhabitant in Jerusalem, you will weep no longer. He will surely be gracious to you at the sound of your cry; when He hears it, He will answer you.

Why did God choose Israel as His favorite nation? Was it because He loved Abraham, Isaac, and Jacob and had entered into a covenant with them? God gave the Holy Land, sometimes called Palestine (which is the center of the Earth, Ezek. 38:12), to Israel, as a permanent possession. She was thus placed on this small portion of the world, the bridge of the nations, in order that she might hold aloft the torch of the revelation of God to all nations of the Earth.

When Abraham and Sarah were beyond the age of childbearing, God performed a biological miracle on their bodies that made possible the birth of Isaac. This miracle is spoken of as an act of creation in such passages as Isaiah 43:1.

But now, thus says the Lord, your Creator, O Jacob,
And He who formed you, O Israel,
"Do not fear, for I have redeemed you;
I have called you by name; you are Mine!

God created Israel. When he did, He injected into the bloodstream of the Jewish race powers and capabilities, both intellectual and spiritual, that account for Israel's special religious endowment and her phenomenal contribution to the world in every realm of human activity and endeavor. The Greeks had a genius for the beautiful. They advanced the arts and sciences. The Romans had a knack for law, order, organization, and government. Thus, the Romans made their contribution to the world in the form of law, order, jurisprudence, government, and administration. On the other hand, the special contribution of the Jewish people is in the field of religion. Through Moses the Lawgiver they brought forward the Ten Commandments written by God. And Jesus was Jewish. It is difficult to understand why the Jewish people could believe in the miraculous birth of Isaac and yet reject the miraculous birth of Jesus. Of course, Jesus was born of a virgin, the only birth of its kind in history.

The Glory of God

The ultimate purpose of the universe is to show the glory of God. God created it all for His glory. Revelation 4:10-11 explains that truth:

The four and twenty elders fall down before him that sat on the throne, and worship him that liveth for ever and ever, and cast their crowns before the throne, saying, Thou art worthy, O Lord, to receive glory and honor and power: for thou hast created all things, and for thy pleasure they are and were created.

Without His glory there would be nothing. But what is the glory of God? It is His honor and dignity (1 Kings 3:13; Heb. 2:7; 1 Pet. 1:24; Ps. 19:1; 29:1). It is manifested in His splendor, brightness, and majesty (Gen. 45:13; Isa. 4:5; Acts 22:11; 2 Cor. 3:7) and it belongs to Him (Jehovah, Yahweh) alone (Isa. 59:19; 60:1; 2 Thess. 1:9). It is also reflected in His glorious moral attributes, His infinite perfections (Isa. 40:5; Acts 7:2; Rom. 1:23; 9:23; Eph. 1:12). Jesus is the "brightness of the Father's glory" (Heb. 1:3; John 1:14; 2:11). And it will be experienced in the bliss of Heaven (Rom. 2:7, 10; 5:2; 8:18; Heb. 2:10; 1 Pet. 5:1, 10).

Glory is who God is, the essence of His nature, the weight of His importance, the radiance of His splendor, the demonstration of His power, and the atmosphere of His patience. God's glory is the expression of His goodness and His other intrinsic, eternal qualities. And where is the glory of God. Simply look around. Everything created by Him, including the sun, the moon, and the stars, reflect His glory. We view it everywhere—from the smallest flower to the vast Milky Way, from sunsets and tides and changing seasons.

God's glory is what He possesses because He is God. The Psalmist exulted, "The heavens declare the glory of God; and the firmament sheweth his handywork" (Ps. 19:1, KJV). All of nature cries out, "God is great. He deserves all of the glory!"

Comments

God created a marvelous world. In spite of chaos in the world, still look at what is good. Not merely the stars at night, the full moon, the sunrise or the sunset. Have you ever considered the wonder of a hermit crab? Or an ant carrying crumbs ten times his size? Or the tiniest flower growing out of a crack in the concrete? Or the teeny sparrow who goes merrily about gathering his "daily bread"?

Focus on God's gift of freedom of choice. Be still and reverence God in His sovereignty. Yet, recognize that Satan and his angels are continually carrying on spiritual warfare. And ask God, through His Holy Spirit, to give you daily victory. We can't help that Adam sinned and introduced the sin nature into the human race, but thank Jesus that He died to remove the sin burden from us.

Believe in Jesus, confess your sins and commit to Him. As Jesus did in the wilderness, rebuke the devil, "Get thee hence, Satan: for it is written, Thou shalt worship the Lord thy God, and him only shalt thou serve" (Matt. 4:10, KJV). The devil is no match for a child of God plus the power of the Holy Spirit.

Remember that God deemed Abraham righteous because he had faith and obeyed God's will. God will grant us as righteous when we accept Jesus' sacrifice and invite Him into our lives. When we think of faith, also remember Noah. It required 120 years for him to build the ark. He was not close to an ocean, and it had never rained. Can you imagine the ridicule he received? However, he listened to God and exercised faith.

So, let us follow in the footsteps of those faithful witnesses.

CHAPTER 5

Christ Our Savior—Redeemer and Mediator

The fellowship between God and humanity was broken by the disobedience of one man, Adam. The human family, in the person of Adam, sinned (Rom. 5:12-13). What could God do to redeem and rescue humanity? Whatever He would do had to be in accordance with His righteousness, holiness, love, and truth. The loss had to be retrieved on the human level and in the realm of God's will.

Since one man sinned under God's government, one man would have to pay for mankind's sins. Who could that be? Who could possibly qualify? There had to be a mediator, a being who could intercede to God for man. God could have created another Adam, perfect and without sin, but since Adam was weak, the second creation would not have been able to withstand Satan. Could a descendant of Adam fill the bill? No! Man had transmitted his fallen nature to all of his descendants. No man was able to redeem his brother or himself. The person making the sacrifice had to be sinless.

Could a celestial creature redeem the race? If one of the angels had offered to champion man's cause and to fight it out with Satan, could he have defeated that enemy of God and humanity and accomplished man's deliverance? The battle had to be fought on the human plane and the realm of God's will. An angel could not have won the battle because Satan, the adversary, was the wisest and most powerful of all creatures under God's moral government. There was left only one avenue of redeeming the race—the God/man, One who could meet the demands of the broken law, who could do the will of God perfectly with reference to the problem of sin, and who could withstand the cunning and onslaughts of the devil.

Such a One would have to enter the human realm not by natural generation but in such a manner that He would not be tainted by the least trace of sin and be affected by Satan, so He could fulfill the demands of the law of God to the nth degree. God's only way was for the God/man to be born of a woman, without an earthly father being involved but through the Godhead's provision of the Holy Spirit's intervention. God would redeem the human family by bringing into the world a Baby by the miraculous virgin birth. We are not to understand it but to accept it because God has clearly revealed it in His Word, the Holy Bible.

Certainly God, who created Adam and breathed into his nostrils the breath of life in order that he became a living soul, could bring a Man into the world in such a supernatural manner. Because of this fact, it was necessary that one of the Divine Persons, who alone could circumvent Satan's diabolical maneuvering, would have to enter the human realm and champion man's cause.

> *Therefore the Lord Himself will give you a sign: Behold, a virgin will be with child and bear a son, and she will call His name Immanuel [meaning "God with us"]. . . . For a child will be born to us, a son will be given to us; And the government will rest on His shoulders; And His name will be called Wonderful Counselor, Mighty God, Eternal Father, Prince of Peace* (Isa. 7:14, 9:6).

God determined that He would create seed—pure, perfect, and holy—in the womb of the woman He chose to be the mother of the Messiah. The Redeemer could not have a human father, a member of the human race, for he would carry the taint of Adam's seed. The Baby would have to be more than a mere man. He would be God-man. There had to be a true, essential blood descent from Mary in order for the Lord Jesus to possess two vitally important factors: one prophetic and the other redemptive. He had to be a true blood descendant in order to be a prophetic son of David.

The Miraculous Virgin Birth

The angel Gabriel announced to the Virgin Mary that she would become the mother of the Messiah (God's "anointed One" in the line of David, the chosen One).

> *The angel said to her, "Do not be afraid, Mary; for you have found favor with God. "And behold, you will conceive in your womb and bear a son, and you shall name Him Jesus. "He will be great and will be called the Son of the Most High; and the Lord God will give Him the throne of His father David; and He will reign over the house of Jacob forever, and His kingdom will have no end." Mary said to the angel, "How can this be, since I am a virgin?"* (Luke 1:30-34).

Micah the prophet had foretold His coming, "But as for you, Bethlehem Ephrathah, Too little to be among the clans of Judah, From you One will go forth for Me to be ruler in Israel. His goings forth are from long ago, From the days of eternity" (5:2). The passage from Luke affirmed that the Virgin Mary would be overshadowed by the Holy Spirit, who would become the father of Jesus. Mary was honored as no other woman in history. Her Child would be totally free from sin. Jesus the Messiah stands on the historic horizon as the only spotless, sinless, perfect man ever, the God-man, "the Lamb of God, which taketh away the sin of the world" (John 1:29, KJV).

He is the Lord and Savior, the Mediator between God and man (the go-between, the bridge who joins them; see 1 Tim. 2:5). He Himself later declared, "I am the way, the truth, and the life: no man cometh unto the Father, but by me" (John 14:6, KJV). The living Word of God (see John 1:1-3), the second Person of the Trinity, the one and only Son of God entered the world through the virgin birth.

Why?

Because God loves mankind. "For God so loved the world, that He gave His only begotten Son, that whoever believes in Him shall not perish, but have eternal life" (John 3:16). Gabriel's message to Mary reinforced the prophecy of the Messiah's endless reign:

> *For a child will be born to us, a son will be given to us; And the government will rest on His shoulders; And His name will be*

called Wonderful Counselor, Mighty God, Eternal Father, Prince of Peace (Isa. 9:6).

He who departed from heaven's glory to assume human form out of His love for mankind offered Himself as a sacrifice for our salvation. The substitution of Himself to pay for our sins was the only acceptable method by which divine justice could be gratified. Jesus "is the propitiation (atonement, satisfaction) for our sins, and not for ours only but all for the whole world" (1 John 2:2, KJV).

The Nativity Story

In Luke's account of the events surrounding the Nativity (the birth of Jesus), God used angelic messengers to announce the birth of two notable persons. The first was John the Baptist. Jesus later declared that of those born to women, none was greater than John the Baptist (Matt. 1:11). The other is Jesus Himself who became flesh. The written Word of God makes it clear that in announcing these births God wanted to impact mankind with the importance of the word "believe."

When the angel of the Lord announced to Zacharias the priest that his prayer would be answered for his barren wife Elizabeth to give birth to a son (John), Zacharias doubted the heavenly messenger, even as Sarah laughed at the angels' prediction. Gabriel identified himself in a manner to emphasize the sin of a man who dares to question God's message: "I am Gabriel, who stands in the presence of God, and I have been sent to speak to you and to bring you this good news. And behold, you shall be silent and unable to speak until the day when these things take place, because you did not believe my words, which will be fulfilled in their proper time" (Luke 1:19-20).

The angel, of course, was giving the message on behalf of the Creator, who arranged the birth of the man who would introduce Jesus to Israel. John's mission would be to lift up the Messiah so people would "believe" in Him (John 1:7). The Virgin Mary, however, contrasted dramatically to Zacharias. When Gabriel informed her that she was chosen to conceive Jesus, she replied, "Let it be to me according to your word." The young woman believed God's message, and her faith was substantiated later when she visited Zacharias and Elizabeth's home. Elizabeth was filled with the Spirit and lauded Mary, "And blessed is she who believed that there would be a fulfillment of what had been spoken to her by the Lord" (Luke 1:45).

Mary was blessed; Zacharias was berated. She believed God's word; he did not. Those two persons symbolize the countless number of people who hear the message of God through the preaching and teaching of the gospel of grace. Some believe; many do not.

This book was written to convince the readers how important it is to believe the Word of God. Jesus warned about a sly enemy who wants no one to believe God. He expressed it through the Parable of the Sower.

> *The sower went out to sow his seed; and as he sowed, some fell beside the road, and it was trampled under foot and the birds of the air ate it up. Other seed fell on rocky soil, and as soon as it grew up, it withered away, because it had no moisture. Other seed fell among the thorns; and the thorns grew up with it and choked it out. Other seed fell into the good soil, and grew up, and produced a crop a hundred times as great. As He said these things, He would call out, "He who has ears to hear, let him hear." . . . Now the parable is this: the seed is the word of God. Those beside the road are those who have heard; then the devil comes and takes away the word from their heart, so that they will not believe and be saved* (Luke 8:5-8, 11-12).

So, Jesus had to explain the parable that warned them of the devil's ploys against men. This passage is highly educative. The devil wants to keep people from believing. In order to believe and have faith, a person must hear the Word of God, and the gospel is that Word.

> *How then shall they call on him in whom they have not believed? and how shall they believe in him of whom they have not heard? and how shall they hear without a preacher? And how shall they preach, except they be sent? as it is written, How beautiful are the feet of them that preach the gospel of peace, and bring glad tidings of good things! But they have not all obeyed the gospel. For Esaias saith, Lord, who hath believed our report? "So then faith cometh by hearing, and hearing by the word of God'* (Rom. 10:14-17, KJV).

Eternal Life Assured

You can know whether or not you have eternal life. Why? Because God's Holy Spirit bears witness and gives us internal assurance: "The Spirit Himself testifies ["bears witness," KJV] with our spirit that we are children of God" (Rom. 8:16). Those who claim they are not sure may in all likelihood not have that life. The Word of God teaches that the true believer has eternal life.

> *And the testimony is this, that God has given us eternal life, and this life is in His Son. He who has the Son has the life; he who does not have the Son of God does not have the life. These things I have written to you who believe in the name of the Son of God, so that you may know that you have eternal life* (1 John 5:11-13).

Persons who have believed the promises transmitted by God's Son through His apostles, and later by subsequent believers, are now on a peaceful journey that will end in the presence of the Lord Jesus. Life for them has new meaning (see 2 Cor. 5:17). Those who are in Christ are no longer terrified by death or tormented for sin. Although evil surrounds them in the world—and although they may fall prey to suffering and setbacks—nothing can be stolen from their eternal inheritance, because the resurrected Lord with all authority and glory has been crowned. He is now their Mediator, Redeemer, and High Priest.

Jesus Christ, Our Savior

In three realms the Lord Jesus Christ wrought eternal results:

On the cross
In hades
In His resurrection

On the cross

Jesus spoke of His death on the cross: "Now is the judgment of this world: now shall the prince of this world be cast out. And I, if I be lifted up from the earth, will draw all men unto me. This he said, signifying what death he should die" (John 12:32-33, KJV).

> *And Jesus answered them, saying, "The hour has come for the Son of Man to be glorified. Truly, truly, I say to you, unless a grain of wheat falls into the earth and dies, it remains alone; but if it dies, it bears much fruit. He who loves his life loses it, and he who hates his life in this world will keep it to life eternal. If anyone serves Me, he must follow Me; and where I am, there My servant will be also; if anyone serves Me, the Father will honor him. Now My soul has become troubled; and what shall I say, 'Father, save Me from this hour'? But for this purpose I came to this hour. "Father, glorify Your name." Then a voice came out of heaven: "I have both glorified it, and will glorify it again." . . . "Now judgment is upon this world; now the ruler of this world [the devil] will be cast out "* (John 12:23-28, 31).

Satan is the prince of this world who has retained permission to have his power a little longer. He has maintained a horrid hold on the world ever since Adam's fall. Presently he is the god of this world, but his sway will come to an ignominious end when he and his followers are cast into the lake of fire. "In whose case the god of this world has blinded the minds of the unbelieving so that they might not see the light of the gospel of the glory of Christ, who is the image of God (2 Cor. 4:4).

Though the devil was potentially conquered at the cross—and was divested of his absolute power over the world—he still exercises tremendous authority. But when Jesus conquered death by being resurrected, Satan no longer had power over death, and he was defeated.

As Jesus was on the cross, having taken upon Himself the sins of the world, God the Father and God the Holy Spirit turned their backs on Him. This was because of their holiness, for they cannot countenance sin in any shape or form, and Jesus had literally become sin for us. "He [God] made Him who knew no sin to be sin on our behalf, so that we might become the righteousness of God in Him" (2 Cor. 5:21). When He took our place, God the Father momentarily forsook Him, even though He was and is God's Son. At that point Deity paid the eternal penalty for man's sin and entered the chambers of death (OT: *sheol*) alone. There and then our Lord and Savior battled Satan and all of his hellish powers.

Yet, the Son of God, by faith, peered through the dark veil that separated Him from the Father and persevered. As He did, all the powers of the unseen world were marshaled against Him. By faith He won the victory over Satan and vanquished his army, disarming them as a conqueror on the field of battle.

On the cross of Calvary Jesus carried out the divine plan through which He can restore fellowship with God to all who accept His atoning sacrifice. His intense love and yearning desire for sinful men were evident, even in His dying agony on the cross when He cried out, "Father, forgive them, for they know not what they do" (Luke 23:34). Christ Jesus, the God-man, laid down His life on the cross, shedding His blood for our salvation. He accomplished the utter defeat of Satan and thus liberated mankind. In doing that He was "the Lamb of God, which taketh away the sin of the world" (John 1:29, KJV).

"In Hades"

Paul wrote in Ephesians 4:8-10 (KJV):

> *Wherefore he saith, When he [Jesus] ascended up on high, he led captivity captive, and gave gifts unto men. (Now that he ascended, what is it but that he also descended first into the lower parts of the earth [hades]? He that descended is the same also that ascended up far above all heavens, that he might fill all things.)*

When the Lord Jesus was put to death on the cross, His body was laid in the tomb, but His spirit descended to the place of departed spirits, referred to as *hades* in the New Testament (translated "hell" in the King James Version) and *sheol* (the grave) in the Old. When the Lord Jesus was released by death from self-imposed limitations of His mortal body, He again was free to exercise His unlimited powers, as He in His wisdom saw fit. When He, in the spirit, passed through the portal of death in the underworld, He abolished death, conquering him who had the power of death, Satan the devil.

This is so profound that most believers do not grasp it. In order to understand the significance of this, we must recall the fact that death primarily means separation from God, the source of all light and life, brought about as we have already seen, through physical death as well as breaking of man's fellowship with God, which culminates in spiritual death. At the end of the millennium, the last vestiges of Satan's power will be destroyed. The last enemy that shall be abolished is death. "For he must reign, till he hath put all enemies under his feet. The last enemy that shall be destroyed is death" (1 Cor. 15:25-26, KJV).

When Jesus cried on the cross, "It is finished," He entered hades and seized the keys of death and hades (hell) from Satan. He put a robe of righteousness around all of the departed who had trusted God. Then He opened the paradise side of hades, where Satan had held them captive, and led them forth to heaven.

In the Resurrection

When Jesus came back from sheol, His spirit re-entered and immortalized His physical body that had been lying in the tomb, He emerged as the glorified Redeemer. When Christ ascended on high, He led away those who had been held captive in sheol. They marched in His triumphal procession into glory! When He re-entered the portals of glory, He sat down on the right hand of the Majesty on high as our Mediator.

Since He conquered Satan and his cohorts, abolished death, and brought life and immortality through the gospel, He had made this provision. When believers die physically, their spirits will go immediately into the presence of God, though their bodies will be separated and await the resurrection. Paul exclaimed: "We are confident, I say, and willing rather to be absent from the body, and to be present with the Lord" (2 Cor. 5:8, KJV).

Jesus' Resurrection—Crucially Important

If our Lord's body had remained in the tomb, there would have been no resurrection for anyone. He "was delivered for our offences, and was raised again for our justification" (Rom. 4:25). In the great resurrection chapter, 1 Corinthians 15, Paul shows that the basis of Christianity is indeed the resurrection of Jesus Christ. His coming forth from the tomb is a guarantee and pledge of our resurrection and fellowship with Him and with the saved throughout eternity.

> *Now if Christ be preached that he rose from the dead, how say some among you that there is no resurrection of the dead? But if there be no resurrection of the dead, then is Christ not risen: And if Christ be not risen, then is our preaching in vain, and your faith is also vain. Yea, and we are found false witnesses of God; because we have testified of God that he raised up Christ: whom he raised*

> *not up, if so be that the dead rise not. For if the dead rise not, then is not Christ raised: And if Christ be not raised, your faith is vain; ye are yet in your sins. Then they also which are fallen asleep in Christ are perished. If in this life only we have hope in Christ, we are of all men most miserable. But now is Christ risen from the dead, and become the firstfruits of them that slept. For since by man came death, by man came also the resurrection of the dead. For as in Adam all die, even so in Christ shall all be made alive* (1 Cor. 15:12-22, KJV).

> *And so it is written, The first man Adam was made a living soul; the last Adam was made a quickening spirit. Howbeit that was not first which is spiritual, but that which is natural; and afterward that which is spiritual. The first man is of the earth, earthy: the second man is the Lord from heaven* (1 Cor. 15:45-48, KJV).

He is able to impart eternal, spiritual life to all who will come to Him and trust Him. His resources, spiritual and otherwise, are unlimited. His power is infinite, and His grace and mercy are boundless. "Therefore He is able also to save forever those who draw near to God through Him, since He always lives to make intercession for them" (Heb. 7:25). He does nothing halfway.

Jesus Existed from the Beginning

The Prologue to the Gospel of John (1:1-18) is one of the most profound statements of Christ's existence in the Word of God. He existed in the beginning, in the eternity prior to the creation of the universe.

> *In the beginning was the Word, and the Word was with God, and the Word was God. He was in the beginning with God. All things came into being through Him, and apart from Him nothing came into being that has come into being* (John 1:1-3).

He is God and is Deity in every sense of the Word. He was the Creator of the universe. In Him was light and life. All living things owe their existence to Him. He was the Light shining in the darkness of the ages past, but men were unable to grasp or understand Him. John the Baptist was sent by God to testify of Him (v. 6). This Word (v. 9) was the true light. Any truth in this world is because of Him. Though He was performing His mission, the world did not know Him (v. 10). He came to His own flesh and blood, the Jews, who should have recognized Him but did not (v. 11). "But as many as received Him, to them He gave the right to become children of God, even to those who believe in His name, who were born, not of blood nor of the will of the flesh nor of the will of man, but of God" (John 1:12-13). That means all of us—if only we will accept Him and have faith in Him.

The Gospel of Matthew presented the genealogy of Jesus, His royal lineage through David back to Abraham. Following that, Matthew gave an account of Jesus' birth (1:18-25), already pointed out in this chapter of my book. Matthew affirmed the virgin birth in fulfillment of prophecy (Matt. 1:23). The God of glory became a Babe in Bethlehem. He laid aside the glory He had with the Father before the foundations of the world (John 17:5). He assumed the form of man that He might redeem us. We must bear in mind, though, that He did not divest Himself of His essential nature. That would have been impossible. He was as much God after He entered human form as He was before. One of the most stirring pictures of the pre-incarnate Word is in Colossians 1:14-18:

> *In whom we have redemption, the forgiveness of sins. He is the image of the invisible God, the firstborn of all creation. For by Him all things were created, both in the heavens and on earth, visible and invisible, whether thrones or dominions or rulers or authorities—all things have been created through Him and for Him. He is before all things, and in Him all things hold together. He is also head of the body, the church; and He is the beginning, the firstborn from the dead, so that He Himself will come to have first place in everything.*

He was the image, the reflection of, the invisible God and the firstborn of all creation. He was the firstborn, not in the sense that He was created, but in His having the preeminence, first place above all others. Only Deity could accomplish what He did. His uniqueness as the God-man is also seen in Philippians 2:5-11:

> *Have this attitude in yourselves which was also in Christ Jesus, who, although He existed in the form of God, did not regard*

equality with God a thing to be grasped, but emptied Himself, taking the form of a bond-servant, and being made in the likeness of men. Being found in appearance as a man, He humbled Himself by becoming obedient to the point of death, even death on a cross. For this reason also, God highly exalted Him, and bestowed on Him the name which is above every name, so that at the name of Jesus every knee will bow, of those who are in heaven and on earth and under the earth, and that every tongue will confess that Jesus Christ is Lord, to the glory of God the Father.

The Four Accounts of Jesus' Life and Ministry

According to the Law of Moses, everything that arose for consideration in the courts of Israel was to be testified to by two or three witnesses (Deut. 17:6; 19:15). This regulation set the precedent for the establishment of facts. If more could testify, of course they were not excluded from giving evidence. In line with this, God has gifted us with the testimony of His servants through the centuries—in both the Old and New testaments. God carried this over to the writers, often called "The Evangelists," of the first five books of the New Testament, the Gospels, which chronicle the life and ministry of our Lord and Savior, Jesus Christ.

MATTHEW: The author of this book was no doubt the Matthew (or Levi), an apostle of our Lord, whose name it bears. As to its time of writing, there is little in the Gospel itself to indicate. It was probably written before the destruction of Jerusalem and a while after the events it records. It was probably written between 60 and 65 A.D.

It is apparent that this Gospel was written for Jewish Christians of Palestine. Matthew's supreme purpose was to prove that Jesus of Nazareth was the promised Messiah, and that in Him the ancient prophecies had their fulfilment. The Gospel is filled with references to those Old Testament passages in which Christ is predicted and foreshadowed. The one overriding aim running through the entire Book is to show that Jesus is he "of whom Moses in the law and the prophets did write."

This Gospel contains no less than 65 references to the Old Testament; 43 of those are word-for-word citations, far more than those found in the other Gospels. The dominant characteristic of this Gospel is summed up in Jesus' expression, "I am not come to destroy, but to fulfil."

The leading characteristic of this Gospel is that it extols the kingly glory of Christ and reveals Him as the true heir to David's throne. It is the Gospel of the kingdom. Matthew uses the expression "kingdom of heaven" (32 times), while Luke employs the expression "kingdom of God" (33 times). Some forms from Latin occur in this Gospel, and it must be remembered that Matthew was a tax collector for the Roman government and thus conversant with Latin.

As the Gospels relate to one another, it is maintained that each writer of the Synoptics (Matthew, Mark, and Luke) wrote independently of the other two. From a total of 1071 verses, Matthew has 387 in common with Mark and Luke, 130 with Mark, 184 with Luke, and only 387 being peculiar to itself. The book is divided into these four parts: 1. Containing the genealogy, the birth, and the infancy of Jesus (Chapters 1—2); 2. The messages and actions of John the Baptist prior to Christ's public ministry (Chapters 3—4:11); 3. The messages and ministry of Christ in Galilee (Chapters 4:12—20:16); and 4. The sufferings, death, and resurrection of our Lord (Chapters 20:17—28:20).

Throughout this record Matthew assumed on the part of his readers a knowledge of and acceptance of the Old Testament as the absolute Word of God. He presented Jesus of Nazareth as being of the royal lineage and heir to the throne of his forefather in the flesh, David. He also recognized Him as "the Son of man," which is no doubt a reference back to Daniel 7:13-14.

> *I kept looking in the night visions, And behold, with the clouds of heaven One like a Son of Man was coming, And He came up to the Ancient of Days And was presented before Him. And to Him was given dominion, Glory and a kingdom, That all the peoples, nations and men of every language Might serve Him. His dominion is an everlasting dominion Which will not pass away; And His kingdom is one Which will not be destroyed.*

This was by all means a Messianic title. An examination of it as it appears in the Synoptics confirms this fact. The Son of God, who is also "A Son of Man" or "The Son of Man," is the Messiah, the Anointed One of Israel. Matthew is exactly the kind of book that would be written by a devout Jew of the first century. Matthew set out to prove the Messiahship of the Lord Jesus—and did it superbly, as directed by the Holy Spirit.

Simon Peter affirmed to the Lord Jesus: "Thou art the Christ [Messiah], the Son of the living God" (Matt. 16:16, KJV). Such a statement demonstrated the fact that the Jews of the first century believed the Messiah to be the Son of God. The Jews seemed to understand the nature and person of the Messiah: i.e., that He would be God in human form, and they were expecting His advent at that time. What they did not process was that He would suffer and die at His first coming. Yet, Isaiah had plainly predicted the Suffering Servant (see Isa. 53, for instance).

They were anticipating a victorious Messiah who would crush the Roman occupation and establish Israel as the preeminent nation on Earth. Why, then, didn't they expect Him to suffer and die at that time as the prophets had foretold? We must recognize that there were four types of Messianic prophecy. One dealt with His first coming only; the second with His second coming altogether; the third blending together elements of the first and second comings; and the fourth giving the entire scope of the Messiah's ministry. Because of the oppression they had undergone, they focused only on the elements of what we consider as the second coming.

When Jesus was crucified the apostles gave up hope. His resurrection, however, made all of the difference. In his First Epistle, Peter exclaimed, "Blessed be the God and Father of our Lord Jesus Christ, who according to His great mercy has caused us to be born again to a living hope through the resurrection of Jesus Christ from the dead" (1 Pet. 1:3). Because the rabbis had this distorted view of His work, the nation turned away from Him and rejected His message.

MARK: Each Gospel account gives a portrait of Jesus' mission and teaching; each of the four is different in style, length, and emphasis. They all have the same common thread and purpose—the proclamation of the good news of Jesus Christ. Among the Gospels, Mark's is unusual from several aspects.

It is the shortest and is probably the earliest. Both Luke and Matthew seem to depend on part of Mark's text, of course being led by the Holy Spirit. Luke's Gospel contains over half of the verses from Mark's account (some 350 verses out of a total 660 verses in Mark). Mark opens his narrative account with Jesus' public ministry and the mission of John the Baptist. He makes it abundantly plain as to who Jesus was. Immediately he stated, "The beginning of the gospel of Jesus Christ, the Son of God" (1:1). Jesus was not merely a man among men but

One who created tremendous amazement among those who encountered Him.

> *"They were amazed at His teaching; for He was teaching them as one having authority, and not as the scribes"* (1:22).
>
> *"They were all amazed, so that they debated among themselves, saying, 'What is this? A new teaching with authority! He commands even the unclean spirits, and they obey Him'"* (1:27).
>
> *"Then He got into the boat with them, and the wind stopped; and they were utterly astonished"* (6:51).
>
> *"The disciples were amazed at His words. But Jesus answered again and said to them, 'Children, how hard it is to enter the kingdom of God!'"* (10:24).

People were amazed and utterly astonished. Mark depicts Jesus' Deity and humanity. Mark relates that Jesus is "the carpenter" (6:3), but Matthew writes that Jesus is the "carpenter's son" (13:55). Mark speaks about Jesus' emotions. He was moved with "compassion" (6:34); he "sighed" (7:34; 8:12); he "marveled" at the unbelief of His own people (6:6); and he "looked" upon the rich young man and "loved him" (10:21).

Mark also gave graphic details the other Gospel writers omitted. For instance, he describes Jesus' tenderness as he took the little children "in his arms and blessed them, laying his hands upon them" (10:16). On another occasion Mark describes Jesus "asleep on a cushion" in the stern of the boat as the apostles feared for their lives when caught in the storm at sea (4:38). The word "again" is employed 26 times which would remind the hearers of an earlier occasion when an event happened. Mark's Gospel is more straightforward in language, even blunt at times. For example, Mark reports: "When His own people heard of this, they went out to take custody of Him; for they were saying, 'He has lost His senses'" (Mark 3:21). In other words, some of them thought he was insane—crazy.

Mark shows Jesus in undelayed action. In chapter 1 the reader becomes aware of Jesus' urgent mission. The word "immediately" is employed no less than eight times. For example, Mark wrote that the

"Spirit immediately drove him out into the wilderness" (1:12). "And immediately he called them" (1:20); "and immediately on the sabbath he entered the synagogue and taught" (1:21).

Mark is referred to some eight times in the New Testament. He was the cousin of Barnabas (Col. 4:10). When the Apostle Paul penned his letter to the Colossians from his prison in Rome, he mentioned that Mark was there with him (Col. 4:10). He also noted in his letter to Philemon that Mark was one of his fellow workers (Philem. 24). Peter called him "my son Mark" (1 Pet. 5:13). It is possible that Peter led Mark to Christ and reared him in the faith. Mark was an associate of Peter and may have written his Gospel in Rome where Peter was based. As did the other Gospel writers, Mark composed it in Greek, the literary language of the day. It was no doubt written for Gentile readers, and more especially for the Christians in Rome.

Mark emphasized Jesus as "Teacher" and as the "Servant of God." Jesus was often called "Teacher" by His disciples (4:38) and by those who desired His aid (5:35). He also utilized the Hebrew form of teacher, "Rabbi" (9:5), though he gave little of Jesus' teaching compared with Luke and Matthew. Mark basically pointed to what Jesus did—for instance, Jesus' endless work and power over sickness, disease, death, and the bane of evil spirits.

Mark often used triads—groups of three—to stress his points: three boat scenes with the disciples (4:35, 6:45, 8:14); three prophecies of His death; and three commands to "keep awake and watch" (8:31, 9:31, 10:32-34), paralleled by the three times the exhausted disciples are mentioned as sleeping. Peter denied Jesus three times; Pilate asked the crowd three questions; and there are three time references at the crucifixion (the third, sixth, and ninth hours in chapter 15). All of these usages emphasize the immediacy of Jesus' task and mission.

He spoke nothing about the virgin birth, perhaps because the Romans were not especially interested in the subject. He wanted to reveal Jesus as a man of action, who ministered to the masses of the common people. This short narrative of our Lord's life grips those who wish to access the facts in the shortest space and time. As Joe Friday of TV fame put it, "Just the facts, Ma'am."

LUKE: The Evangelist was a Gentile. The date and circumstances of his conversion are unknown. It is probable that he was a physician in Troas, and was there won to the Lord by Paul. He became attached to Paul as physician and fellow missionary. He accompanied him to Philippi but did not there share Paul's imprisonment. He did not accompany Paul further in his missionary journey at that time (see Acts 17:1). On Paul's third visit to Philippi (Acts 20:5-6), Luke is again introduced. He had more than likely spent all the intervening time in that city—a time of seven or eight years.

From that juncture forward Luke was Paul's constant companion during his journey to Jerusalem (20:6—21:18). He dropped out of sight during Paul's imprisonment at Jerusalem and Caesarea but reappeared when Paul set out for Rome (27:1) where he accompanied him (28:2, 12–16), and where he remained with him until the close of his first imprisonment (Philemon 1:24; Col. 4:14). The last notice of the "beloved physician" was in 2 Timothy 4:11. Biblical scholars agree that Luke wrote both the Gospel and the Acts, often called "The Acts of the Apostles." The "we" passages of Acts reveal when Luke was in Paul's company.

He did not claim to be an eyewitness of Jesus' ministry, but he had first-hand involvement in Paul's missions. He considered the best sources, under the Spirit's leadership, in writing an orderly account of our Lord's ministry (Luke 1:1-4). The authors of the first three Gospels, the Synoptics, wrote independently of each other.

Luke's Gospel has been referred to as the Gospel of the nations; the Gospel of the saintly life; the Gospel for the Greeks; the Gospel of the future; the Gospel of progressive Christianity; the historic Gospel; the Gospel of Jesus as the good Physician and the Savior of mankind; the Gospel of the outcast, of the Samaritan, the publican, the harlot, and the prodigal; and the Gospel of tolerance. The main attribute of this Gospel is aptly put forth in Acts 10:38: "You know of Jesus of Nazareth, how God anointed Him with the Holy Spirit and with power, and how He went about doing good and healing all who were oppressed by the devil, for God was with Him" (see also Luke 4:18).

Out of a total of 1,151 verses, Luke contains 389 in common with Matthew and Mark, 176 in common with Matthew alone. From all evidence, it appears that Luke had a particular appeal to the Greeks, representing the Gentiles. He presented Jesus as the perfect man. He recognized, too, that He was the God-man. In His Prologue (1:1-4) he explained: "Inasmuch as many have undertaken to compile an account of the things accomplished among us, just as they were handed down to us by those who from the beginning were eyewitnesses and servants of the word, it seemed fitting for me as well, having investigated everything carefully from the beginning, to write it out for you in consecutive order, most excellent Theophilus; so that you may know the exact truth about the things you have been taught."

Whether Theophilus (meaning "lover of God" in Greek) was an actual person, or representative of lovers of God, we are not sure. Thus, Luke drew up, in an orderly narrative, a powerful account of the Lord Jesus' life. He pointed out why he wrote, his procedure, and his ultimate object. When one compares Luke with Mark, it is seen that both of these Gospels are in chronological order. Luke starts out with the birth narrative and genealogy of Jesus, which he carries clear back to Adam. He relates the miraculous virgin birth of Jesus but does not tie it to Old Testament prophecy, for he may not have had a Hebrew audience in mind. Since Jesus was begotten of the Holy Spirit, and was born of the virgin, the portrait appearing throughout the Book confirms to the facts of chapters 1 and 2.

Some commentators have called the Gospel of Luke the most beautiful book ever written; others have spoken the same about the Gospel of John. In chapters 9:51—18:34, Luke presents a treasure trove of information not given by the other Gospel writers. His account of the last week of our Lord's life is of inestimable value.

JOHN: John the Evangelist (and author of this Gospel and the Epistles of 1, 2, and 3 John) was one of Jesus' original apostles, as was his brother James. They were the sons of Zebedee and before their conversion were called "the sons of thunder," perhaps because of their violent temperament. A close examination of this Gospel shows that John's aim was to reveal Jesus Christ as the God-man. His Prologue (chapter 1:1-18) is a virtual textbook of Christology. He supplemented the material left uncovered by the other three Gospels, the Synoptics. Notice the overwhelming power of 1:1-3:

> *In the beginning was the Word [Jesus Christ], and the Word was with God, and the Word was God. He was in the beginning with God. All things came into being through Him, and apart from Him nothing came into being that has come into being.*

What was lightly touched upon by the Synoptics is boldly asserted by John. The Spirit of God led John to record Jesus' amazing discourses He delivered to the authorities in Jerusalem. Those centered around His person and His claim to being the Son of God and God Himself. Prominent among His declarations was John 14:6:

> *Jesus said to him, "I am the way, and the truth, and the life; no one comes to the Father but through Me."*

John stressed not so much what Jesus did as Who He was. Our Lord was and is holy and righteous, the only man in history without sin. John viewed Him as the perfect Lamb of God. Another John, the Baptist, cried out, "Behold the lamb of God that taketh away the sin of the world" (John 1:29, KJV). "For it was fitting for us to have such a high priest, holy, innocent, undefiled, separated from sinners and exalted above the heavens; who does not need daily, like those high priests, to offer up sacrifices, first for His own sins and then for the sins of the people, because this He did once for all when He offered up Himself (Heb. 7:26-27).

In this passage the apostle asserted that Christ as a man was holy, guileless, undefiled, and separated from sinners—higher than the heavens. The only interpretation of this must be that Jesus Christ was different from all other people. He entered the world differently in that He was begotten by the Holy Spirit who moved through a virgin. He had no sin in the flesh; neither did He ever commit sin. However, He became identified with our sins in His sufferings on the cross. "For He [God the Father] made Him [God the Son, Jesus] who knew no sin to be sin on our behalf, so that we might become the righteousness of God in Him" (2 Cor. 5:21). The Apostle John in his first Epistle (3:5) wrote: "You know that He [Jesus] appeared in order to take away sins; and in Him there is no sin."

These and other passages prove conclusively that Jesus of Nazareth was the only man in history without sin. He was apart from all sin. He is on a plane infinitely higher than all other men. Let us focus on John 1:1-3 that plainly calls the Word [Jesus] God. He was and is God but also God incarnate, in the flesh. "And the Word became flesh, and dwelt among us, and we saw His glory, glory as of the only begotten from the Father, full of grace and truth. No one has seen God at any time; the only begotten God who is in the bosom of the Father, He has explained Him" (John 1:14, 18).

The psalmist in a vision, upon viewing the Messiah, praised Him:

"You are fairer than the sons of men; Grace is poured upon Your lips; Therefore God has blessed You forever" (Ps. 45:2). The psalmist beheld the Messiah in His unique character, and he could not classify Him with the sons of men. He is the spotless Lamb of God.

Statements About Christ's Human Nature

His Body

That Christ had an actual human body is seen from John's record that the Word became flesh. "Flesh" there meant His actual human body consisting of flesh and bones. He "dwelt among us," meaning that He had a real body. He did not merely "seem" to exist in flesh, as certain false teachers, called Gnostics, contended in the first century (also see 1 John 1:1-4). It is a heresy not only to reject His Deity but a heresy to dispute His manhood. John pointedly refuted the Gnostics in his Epistles of 1, 2, and 3 John.

> *By this you know the Spirit of God: every spirit that confesses that Jesus Christ has come in the flesh is from God; and every spirit that does not confess Jesus is not from God; this is the spirit of the antichrist, of which you have heard that it is coming, and now it is already in the world* (1 John 4:2-3).

His Spirit

That Jesus had a human spirit is evident from this statement: "And Jesus kept increasing in wisdom and stature, and in favor with God and men" (Luke 2:52). According to this quotation, Jesus advanced in wisdom, as well as growing in physical stature. His increase of wisdom and stature could only have been in the arena of the human spirit. Further proof of His human spirit is seen in his statement to three of His disciples: "My soul is exceeding sorrowful, even unto death: abide ye here, and watch with me" (Matt. 26:38, KJV).

Pay attention to the following:

> *When Jesus therefore saw her weeping, and the Jews who came with her also weeping, He was deeply moved in spirit and was troubled, and said, "Where have you laid him?" They said to Him, "Lord, come and see." Jesus wept. So the Jews were saying, "See how He loved him!"* (John 11:33-36).

Jesus was deeply moved {"groaned," KJV) in His spirit and wept. This is another proof of His human spirit. John 12:27 further enforces this fact: "Now My soul has become troubled; and what shall I say, 'Father, save Me from this hour'? But for this purpose I came to this hour." Jesus had a human spirit as well as a human body.

The Man Christ Jesus

Before the condemning crowd Pontius Pilate pointed to Jesus and declared, "Behold, the Man!" (John 19:5). Jesus spoke of Himself not only as a man but also the Son of Man. The leaders had become enraged against Him to the point they wanted to kill Him. He answered them, "But now ye seek to kill me, a man that hath told you the truth, which I heard from God: this did not Abraham" (John 8:40). If He were not a man in a proper sense, He would not have used that language in reference to Himself. What constitutes a real man? Spirit and body.

On the Day of Pentecost Peter preached to a massive audience (see Acts 2). He proclaimed:

> *Men of Israel, listen to these words: Jesus the Nazarene, a man attested to you by God with miracles and wonders and signs which God performed through Him in your midst, just as you yourselves know—this Man, delivered over by the predetermined plan and foreknowledge of God, you nailed to a cross by the hands of godless men and put Him to death* (Acts 2:22-23).

He and the apostles recognized Him as a man but more than a mere man. He was and is The Man. He was thoroughly human but apart from sin. At the same time He was and is God, in the fullest sense of the term. The union of the divine with the human constituted Him as the spiritual Head of a new race, the redeemed, born-again, saved people (see 1 Cor. 15:45). He is a life-giving spirit. Thus, by the union of the divine and human in Him, He is the Giver of eternal life. He communicates His own spiritual life to those who accept Him as Lord and Savior.

Isaiah no doubt had this in mind when he stated that the Messiah would be called "the everlasting Father" (Isa. 9:6). In Revelation 22:16 speaks of Himself not merely as the offspring of David but as the root of David, the one from whom David derived His life. Jesus declared that He gave life to those whom He would (John 5:21). He referred to Himself as the vine and His followers as branches. "Abide in Me, and I in you. As the branch cannot bear fruit of itself unless it abides in the vine, so neither can you unless you abide in Me. I am the vine, you are the branches; he who abides in Me and I in him, he bears much fruit, for apart from Me you can do nothing" (John 15:4-5). His disciples derive their life from Him.

It is not sufficient for us to have an intellectual understanding of these magnificent truths about Jesus Christ of Nazareth, the God-man. He extends life to one and all. As lost sinners, we must come to Him in humility and trust Him as our Lord and Savior. Then we will have eternal life. "The thief comes only to steal and kill and destroy; I came that they may have life, and have it abundantly" (John 10:10). The apostle Paul in Romans 5:15 penned: "But the free gift is not like the transgression. For if by the transgression of the one the many died, much more did the grace of God and the gift by the grace of the one Man, Jesus Christ, abound to the many." "The one Man, Jesus Christ." To Timothy he wrote, "For there is one God, and one mediator also between God and men, the man Christ Jesus" (1 Tim. 2:5). The apostles considered Jesus as a man, The Man, perfect in every particular.

The Word of God reveals Jesus as a normal human being, acting and reacting to people and circumstances as a man does, only without sin and spot. He became hungry (Matt. 4:2); thirsty (John 19:28); and weary (John 4:6). He needed sleep (Matt. 8:24). He looked upon a young man and loved Him, even as He loves us all (Mark 10:21). He was "moved with compassion" (Matt. 9:36, KJV). At Nazareth He looked upon His hearers with righteous indignation because He was smitten with the hardness of their hearts (Mark 3:5). Throughout His life He made pleadings and prayers to the Father with tears and groanings (Heb. 5:7).

As He neared the cross, His holy being recoiled from it, and He prayed, "Now My soul has become troubled; and what shall I say, 'Father, save Me from this hour'? But for this purpose I came to this hour" (John 12:27). In the Garden of Gethsemane, He poured out His soul before the disciples and the Heavenly Father:

> *Then saith he unto them, My soul is exceeding sorrowful, even unto death: tarry ye here, and watch with me. And he went a little further, and fell on his face, and prayed, saying, O my Father, if it*

> *be possible, let this cup pass from me: nevertheless not as I will, but as thou wilt* (Matt. 26:38-39, KJV).

From these instances and numerous others, we recognize that our Lord was a man, perfect in every particular.

Expressions of Christ's Divine Nature

We have seen ample evidence of Jesus' being God in human form. John 1:1-18 might be called "The Biography of the Living Word." He was with God and was and is God. As we have learned from the Old Testament He often appeared to the patriarchs—I. e., Abraham, Isaac, Jacob, Joseph, Moses—as "the angel of Jehovah." He was God's one and only "begotten," who is the embodiment of grace and truth. He is the incarnation of truth.

I would direct you to three brilliant passages that speak of His divine nature: Philippians 2:5-11; Colossians 1:14-17; and Hebrews chapter 1.

The Death of Jesus

The major note of the atonement, Christ's saving death on the cross, was sounded by John the Baptist: "Behold the lamb of God that taketh away the sin of the world" (John 1:29). Christ is the great Sin-bearer of the world. Many so-called believers have tended to tone down their preaching and teaching concerning Christ's substitutionary death for us. Liberals have called this doctrine "a gospel of gore," "a bloodthirsty aberration," and even worse. Yet, Christ's death on the cross and His resurrection from the dead are the core, the essence of Christianity. Without those all mankind is sunk!

According to Isaiah 53:10, Jehovah the Father was pleased to bruise King Messiah and to put Him to grief. "But the Lord was pleased To crush Him, putting Him to grief; He would render Himself as a guilt offering, He will see His offspring, He will prolong His days, And the good pleasure of the Lord will prosper in His hand."

On the Day of Pentecost, Peter preached to a huge throng and proclaimed

> *Men of Israel, listen to these words: Jesus the Nazarene, a man attested to you by God with miracles and wonders and signs which*

> *God performed through Him in your midst, just as you yourselves know—this Man, delivered over by the predetermined plan and foreknowledge of God, you nailed to a cross by the hands of godless men and put Him to death* (Acts 2:22-23).

Before the foundation of the world, the Godhead—Father, Son, and Holy Spirit—planned for the Son to offer His life as a sacrifice for mankind's sin. Peter later wrote in his First Epistle:

> *. . . but with precious blood, as of a lamb unblemished and spotless, the blood of Christ. For He was foreknown before the foundation of the world, but has appeared in these last times for the sake of you* (1 Pet. 1:19-20).

Although the Jewish leaders and the Roman officials had a hand in His crucifixion, so did you and I. The apostle John summed it up:

> *My little children, I am writing these things to you so that you may not sin. And if anyone sins, we have an Advocate with the Father, Jesus Christ the righteous; and He Himself is the propitiation for our sins; and not for ours only, but also for those of the whole world. By this we know that we have come to know Him, if we keep His commandments* (1 John 2:1-3).

The Messiah was rejected by Israel, His own people in the flesh.

> *He came to His own, and those who were His own did not receive Him. But as many as received Him, to them He gave the right to become children of God, even to those who believe in His name, who were born, not of blood nor of the will of the flesh nor of the will of man, but of God* (John 1:11-13).

The leaders in the rejection of the Messiah acted in blind ignorance, but that was still no excuse. They considered Jesus an imposter who would have led the nation astray. As He died on the cross, He prayed, "Father, forgive them; for they know not what they do" (Luke 23:34, KJV). The apostle Peter stated to an audience in Jerusalem: "And now, brethren, I know that you acted in ignorance, just as your rulers did also" (Acts 3:17). In Antioch of Pisidia, Paul proclaimed essentially the same:

> *For they that dwell at Jerusalem, and their rulers, because they knew him not, nor yet the voices of the prophets which are read every sabbath day, they have fulfilled them in condemning him. And though they found no cause of death in him, yet desired they Pilate that he should be slain. And when they had fulfilled all that was written of him, they took him down from the tree, and laid him in a sepulchre. But God raised him from the dead* (Acts 13:27-30, KJV).

When Jesus established the Lord's Supper, He made it plain that our salvation is tied to the shedding of His blood:

> *While they were eating, Jesus took some bread, and after a blessing, He broke it and gave it to the disciples, and said, "Take, eat; this is My body. And when He had taken a cup and given thanks, He gave it to them, saying, "Drink from it, all of you; for this is My blood of the covenant, which is poured out for many for forgiveness of sins"* (Matt. 26:26-28).

Every time our Lord spoke of His death on our behalf, He presented this truth as cause and effect.

> *And He said to them, '"Thus it is written, that the Christ would suffer and rise again from the dead the third day, and that repentance for forgiveness of sins would be proclaimed in His name to all the nations, beginning from Jerusalem"* (Luke 24:46-47).

At Jesus' Transfiguration, when the glory of God enveloped Him, the Heavenly Father expressed His approval: "This is my beloved Son, in whom I am well pleased" (Matt. 17:5; see the same expression in Matt. 3:17). God repeatedly showed His approval of His only begotten Son, Jesus, through signs, wonders, and miracles. Despite Jesus' credentials, the religious leaders rejected Him and turned Him over to the Roman executioners. Peter preached on the Day of Pentecost:

> *Ye men of Israel, hear these words; Jesus of Nazareth, a man approved of God among you by miracles and wonders and signs,*

> *which God did by him in the midst of you, as ye yourselves also know: Him, being delivered by the determinate counsel and foreknowledge of God, ye have taken, and by wicked hands have crucified and slain* (Acts 2:22-23, KJV).

Those leaders were simply carrying out God's providential plans from the foundation of the world. Wicked men often help accomplish God's will and have no idea they are doing it. As J. B. Gambrell, a Baptist leader, expressed it: "God hits straight licks with crooked sticks." Yes, they are still held accountable for their deeds, but God makes their evil actions contribute to the advancement of His cause. Though Christ was delivered up to death, He would not remain in that condition. I repeat Peter's affirmation: "And when they had fulfilled all that was written of him, they took him down from the tree, and laid him in a sepulchre. But God raised him from the dead" (see Acts 13:27-30, KJV). God raised Him from the dead!

After His resurrection Jesus appeared ten recorded times to different ones of His disciples (1 Cor. 15:1-8). The apostle John exclaimed:

> *What was from the beginning, what we have heard, what we have seen with our eyes, what we have looked at and touched with our hands, concerning the Word of Life—and the life was manifested, and we have seen and testify and proclaim to you the eternal life, which was with the Father and was manifested to us—what we have seen and heard we proclaim to you also, so that you too may have fellowship with us; and indeed our fellowship is with the Father, and with His Son Jesus Christ. These things we write, so that our joy may be made complete* (1 John 1:1-4).

The early disciples were emboldened by the power of their Lord's resurrection. They were ready to lay down their lives, and many of them did. Jesus was seen by chosen witnesses. In Peter's second recorded sermon (in Acts 3) he identified Jesus as "the servant of Jehovah" of whom Isaiah prophesied.

> *The God of Abraham, Isaac and Jacob, the God of our fathers, has glorified His servant Jesus, the one whom you delivered and disowned in the presence of Pilate, when he had decided to release Him. But you disowned the Holy and Righteous One and asked for*

> *a murderer [Barabbas] to be granted to you, but put to death the Prince of life, the one whom God raised from the dead, a fact to which we are witnesses. And on the basis of faith in His name, it is the name of Jesus which has strengthened this man whom you see and know; and the faith which comes through Him has given him this perfect health in the presence of you all* (Acts 3:13-16).

The Servant of Isaiah 53 is none other than King Messiah, who makes His soul an offering for the sins of many. Later Peter wrote in his First Epistle:

> *If you address as Father the One who impartially judges according to each one's work, conduct yourselves in fear during the time of your stay on earth; knowing that you were not redeemed with perishable things like silver or gold from your futile way of life inherited from your forefathers, but with precious blood, as of a lamb unblemished and spotless, the blood of Christ. For He was foreknown before the foundation of the world, but has appeared in these last times for the sake of you who through Him are believers in God, who raised Him from the dead and gave Him glory, so that your faith and hope are in God* (1 Pet. 1:17-21).

Peter affirmed that Christ in His sufferings fulfilled the sacrifices offered under the law and that His blood actually made atonement for their sins. Christ carried the payment, penalty, and punishment for our sins on the cross. He liberated us from the penalty of sin and He is "able also to save them to the uttermost that come unto God by him, seeing he ever liveth to make intercession for them" (Heb. 7:25). One preacher aptly commented, "Jesus is able to save us from the guttermost to the uttermost!" Amen.

The Apostle Paul, of course, penned classic statements about Jesus' atoning death.

For the love of Christ controls us, having concluded this, that one died for all, therefore all died; and He died for all, so that they who live might no longer live for themselves, but for Him who died and rose again on their behalf. Therefore from now on we recognize no one according to the flesh; even though we have known Christ according to the flesh, yet now we know Him in this way no longer. Therefore if anyone is in Christ, he is a new creature; the old things passed away;

behold, new things have come. Now all these things are from God, who reconciled us to Himself through Christ and gave us the ministry of reconciliation, namely, that God was in Christ reconciling the world to Himself, not counting their trespasses against them, and He has committed to us the word of reconciliation. Therefore, we are ambassadors for Christ, as though God were making an appeal through us; we beg you on behalf of Christ, be reconciled to God. He made Him who knew no sin to be sin on our behalf, so that we might become the righteousness of God in Him (2 Cor. 5:14-21)

Here the apostle declared that One died for all, so all died. In Christ's dying, we died potentially. By His dying for us and our dying in Him, it is now possible for us who accept Him to live for Him. That is further what Paul meant when he testified "I have been crucified with Christ; and it is no longer I who live, but Christ lives in me; and the life which I now live in the flesh I live by faith in the Son of God, who loved me and gave Himself up for me" (Gal. 2:20). To the church at Corinth, the apostle explained that "Christ did not send me to baptize, but to preach the gospel, not in cleverness of speech, so that the cross of Christ would not be made void" (1 Cor. 1:17). To the same church he emphasized: For I determined to know nothing among you except Jesus Christ, and Him crucified" (1 Cor. 2:22). The apostles showed beyond a doubt the centrality of Jesus' sacrificial death on mankind's behalf.

In the Prison Epistles—Ephesians, Philippians, and Colossians—Paul continues to exalt the death of Christ not only to redeem mankind but to reconcile to God all things in heaven and on Earth.

> *For it was the Father's good pleasure for all the fullness to dwell in Him, and through Him to reconcile all things to Himself, having made peace through the blood of His cross; through Him, I say, whether things on earth or things in heaven* (Col. 1:19-20).

The Cross—Symbol of the Savior's Death

The cross is the symbol of the Lord's substitutionary death on Calvary (also called Golgotha, meaning "the place of the skull"). The enemies of the Lord Jesus Christ hate the cross and all it stands for. It was demanded by the holiness of God and dictated by His love. He died in our place. "For God so loved the world, that He gave His only begotten Son, that whoever believes in Him shall not perish, but have eternal life" (John 3:16).

We must remember that man was given authority over the entire Earth (Gen. chapter 1) but by his disobedience he gave up all rights to Satan. Yet, Satan has operated with certain limitations. One person, filled with God's Holy Spirit, is more powerful than Satan and all of his demons! "You are from God, little children, and have overcome them; because greater is He who is in you than he who is in the world" (1 John 4:4).

After Jesus' water baptism, the Spirit led Him into the wilderness where He was tempted for 40 days. The third temptation, according to Luke, was the devil's offer to give Christ all the kingdoms of the Earth if He would fall down and worship him.

> *And he led Him up and showed Him all the kingdoms of the world in a moment of time. And the devil said to Him, "I will give You all this domain and its glory; for it has been handed over to me, and I give it to whomever I wish. Therefore if You worship before me, it shall all be Yours"* (Luke 4:5-7).

Christ did not deny Satan's claim. Satan could have given those kingdoms to whomever he pleased. Jesus later referred to Satan as "the prince of this world" (see John 12:30-31; 16:8-11). Paul called Satan "the god of this world" (2 Cor. 4:4). The intensity of that temptation lay in the fact that Jesus came to wrench the world out of Satan's grisly grip, and that could be done only by His death on the cross. Thus, Satan tried to steer Christ away from His life's purpose by offering Him the world without His having to suffer and die for it.

In the grandeur of His holy nature, Jesus rejected Satan's insidious offer. Though Satan left Him for a short period of time, he reappeared to attack Him during His ministry. That is true with Jesus' true believers. As they stand against the onslaught of the devil, and are victorious over temptations, the devil will leave them alone for a while—but then he rears his ugly head and returns. That is why the Christian must remain vigilant. When the time of His crucifixion drew nearer, the more his soul was troubled and the more He recoiled from the conflict. After all, the pure, spotless Son of God would have all of the sins of the world—past, present, and future—heaped upon Him as He died on the cross! I repeat a previously quoted verse: "He [God] made Him who knew no sin to be sin on our behalf, so that we might become the righteousness of God in Him" (2 Cor. 5:21).

On the Sunday (Palm Sunday) before His crucifixion on Friday (Good Friday), He showed the necessity of His death, illustrating it by a grain of seed that falls into the ground, dies, and then comes up into new life as a growing plant. "Truly, truly, I say to you, unless a grain of wheat falls into the earth and dies, it remains alone; but if it dies, it bears much fruit" (John 12:24). Those around Him did not understand. He recognized the horrors of His impending death and was agonizing before the Father, even as He did in the Garden of Gethsemane before His arrest by the Roman soldiers and temple guards. He then gave this momentous prophecy: "Jesus answered and said, 'This voice has not come for My sake, but for your sakes. Now judgment is upon this world; now the ruler of this world will be cast out. And I, if I am lifted up from the earth, will draw all men to Myself'" (John 12:30-32).

By His death, Jesus would diminish Satan's power, and the prince of this world would realize his was a losing cause. On Thursday night, as Jesus was establishing the Lord's Supper with His disciples, the devil entered into Judas Iscariot, who would betray Him. Of course, our Lord was well aware of all that was going on; the disciples were not. After the Supper, He had a quiet talk with the disciples (John chapters 14—16). He said, "I will not speak much more with you, for the ruler of the world is coming, and he has nothing in Me; but so that the world may know that I love the Father, I do exactly as the Father commanded Me. Get up, let us go from here" (John 14:30-31). The Lord boldly predicted that Satan was coming but that he had nothing in Him, that is, there was nothing of a sinful nature or actions that the devil could accuse Him of. This was His declaration of sinlessness.

En route to Gethsemane, Jesus taught His disciples about the coming of the Holy Spirit. He would convict or reprove concerning three matters.

> *And He, when He comes, will convict the world concerning sin and righteousness and judgment; concerning sin, because they do not believe in Me; and concerning righteousness, because I go to the Father and you no longer see Me; and concerning judgment, because the ruler of this world has been judged* (John 16:8-11).

The number-one sin is not to believe, not to have faith in the Lord Jesus Christ. That is the sin which separates people from God and ultimately determines their eternal destiny, whether in heaven or in hell. Jesus put it plainly:

> *For God did not send the Son into the world to judge the world, but that the world might be saved through Him. He who believes in Him is not judged; he who does not believe has been judged already, because he has not believed in the name of the only begotten Son of God. This is the judgment, that the Light has come into the world, and men loved the darkness rather than the Light, for their deeds were evil* (John 3:17-19).

The second item of the Spirit's conviction is righteousness. When the Spirit descended, He testified that Jesus was the righteous, sinless Messiah who suffered, died, and was raised from the dead in fulfillment of the Old Testament predictions. The Jews of our Lord's day thought Jesus was an imposter. When the showdown came the Jewish leaders rejected Him as being a pretender to Messianic honors. When the Holy Spirit came He emphasized that Jesus was indeed the Messiah, the anointed One: that He, at the invitation of God according to Psalm 110, ascended into heaven, and that He is now at the right hand of the throne of God. Thus, the Holy Spirit demonstrated that Jesus Christ is the true Son of God, Savior of all who call on Him, and the embodiment of God's righteousness that all must have to stand acceptably in the sight of God.

The third major point on which the Holy Spirit would give His testimony in convicting power was judgment, "because the ruler of this world has been judged." When the Day of Pentecost arrived, Satan had already been judged and could bring no legitimate charge against the Lord Jesus, even as Pontius Pilate washed his hands in a basin and declared before the multitude, "I find no fault in this man" (John 19:4). Christ, the perfect, sinless God-man condemned Satan by His death on the cross.

Upon His death the Lord Jesus was well aware that Satan would be cast from his earthly throne and shorn of his power. At the cross he was struck a death blow. He is still kicking, but he is totally doomed! At one of His post-resurrection appearances Jesus attested that,

> *All authority hath been given unto me in heaven and on earth. Go ye therefore, and make disciples of all the nations, baptizing them in the name of the Father and of the Son and of the Holy Spirit: teaching them to observe all things whatsoever I command you: and lo, I am with you always, even unto the end of the world* (Matt. 28:18-20).

From the predicted we just looked at (see also John 12:31) we note that Satan would be cast out. From our Lord's statement after His resurrection, we also recognize that He had all power and authority, even that which Satan might have formerly possessed. These are proofs that the devil was defeated by Jesus' death and resurrection. He still attempts to intimidate us and deceive us—but he is a coward, realizing he cannot stand against even one pitiful Christian who is energized by the resurrection power of the Lord Jesus and the infilling of the Holy Spirit. The apostle Peter expressed it well:

> *Be of sober spirit, be on the alert. Your adversary, the devil, prowls around like a roaring lion, seeking someone to devour. But resist him, firm in your faith, knowing that the same experiences of suffering are being accomplished by your brethren who are in the world. After you have suffered for a little while, the God of all grace, who called you to His eternal glory in Christ, will Himself perfect, confirm, strengthen and establish you* (1 Pet. 5:8-10).

James encourages us: "Submit therefore to God. Resist the devil and he will flee from you" (Jas. 4:7). That Christ did by and through His death break the power of Satan is clear from 1 John 3:8: "The one who practices sin is of the devil; for the devil has sinned from the beginning. The Son of God appeared for this purpose, to destroy the works of the devil." This is further verified in Hebrews 2:14-15:

> *Therefore, since the children share in flesh and blood, He Himself likewise also partook of the same, that through death He might render powerless him who had the power of death, that is, the devil, and might free those who through fear of death were subject to slavery all their lives.*

Paul writing to Timothy cried out: "But now has been revealed by the appearing of our Savior Christ Jesus, who abolished death and brought life and immortality to light through the gospel" (2 Tim. 1:10). Hallelujah! Christ has already conquered Satan, the old devil!!!

Speaking of Paul

Saul of Tarsus, later renamed Paul by the Lord, was an ardent opponent of Christ and His followers. Later in his ministry he testified: "I persecuted this Way [the Christians] to the death, binding and putting both men and women into prisons (Acts 22:4). "And as I punished them often in all the synagogues, I tried to force them to blaspheme; and being furiously enraged at them, I kept pursuing them even to foreign cities" (Acts 26:11).

That changed when he encountered the Lord on the Road to Damascus. Backed by authority of the high priest in Jerusalem, he was going to that city to persecute the Christians there. Read the text:

> *And as he journeyed, he came near Damascus: and suddenly there shined round about him a light from heaven: And he fell to the earth, and heard a voice saying unto him, Saul, Saul, why persecutest thou me? And he said, Who art thou, Lord? And the Lord said, I am Jesus whom thou persecutest: it is hard for thee to kick against the pricks [twinges of conviction]. And he trembling and astonished said, Lord, what wilt thou have me to do? And the Lord said unto him, Arise, and go into the city, and it shall be told thee what thou must do* (Acts 9:3-6, KJV).

There is no question about Saul's conversion. He was transformed from the persecutor of Christians to a prince of apostles, not one of the original Twelve but a qualified apostle, for he had seen the Lord in person. Why did Paul embrace the faith he had despised and rejected? When his situation is carefully analyzed, we must agree that there was only one possible motive that changed him from being a violent hater of Christ and Christians to a lover of both with all of his heart. The deciding factor was the conviction that he was wrong to reject Jesus and that the only logical course was for him to repent and embrace Him as His Messiah—and, yes, he beheld Jesus Himself on that road.

Saul was an intellectual giant who gave up all of his religious, scholarly, and social standing to follow the Man of Galilee. He became a firebrand covering the Roman Empire with the glorious gospel of his Savior, pointing out that Jesus was the fulfillment of Old Testament prophecies and that He was the genuine Messiah and Savior. He preached that he had seen Jesus in heaven and that Jesus had spoken to him on the Damascus Road. Paul was in the prime of his life, was in possession of his mental powers, and stood for the same testimony through a ministry of over 30 years. He became the Spirit-led author of 13 New Testament Books and was the leader in at least three extensive missionary journeys of the Mediterranean world. His long-term mission was to preach the gospel in Rome which he did to "Caesar's family" and possibly even to Caesar himself. "All the saints greet you, especially those of Caesar's household" (Phil. 4:22).

We are used to considering the atonement in reference to the death of Christ. However, that is a partial position. As he wrote of Christ, Paul declared, "He was delivered up for our trespasses, and was raised for our justification" (Rom. 4:25, KJV). Our salvation also is dependent on Jesus' resurrection.

The Ascension of Christ

The psalmist prophesied about Christ's ascension:

The Lord says to my Lord:
"Sit at My right hand
Until I make Your enemies a footstool for Your feet."
The Lord will stretch forth Your strong scepter from Zion,
saying, "Rule in the midst of Your enemies."
(Ps. 11:1-2).

In these verses David predicted the ascension of the risen Christ into heaven. Through the Spirit he was enabled to gaze ahead to a time when the Messiah, whom he called the Lord, would appear incarnate. Instead of receiving Him with enthusiasm and respect, the inhabitants of Jerusalem became His enemies. When they assumed that attitude, God in heaven invited Him to leave earth and to ascend into heaven, there to sit at the right hand of the Father until He, the Almighty, makes Messiah's enemies—the Jews who rejected Him—the footstool of His feet (see Luke 24:50-33).

Luke wrote about Jesus' ascension into heaven in Acts 1:

> *So when they had come together, they were asking Him, saying, "Lord, is it at this time You are restoring the kingdom to Israel?" He said to them, "It is not for you to know times or epochs which the Father has fixed by His own authority; but you will receive power when the Holy Spirit has come upon you; and you shall be My witnesses both in Jerusalem, and in all Judea and Samaria, and even to the remotest part of the earth." And after He had said these things, He was lifted up while they were looking on, and a cloud received Him out of their sight. And as they were gazing intently into the sky while He was going, behold, two men in white clothing stood beside them. They also said, "Men of Galilee, why do you stand looking into the sky? This Jesus, who has been taken up from you into heaven, will come in just the same way as you have watched Him go into heaven"* (Acts 1:6-11).

According to Psalm 110:3 and other passages the Jewish nation will surrender to the Messiah they have long rejected and will plead for His second coming. The New Testament is filled with passages that speak of the exaltation of the man Christ Jesus, who has ascended to heaven and who is the great High Priest there, carrying out His work of mediation on behalf of those who have trusted Him as Lord and Savior.

The Mediation of the Messiah

Adam and Eve felt their sinfulness to enter the presence of God. Since then mankind has experienced this feeling. No person is worthy to approach God in a sinful state. The prophet Habakkuk prayed to God: "Your eyes are too pure to approve evil, And You can not look on wickedness with favor. Why do You look with favor On those who deal treacherously? Why are You silent when the wicked swallow up Those more righteous than they?" (Hab. 1:13). The King James Version renders it: "Thou art of purer eyes than to behold evil, and canst not look on iniquity." Mankind needs a mediator, a go-between, someone who is able to present his case to the Lord and represent him.

In the Old Testament a priest interceded for the people of Israel and made offerings. But, according to Genesis 14, there was to arise in Israel a priest "after the order of Melchizedek," the extraordinary priest-king of Salem (later called Jerusalem), who would be unlike any other priests. Melchizedek was undoubtedly Jesus in what is called a "theophany," an appearance of God in human form.

The writer of the Epistle to the Hebrews shows that He was a sinless man, the God-man, who did not have to make sacrifices and offerings for Himself as the priests of Israel did. Peter proclaimed: "Who [in reference to Jesus] did no sin, neither was guile found in his mouth" (1 Pet. 2:22).

> *For it was fitting for us to have such a high priest, holy, innocent, undefiled, separated from sinners and exalted above the heavens; who does not need daily, like those high priests, to offer up sacrifices, first for His own sins and then for the sins of the people, because this He did once for all when He offered up Himself. For the Law appoints men as high priests who are weak, but the word of the oath, which came after the Law, appoints a Son, made perfect forever* (Heb 7:26-28).

Jesus became our great High Priest. Since He has made purification for our sin, He has sat down at the right hand of the Majesty on high. He was in all points tempted as we, yet without sin. He is able to empathize with all those who come to God through Him. He has never rejected anyone who has sincerely approached Him (see Heb. 7:25). Through His blood we have free access to Him. "Let us therefore come boldly unto the throne of grace, that we may obtain mercy, and find grace to help in time of need" (Heb. 4:16, KJV).

A Summary of the Atonement

The word "atonement" does not occur in the King James Version of the New Testament except in Romans 5:11, where in some other versions the word "reconciliation" is used. In the Old Testament it is of frequent occurrence. The meaning of the word is simply at-one-ment, i.e., the state of being at one or being reconciled, so that atonement is reconciliation. It denotes the effect that emanates from the death of Christ. The word is also employed to betoken that by which this reconciliation is effected, the death of Christ itself. It can mean satisfaction—in this sense to make an atonement for one is to make satisfaction for the grievances he has created (see Ex. 32:30; Lev. 4:26; 5:16; Num. 6:11).

By the atonement of Christ is meant His work by which He paid for our sins. In Scripture usage the word refers to the reconciliation itself, and not the means by which it is carried out. "Satisfaction" is the word often used in relation to the atonement. Christ's satisfaction is all He did on behalf of sinners to satisfy, or fulfill, the demands of the law and the justice of God. Christ's atoning death was comprised of suffering and obedience, and these were substitutionary, not simply for our benefit, but were in our stead as the suffering and obedience of our substitute. Our guilt is propitiated [some refer to it as "expiated"] by the punishment our substitute, the Lord Jesus Christ, bore.

It is now in keeping with His justice to manifest His love to sinners. Yes, "Jesus Paid It All," to quote an old hymn title by Mrs. H.M. Hall. Jesus through His death made satisfaction for sin, and our sins are covered when we accept the benefits of His shed blood. Our sins are covered. In Him. The means by which they are covered is vicarious satisfaction. The end of their being covered is atonement or reconciliation. Christ's mediatorial work and sufferings are the bases of reconciliation with God. They repair the disrupted relations between God and man, removing the barriers presented by sin to their fellowship. The reconciliation is in two directions: it is not only that of sinners toward God, but basically that of God toward sinners, carried out by the sin offering He himself provided.

The main concept revealed throughout the Scripture is: the death of Christ is a satisfaction of measureless worth supplied to the law and justice of God and accepted by Him. We must remember that the atonement is the consequence of God's love to guilty men (John 3:16; Rom. 3:24, 25; Eph. 1:7; 1 John 1:9; 4:9). There is no other way to salvation, for this is God's plan wrought out before the foundation of the world (Ex. 34:7; Josh. 24:19; Ps. 5:4; 7:11; Nah. 1:2, 6; Rom. 3:5).

> *Forasmuch as ye know that ye were not redeemed with corruptible things, as silver and gold, from your vain conversation received by tradition from your fathers; But with the precious blood of Christ, as of a lamb without blemish and without spot: Who verily was foreordained before the foundation of the world, but was manifest in these last times for you, Who by him do believe in God, that raised him up from the dead, and gave him glory; that your faith and hope might be in God* (1 Pet. 1:18-21, KJV).

This is God's plan, and that is more than sufficient for us to know. The writer of Hebrews explained his reason for writing:

> *God, after He spoke long ago to the fathers in the prophets in many portions and in many ways, in these last days has spoken to us in His Son, whom He appointed heir of all things, through whom also He made the world. And He is the radiance of His glory and the exact representation of His nature, and upholds all things by the word of His power. When He had made purification of sins, He sat down at the right hand of the Majesty on high, having become as much better than the angels, as He has inherited a more excellent name than they* (Heb. 1:1-4).

God the Father sent the Son into the world to purchase redemption, reconciliation, salvation for us. In Hebrews 1:5—2:4 the writer contrasted the position Jesus now commands with that held by angels. In contrast with Him the angels are merely servants sent forth at His command to give assistance to those who inherit salvation. But Christ the God-man will fulfill the destiny of the human race by subjecting the inhabited Earth to man. In Hebrews 2:6 is a prophecy based on Psalm 8 predicting the time when this Earth will revert to man as its lawful master. This promise has not been fulfilled to men in general. It has, though, been fulfilled in the case of one man, the Man Christ Jesus. So, the promise of Psalm 8 has been only partly fulfilled, but it has not been made good to man in general.

How will this be carried out? The author of Hebrews answered: "For it was fitting for Him, for whom are all things, and through whom are all things, in bringing many sons to glory, to perfect the author of their salvation through sufferings" (Heb. 2:10). The Captain of our salvation was made perfect? What can that mean? It means He fulfilled and completed His mission of providing salvation for mankind. During life His body was in what we might call a state of humiliation. After His resurrection, though, His body was in a glorified form. Having walked this earthly path before us, He beckons us to follow Him. He will lead us into the same glorious state. At the time of the rapture God will raise those who have died with Christ as their Savior, and He will change the bodies of living believers. Paul exclaimed:

> *For if we believe that Jesus died and rose again, even so God will bring with Him those who have fallen asleep in Jesus. For this we say to you by the word of the Lord, that we who are alive and remain until the coming of the Lord, will not precede those who have*

> *fallen asleep. For the Lord Himself will descend from heaven with a shout, with the voice of the archangel and with the trumpet of God, and the dead in Christ will rise first. Then we who are alive and remain will be caught up together with them in the clouds to meet the Lord in the air, and so we shall always be with the Lord. Therefore comfort one another with these words* (1 Thes. 4:14-18).

When our Lord was on the Earth, He had a real physical, material body. One of His purposes for assuming the form of man was to accomplish our sanctification, that is, making us holy and righteous and being conformed to His spiritual image. Sanctification is more than a moral reformation of character caused by the power of the truth. It is the work of the Holy Spirit bringing one's nature more and more under God's spiritual influences following one's being born again and converted. It is maintaining on to perfection the work begun when one is born again (Rom. 6:13; 2 Cor. 4:6; Col. 3:10; 1 John 4:7; 1 Cor. 6:19). The Holy Spirit is the agent of this continuing process, which is sometimes called "growing in grace."

"But grow in the grace and knowledge of our Lord and Savior Jesus Christ. To Him be the glory, both now and to the day of eternity. Amen" (2 Pet. 3:18; see also 1 Cor. 6:11; 2 Thes. 2:13). Perfect sanctification is not reachable in this life (1 Kings 8:46; Prov. 20:9; Eccl. 7:20; James 3:2; 1 John 1:8). Pay attention to Paul's account of himself in Romans 7:14–25; Phil. 3:12–14; and 1 Tim. 1:15; also the confessions of David (Ps. 19:12, 13; Ps. 51), of Moses (Ps. 90:8), of Job (42:5, 6), and of Daniel (9:3–20).

I repeat: Christ's reason for leaving heaven, becoming flesh, and dwelling among humans is laid out in Hebrews 2:14-15.

> *Therefore, since the children share in flesh and blood, He Himself likewise also partook of the same, that through death He might render powerless him who had the power of death, that is, the devil, and might free those who through fear of death were subject to slavery all their lives.*

As pointed out earlier, Christ has defeated the power of Satan. Only Deity could accomplish the daunting task of putting Satan to flight. The second person of the Trinity, God the Son, volunteered to take upon Himself a body, to come to Earth, and to duel with the devil. Paul extolled our Lord in this classic passage:

> *And being found in fashion as a man, he humbled himself, and became obedient unto death, even the death of the cross. Wherefore God also hath highly exalted him, and given him a name which is above every name: That at the name of Jesus every knee should bow, of things in heaven, and things in earth, and things under the earth; And that every tongue should confess that Jesus Christ is Lord, to the glory of God the Father* (Phil. 2:8-11, KJV).

Jesus conquered Satan, death, hell, and sin. But why did One of the eternal Trinity have to die in order to break Satan's power and liberate mankind? It was because God had pronounced the death sentence on man in Eden. God warned: "But of the tree of the knowledge of good and evil, thou shalt not eat of it: for in the day that thou eatest thereof thou shalt surely die" (Gen. 2:17, KJV). "Behold, all souls are Mine; the soul of the father as well as the soul of the son is Mine. The soul who sins will die" (Ezek. 18:4). The first Adam in his contact with Satan was defeated through his disobedience to God. It was essential in God's plan that the second Adam, the God-man, through His obedience should defeat the devil.

Were it not for Christ's sacrificial death, every person in history would spend eternity separated from God in a place the Bible refers to as hell and ultimately gehenna, the lake of fire. The great hymnist of Methodism, Charles Wesley, wrote:

> *'Tis finished! The Messiah dies,—*
> *Cut off for sins, but not His own;*
> *Accomplished is the sacrifice,*
> *The great redeeming work is done.*
> *'Tis finished! All the debt is paid;*
> *Justice divine is satisfied;*
> *The grand and full atonement made;*
> *Christ for a guilty world hath died.*
> *The veil is rent; in Him alone*
> *The living way to heaven is seen;*
> *The middle wall is broken down,*
> *And all mankind may enter in.*

The types and figures are fulfilled;
Exacted is the legal pain;
The precious promises are sealed;
The spotless Lamb of God is slain.
Death, hell, and sin are now subdued;
All grace is now to sinners given;
And, lo, I plead the atoning blood,
And in Thy right I claim my heaven.
Appropriating the Atonement.

Since Jesus has provided the atonement, and God the Father has accepted it, God has sent forth messengers of the cross as ambassadors. "Therefore, we are ambassadors for Christ, as though God were making an appeal through us; we beg you on behalf of Christ, be reconciled to God. He made Him who knew no sin to be sin on our behalf, so that we might become the righteousness of God in Him" (2 Cor. 5:20-21).

By the Individual

One's faith must be decided by the individual. An old song's lyrics went: "Not my brother, not my sister, but it's me, O Lord, standing in the need of prayer." "Proxy religion" does not really exist. Each person must deal with God individually. God sent His Son into the world that "whosoever will" may believe and have eternal life. There was a time when the majority of Americans may have known John 3:16—sadly no more. "For God so loved the world, that He gave His only begotten Son, that whoever believes in Him shall not perish, but have eternal life."

Jesus declared: "Truly, truly, I say to you, he who hears My word, and believes Him who sent Me, has eternal life, and does not come into judgment, but has passed out of death into life" (John 5:24).

> *But now apart from the Law the righteousness of God has been manifested, being witnessed by the Law and the Prophets, even the righteousness of God through faith in Jesus Christ for all those who believe; for there is no distinction; for all have sinned and fall short of the glory of God, being justified as a gift by His grace through the redemption which is in Christ Jesus; whom God displayed publicly as a propitiation in His blood through faith. This was to demonstrate His righteousness, because in the forbearance of God He*

> *passed over the sins previously committed; for the demonstration, I say, of His righteousness at the present time, so that He would be just and the justifier of the one who has faith in Jesus* (Rom. 3:21-26).

Since Christ has met the demands of the broken law and has died in our stead, becoming a curse for us (Gal. 3:13), now the disciples of the Lord must go and proclaim redemption through His blood. Jesus has all authority [*exousia* in the Greek, sometimes translated as power] in heaven and Earth. So, we are to follow His leading in the Great Commission:

> *And Jesus came up and spoke to them, saying, "All authority has been given to Me in heaven and on earth. Go therefore and make disciples of all the nations, baptizing them in the name of the Father and the Son and the Holy Spirit, teaching them to observe all that I commanded you; and lo, I am with you always, even to the end of the age"* (Matt. 28:18-20).

Salvation is a free gift from God which He offers to all who will accept Christ as their sacrifice, their stand-in. In other words, either we will die for our sins or accept His substitution on our behalf. Ephesians 2:8-9 makes it plain: "For by grace you have been saved through faith; and that not of yourselves, it is the gift of God; not as a result of works, so that no one may boast." Salvation is free, but the Christian is to live a life of good works—not to be saved but because he is saved. He will receive rewards, but they are not to be confused with salvation. Rewards are given for the good we do after we are saved. "If any man's work which he has built on it remains, he will receive a reward. If any man's work is burned up, he will suffer loss; but he himself will be saved, yet so as through fire" (1 Cor. 3:14-15).

We shall be rewarded according to our works. "For the Son of Man is going to come in the glory of His Father with His angels, and will then repay every man according to his deeds" (Matt. 16:27).

By Israel Nationally

God has always dealt with Israel nationally. At the same time, though, He deals with each person as an individual. "So then each one of us will give an account of himself to God" (Rom. 14:12). God has preserved and kept Israel intact through the centuries, an historical fact that is difficult for the biblically illiterate to fathom. Other groups as political entities will pass away—but not Israel. Israel remains, even though the Jews have been persecuted as no other nation in history. The Nazis exterminated at least 6 million of them; it is thought the Russians under Joseph Stalin did away with at least that many. The Inquisition, which was religious persecution, annihilated thousands. The Old Testament records their enslavement and mistreatment at the hands of warring tribes in Canaan and the Syrians, Assyrians, Egyptians, Medes and Persians, Babylonians, Greeks, and Romans, ad infinitum. Yet, Israel will never cease to exist as a nation. (Jer. 30:11).

After 15 centuries of supposed non-existence, Israel was reestablished as a nation in 1948, yet it was there all the time, watched over by Yahweh (Jehovah), the God of the covenant. God has not overlooked His promises to Abraham, Isaac, and Jacob. Hosea the prophet foresaw the era when Israel would sin against Jehovah upon His appearance in her midst. When she thus sins, He leaves her and returns to His place, saying He will stay there until she confesses her sin and sincerely seeks His face. "I will go away and return to My place Until they acknowledge their guilt and seek My face; In their affliction they will earnestly seek Me" (Hos. 5:15).

Israel's national confession of sin is seen in the passion of Isaiah 53:1-9:

> *Who has believed our message? And to whom has the arm of the Lord been revealed? For He grew up before Him like a tender shoot, And like a root out of parched ground; He has no stately form or majesty That we should look upon Him, Nor appearance that we should be attracted to Him. He was despised and forsaken of men, A man of sorrows and acquainted with grief; And like one from whom men hide their face He was despised, and we did not esteem Him. Surely our griefs He Himself bore, And our sorrows He carried; Yet we ourselves esteemed Him stricken, Smitten of God, and afflicted. But He was pierced through for our transgressions, He was crushed for our iniquities; The chastening for our well-being fell upon Him, And by His scourging we are healed. All of us like sheep have gone astray, Each of us has turned to his own way; But the Lord has caused the iniquity of us all To fall on Him.*

> *He was oppressed and He was afflicted, Yet He did not open His mouth; Like a lamb that is led to slaughter, And like a sheep that is silent before its shearers, So He did not open His mouth. By oppression and judgment He was taken away; And as for His generation, who considered That He was cut off out of the land of the living For the transgression of my people, to whom the stroke was due? His grave was assigned with wicked men, Yet He was with a rich man in His death, Because He had done no violence, Nor was there any deceit in His mouth* (Isa. 53:1-9).

That is an unmistakable prophecy about the Lord Jesus Christ as the Suffering Servant, the Messiah of Israel. He made a similar announcement to the Jewish Sanhedrin:

> *Jerusalem, Jerusalem, who kills the prophets and stones those who are sent to her! How often I wanted to gather your children together, the way a hen gathers her chicks under her wings, and you were unwilling. Behold, your house is being left to you desolate! For I say to you, from now on you will not see Me until you say, "Blessed is He who comes in the name of the Lord!"* (Matt. 23:37-39).

According to certain predictions the leaders of Israel will first learn and then understand the facts regarding the Messiah and will accept Him. "The stone which the builders refused is become the head of the corner. This is the LORD'S doing; it is marvellous in our eyes" (Ps. 118:22-23, KJV). Upon studying this prophecy, it is apparent that the leaders of the Jews will learn about the stone (King Messiah) who was rejected by the great men of Israel 2,000 years ago. They will recognize their grievous mistake and will then point the nation to Him (Hos. 5:15—6:3). There will be a widespread acceptance of the Christ as their Messiah. The Deliverer, Jesus, will come to Zion and turn ungodliness from Jacob (Isa. 59:20ff.; Rom. 11:25-27). Then will be ushered in the perfect day of 2 Samuel 23:1-7 and Proverbs 4:18.

The coming to them who wait for Him unto salvation is known as the second coming of our Lord, which occurs at the end of the tribulation. We must not confuse this with the rapture of the church , an event that occurs before the tribulation period, "the time of Jacob's trouble."

The Role of Sin

The Word of God often recognizes the prospect of persons' committing sin unwittingly. In Numbers 15:28 provision is set forth for such sins." The priest shall make atonement before the Lord for the person who goes astray when he sins unintentionally, making atonement for him that he may be forgiven." David realized there are sins one may not be aware of. In Psalm he sang, "Who can discern his errors? Acquit me of hidden [secret, KJV] faults" (Ps. 19:12). Those types of sins are subtle, hard to pin down. No one except Jesus is free of those. There are sins of omission and commission. Commission sins are those done deliberately and willfully. Omission ones are those when a person simply, for one reason or another, fails to do that which is good and right. James emphasized, "Therefore, to one who knows the right thing to do and does not do it, to him it is sin" (Jas. 4:17).

The all-seeing eyes of the omniscient God see everything we do, say, think, and feel. Nothing is hid from Him. In Psalm 14 and 53 the psalmist concluded that there is not a single righteous person (with the exception of the perfect Son of God, of course). All are guilty before God.

> *The fool has said in his heart, "There is no God." They are corrupt, they have committed abominable deeds; There is no one who does good. The Lord has looked down from heaven upon the sons of men To see if there are any who understand, Who seek after God. They have all turned aside, together they have become corrupt; There is no one who does good, not even one. Do all the workers of wickedness not know, Who eat up my people as they eat bread, And do not call upon the Lord?* (Ps. 14:1-4).

The Word of God continually speaks of mankind's sinning. Sin is variously described as a violation of and lack of conformity to the laws and precepts of God (1 John 3:4; Rom. 4:15). It is in and inner state of man's soul, as well as in the outward conduct of the life, either by omission or commission (Rom. 6:12–17; 7:5–24). Sin is inherently vile and filthy, deserves punishment, and evokes the righteous wrath of God.

Certain words in both Old and New testaments denote sin as "missing the mark" or "the target." An Old Testament term is the word rendered "transgression." It basically means to separate, to pull apart, to revolt, and to disobey. Moab, for instance, is said to have transgressed against Israel in breaking a treaty between the two entities (2 Ki. 1:1). The moral nature of a man's actions is determined by the moral condition of his heart, his inward being. The inclination to sin, or the habit of the soul leading to the sinful act, is itself also sin (Rom. 6:12–17; Gal. 5:17; James 1:14, 15).

Adam's sin (Gen. 3:1–6) consisted of his giving in to the assaults of temptation and eating the taboo fruit. His sin included unbelief, actually making God a liar, and the transgression of disobedience to a clear command. By this sin he became estranged from God, a rebel against the Creator. He departed from favor with God and was cut off from communion with Him. When Adam fell, subsequently all mankind would fall with him (Rom. 5:12–21; 1 Cor. 15:22–45). Because of Adam's first sin, all his descendants entered the world in a state of sin and condemnation.

"Original sin" is often used to describe the moral corruption of their entire nature inherited by all men from Adam. This moral degeneracy entails the loss of original righteousness and constant inclination to evil, which is the root of all actual sin. It is referred to as "sin" (Rom. 6:12, 14, 17; 7:5–17); the "flesh" (Gal. 5:17, 24); "lust" (James 1:14, 15); the "body of sin" (Rom. 6:6); "ignorance," "blindness of heart," and "alienation from the life of God" (Eph. 4:18, 19). It influences and corrupts the whole person, and its tendency is downward to worse and worse.

It is a "total depravity," inherited by all the descendants of Adam (Rom. 3:10–23; 5:12–21; 8:7). Man is spiritually dead (Eph. 2:1; 1 John 3:14). Original sin is proved from the universal sinfulness of persons. "There is no man that sinneth not" (1 Kings 8:46; Isa. 53:6; Ps. 130:3; Rom. 3:19, 22, 23; Gal. 3:22). (2.) From the total depravity of man. All men are declared to be destitute of any principle of spiritual life; man's apostasy from God is total and complete (Job 15:14–16; Gen. 6:5,6). (3.) From its early manifestation (Ps. 58:3; Prov. 22:15). (4.) It is proved also from the necessity, absolutely and universally, of regeneration (John 3:3; 2 Cor. 5:17). (5.) From the universality of death (Rom. 5:12–20).

Various kinds of sin are referred to in God's Word: "Presumptuous sins," i.e., insolent acts of sin over against inadvertent errors (Ps. 19:13); "secret," i.e., hidden sins (19:12) that escape the notice of the soul; "sin against the Holy Ghost," often called "the unpardonable sin," which is a hardened, final rejection of the Holy Spirit who convicts concerning Christ (Matt. 12:31); and "the sin unto death," which is often interpreted as an obstinate sin of a Christian (1 John 5:16).

Conclusions About the Kingdom

How can a person enter the kingdom of God, sometimes also called the kingdom of heaven? Only through Jesus Christ, of course. Only through His shed blood. Only by receiving Him as one's personal Lord and Savior. "Testifying both to the Jews, and also to the Greeks, repentance toward God, and faith toward our Lord Jesus Christ" (Acts 20:21). Repentance means not only to feel sorrow for one's sins but to turn away from them and to trust the Lord Jesus for salvation. But what happens at the moment one trusts Christ and yields to Him?

One is "born again" or "anew"—literally "born from above" in the Greek. Jesus had numerous conversations with "inquiring minds." One of the most memorable was when a Jewish religious leader, Nicodemus, visited Him. Let the Scripture speak.

> *Jesus answered and said to him, "Truly, truly, I say to you, unless one is born again he cannot see the kingdom of God." Nicodemus said to Him, "How can a man be born when he is old? He cannot enter a second time into his mother's womb and be born, can he?" Jesus answered, "Truly, truly, I say to you, unless one is born of water and the Spirit he cannot enter into the kingdom of God. That which is born of the flesh is flesh, and that which is born of the Spirit is spirit. Do not be amazed that I said to you, 'You must be born again.' The wind blows where it wishes and you hear the sound of it, but do not know where it comes from and where it is going; so is everyone who is born of the Spirit." Nicodemus said to Him, "How can these things be?"* (John 3:3-9).

Jesus used water with a symbolic meaning, signifying the Spirit. Jesus further explained: "That which is born of the flesh is flesh, and that which is born of the Spirit is spirit." In other words there is the natural birth (a human consists of 80 percent water, and a baby in his mother's womb is surrounded by her "bag of waters"), and there is the supernatural, the spiritual birth when one is born into the Kingdom of God. Although "born of water" does not refer to water baptism, that ordinance is essential to one's obedience. The Lord Jesus traveled from

Nazareth to the Jordan River to be baptized by John the Baptist (Matt. 3:13-17). Jesus' baptism was an example for His followers. "But Jesus answering said to him, 'Permit it at this time; for in this way it is fitting for us to fulfill all righteousness'" (Matt. 3:15). After His resurrection He charged His disciples to go into all the world, make disciples, baptize them, and teach them "even to the end of the age" (see Matt. 28:18-20). All who accept the Lord Jesus should submit to water baptism, not to be saved but because they are already saved.

Since to be "born of water" does not mean water baptism, what on earth or heaven does it mean? Let's examine John 7:37-39:

> *Now on the last day, the great day of the feast, Jesus stood and cried out, saying, "If anyone is thirsty, let him come to Me and drink. He who believes in Me, as the Scripture said, 'From his innermost being will flow rivers of living water.'" By this He spoke of the Spirit, whom those who believed in Him were to receive; for the Spirit was not yet given, because Jesus was not yet glorified.*

On that occasion Jesus spoke of the Holy Spirit in terms of water. The kingdom of God Jesus talked to Nicodemus about is the spiritual Kingdom into which all believers enter and which is known as the Church, the Body of Christ. Both John the Baptist and Jesus announced that "the kingdom of heaven is at hand." In the 13th chapter of Matthew the Lord explained what He meant by the kingdom of heaven. An examination of the seven parables of the kingdom reveals that it, preached by Jesus and John, is the spiritual kingdom that is in existence during this present age.

The kingdom of God, which was coextensive with the kingdom of Israel, was taken from the Jews and given to a nation bearing fruit—believers from both Jews and Gentiles—the present spiritual kingdom. "Therefore I say to you, the kingdom of God will be taken away from you and given to a people, producing the fruit of it" (Matt. 21:43). At the end of this Church-age dispensation, as we understand from the parable of the dragnet (Matt. 13:47-50), the kingdom of heaven will be purged of all the wicked and will be merged into the great kingdom of God which the Lord Jesus will set up when He comes back. All who enter the kingdom will be ready for the kingdom of glory when Jesus returns in power and glory.

So, one must be born again, or he/she cannot enter the kingdom of God.

The Law of God and Grace

> *Then the Lord passed by in front of him and proclaimed, "The Lord, the Lord God, compassionate and gracious, slow to anger, and abounding in lovingkindness and truth; who keeps lovingkindness for thousands, who forgives iniquity, transgression and sin; yet He will by no means leave the guilty unpunished, visiting the iniquity of fathers on the children and on the grandchildren to the third and fourth generations"* (Ex. 34:6-7).

The LORD declared His name to Moses. Thus, He set forth the characteristics of His being. This divine statement revealed the basis for all legal requirements and also the foundation for the grace of God through the gospel. First of all, God is seen as kind, loving, filled with compassion, and forgiving every stripe of evil against God and man—iniquity, transgression, and sin. At the same time, though, He punishes the unrepentant sinner. Interwoven into man's makeup are the elements of justice, righteousness, and a sense of responsibility toward his Creator. In God's code of morals and ethics given to Moses, including the Ten Commandments

THE TEN COMMANDMENTS

> *Thou shalt have no other gods before me. Thou shalt not make unto thee any graven image, or any likeness of any thing that is in heaven above, or that is in the earth beneath, or that is in the water under the earth: Thou shalt not bow down thyself to them, nor serve them: for I the LORD thy God am a jealous God, visiting the iniquity of the fathers upon the children unto the third and fourth generation of them that hate me; And shewing mercy unto thousands of them that love me, and keep my commandments. Thou shalt not take the name of the LORD thy God in vain; for the LORD will not hold him guiltless that taketh his name in vain. Remember the sabbath day, to keep it holy. Six days shalt thou labour, and do all thy work: But the seventh day is the sabbath of the LORD thy God: in it thou shalt not do any work, thou, nor thy son, nor thy daughter, thy manservant, nor thy maidser-*

> *vant, nor thy cattle, nor thy stranger that is within thy gates: For in six days the LORD made heaven and earth, the sea, and all that in them is, and rested the seventh day: wherefore the LORD blessed the sabbath day, and hallowed it. Honour thy father and thy mother: that thy days may be long upon the land which the LORD thy God giveth thee. Thou shalt not kill. Thou shalt not commit adultery. Thou shalt not steal. Thou shalt not bear false witness against thy neighbour. Thou shalt not covet thy neighbour's house, thou shalt not covet thy neighbour's wife, nor his manservant, nor his maidservant, nor his ox, nor his ass, nor any thing that is thy neighbour's* (Ex. 20:3-17).

In the Mosaic Code and legislation there are displayed God's legal, righteous expectations. However, all of those are only a partial revelation of the Almighty's integral character. Only through God's one and only Son, the Lord Jesus Christ, could mankind view the love and compassionate mercy of the Heavenly Father. "But when the fullness of the time came, God sent forth His Son, born of a woman, born under the Law, so that He might redeem those who were under the Law, that we might receive the adoption as sons" (Gal. 4:4-5).

During Jesus' earthly ministry, manmade, rabbinic traditions had built a "hedge" about the Old Testament Law. So, the real core of the Law was obscured. Only those with keen perception, through the Holy Spirit's insight, could recognize the divine content of the Law. At the appointed time in His ministry the Lord Jesus delivered His Sermon on the Mount (Matt. chapters 5—7; Luke 6:20-49). He reinterpreted Psalm 37, which was David's explanation of the Law.

Jesus' teachings laid bare the heart of God's will as revealed in Law and precept. Our Lord emphasized not performing outward acts but the inward condition of the heart. He introduced His message with the Beatitudes.

THE BEATITUDES

> *Blessed are the poor in spirit: for theirs is the kingdom of heaven. Blessed are they that mourn: for they shall be comforted. Blessed are the meek: for they shall inherit the earth. Blessed are they which do hunger and thirst after righteousness: for they shall be filled. Blessed are the merciful: for they shall obtain mercy. Blessed are the pure in heart: for they shall see God. Blessed are the peace-*

> *makers: for they shall be called the children of God. Blessed are they which are persecuted for righteousness' sake: for theirs is the kingdom of heaven. Blessed are ye, when men shall revile you, and persecute you, and shall say all manner of evil against you falsely, for my sake. Rejoice, and be exceeding glad: for great is your reward in heaven: for so persecuted they the prophets which were before you* (Matt. 5:3-12).

"Blessed" literally means "exceedingly happy." Jesus moved on from an examination of the heart's spiritual condition to the basic attitudes of the soul expressed in one's actions. The central message of all His preaching was that He did not come to destroy the Law and the Prophets—but to fulfill them. "For the Law was given through Moses; grace and truth were realized through Jesus Christ" (John 1:17). John well summed it up. Every word, act, and teaching of our Lord was an expression of love, grace, mercy, and truth. No man every lived and spoke as He did. "The officers answered, 'Never has a man spoken the way this man speaks'" (John 7:46).

Chapter 6

Christ's Life and Ministry

And Jesus came up and spoke to them, saying, "All authority has been given to Me in heaven and on earth. Go therefore and make disciples of all the nations, baptizing them in the name of the Father and the Son and the Holy Spirit, teaching them to observe all that I commanded you; and lo, I am with you always, even to the end of the age" (Matt. 28:18-20).

For God so loved the world, that he gave his only begotten Son, that whosoever believeth in him should not perish, but have everlasting life. For God sent not his Son into the world to condemn the world; but that the world through him might be saved. He that believeth not is condemned already, because he hath not believed in the name of the only begotten Son of God (John 3:16-18, KJV). **(Also see Chapter 5 of this book.)**

Jesus Christ traveled throughout Palestine to fulfill His purpose for entering the world. "I am come that they might have life, and that they might have it more abundantly," He explained (John 10:10, KJV), pointing out, "For the Son of man is come to seek and to save that which was lost (Luke 19:10, KJV). He identified Himself with the people He purposed to save. He even called them "friends" and "brethren," though He is the God-man, "Emmanual," meaning "God with us" (see Matthew 1:23).

Jesus lived by the highest ethical and moral standards. Of course, it seems that most, even His apostles, were not onto the fact of His Deity and sinlessness. "For we do not have a high priest who is unable to sympathize with our weakness, but we have one who has been tempted in every way, just as we are—yet without sin (Heb. 4:15). He had compassion on people (see Matt. 9:35-38) and taught as no other man had ever done (see John 7:46). The masses loved Him, but the religious and political leaders were jealous of Him and determined to snuff Him out.

> *Jesus is the image of the invisible God, the firstborn over all creation, for by Him all things were created that are in heaven and that are on earth, visible and invisible, whether thrones or dimensions or principalities or power. All things were created through Him and for Him* (Col. 1:15-16, KJV).

In heaven we will have an eternal, never-ending existence to learn of and worship God. Heaven will be beyond anything we can imagine. God the Son submitted to incarnation by becoming a God-man, so He could secure our redemption by bearing our sins at His crucification. He agreed to set aside His glory and to limit His divine power by coming to earth and becoming God/man by entering the human sphere by miraculous conception and virgin birth.

The Scripture teachings of both the Old and New testaments show that the Almighty God would enter the human realm by being born of a virgin and becoming a helpless little baby. He grew to manhood to lay down His life for man's redemption.

The Virgin Mary

> *And the angel [Gabriel] said unto her, fear not Mary for you have found favor with God and, behold you shall conceive in your womb, and bring forth a son, and shall call His name Jesus. He shall be great and shall be called the Son of the Most High: and the Lord shall give unto him the throne of His father David, and shall reign over the house of Jacob for ever. And his kingdom there shall be no end. The Holy Spirit shall come upon thee, and the power of the Most High shall overshadow thee. Also the Holy thing which is begotten shall be called the Son of God* (Luke 1:30-35, KJV).

The Holy Spirit is revealed, and the part He was to play in the birth of the Son of God is foretold. In this passage there are three divine personalities: God the Father, the Son of the Most High, and the Holy Spirit.

The Necessity of the Virgin Birth (also see Chapter 5 of this book)

If Jesus were to become our sin bearer, He could not possibly have an earthly Father, because He would have been a sinner just like you and I—and unfit to sacrifice. Jesus had to be God because only God is perfect, without sin. The sacrifice had to be without spot and blemish." But with precious blood, as of a lamb unblemished and spotless" (1 Pet. 1:19).

However, God cannot die, and that is why He needed a mortal body that could die, rise from the dead, and could come again someday to restore the Divided Kingdom and reign on the throne of King David of Israel forever.

Animal blood never was intended to remove the sin of man, only to cover it temporarily. It was temporary until the time was right for a perfect sacrifice to be made once and for all. That perfect sacrifice was the Messiah of Israel who died to remove not only the sins of the Jewish people, but of all people everywhere—Jew and Gentile alike. But each individual must receive God's gift by faith and accept Christ into his life. At the moment we believe in God, He converts us and gives us a new heart, and our sin debt is paid in full never to be held against us.

The prophet Isaiah in the Old Testament had written that God would come to earth and be born of a virgin. The God/man Jesus was born into a working-class family and Joseph, His stepfather, was a carpenter. Joseph was a hard worker and no doubt a good provider for his family.

Infancy and Youth of Jesus

Augustus, ruler of the Roman Empire, decreed that there would be a census of the population for the purpose of taxation. Joseph and Mary traveled to Bethlehem from Nazareth and slept in a stable with the livestock. There baby Jesus was born. Joseph and Mary alone recognized the tremendous secret that on her, the peasant maiden and carpenter's bride, had been conferred the honor of being the mother of Him who was to be the Messiah, the Savior of the world.

Jesus was well-educated as a result of school at the temple and home study. He was well-informed. When He was 12 years of age, Jesus traveled with his parents to the Passover at Jerusalem (see Luke chapter 2). Jesus went to the temple where the rabbis of wisdom taught. His mind was teeming with questions. His anxious parents were returning home, thinking Jesus was in the caravan. After a day's journey they returned to search for Him. They found Him listening with excitement to the oracles of the day. Upon questioning by his parents, "He said to them, 'Why is it that you were looking for Me? Did you not know that I had to be in My Father's house?'" (Luke 2:49).

After 30 years of silence and obscurity in Nazareth, Jesus stepped forth onto the biblical stage.

John the Baptist

The Jewish leaders of Jerusalem sent priests and Levites to ask John who he was, to which he answered, "I am not the Christ. I am the forerunner." "The voice of one crying in the wilderness, Prepare ye the way of the Lord, make his paths straight. John did baptize in the wilderness, and preached the baptism of repentance for the remission of sins" (Mark 1:3-4). John the Baptist declared, "As for me, I baptize you with water for repentance, but He who is coming after me is mightier than I, and I am not fit to remove His sandals; He will baptize you with the Holy Spirit and fire" (Matt. 3:11).

John Baptizes Jesus

John the Baptist was baptizing in the river Jordan, looked up, and announced, "Behold the Lamb of God.' Jesus presented himself for baptism but John was reluctant to baptize Him. He was no subject for the baptism of repentance that he had administered to all others. John recognized that Jesus was without sin and that he had no right to baptize Him. But Jesus wanted to begin His personal ministry by being baptized by John (Matt. 3:13-17; Mark 1:9-11; Luke 3:21-22). A study of these passages indicates that on that occasion three divine personalities were present. God the Father was in heaven. God the Son was baptized by John in the presence of vast multitudes of people. God the Holy Spirit in the form of a dove descended out of heaven and lit on

Jesus. At that time the voice of The Father from heaven announced, "This is my beloved Son, in whom I am well pleased."

God the Father sent the Holy Spirit to God the Son to empower Him for His mission on earth and to crown His miraculous powers. He was filled with the Holy Spirit without measure.

As he talked with Jewish leaders, John stated, "I did not recognize Him, but He who sent me to baptize in water said to me, 'He upon whom you see the Spirit descending and remaining upon Him, this is the One who baptizes in the Holy Spirit.' I myself have seen, and have testified that this is the Son of God" (John 1:33-34).

Jesus Christ had only three years to accomplish His life's work. Two events prepared Him for His ministry: the baptism by John and the temptation by Satan.

Christ Tempted by Satan

Now the Lord Jesus felt Himself in possession of supernatural powers essential to effect God's plan. The Holy Spirit led Him into the wilderness for 40 days, where He fasted without food. At the end of those days, His soul was tempted (tried) by Satan. Since Jesus was hungry from fasting, Satan suggested He turn rocks into bread. Jesus answered every temptation with Scripture from the Book of Deuteronomy.

> *It is written, Man shall not live by bread alone, but by every word that proceedeth out of the mouth of God. Then the devil taketh him up into the holy city, and setteth him on a pinnacle of the temple, And saith unto him, If thou be the Son of God, cast thyself down: for it is written, He shall give his angels charge concerning thee: and in their hands they shall bear thee up, lest at any time thou dash thy foot against a stone. Jesus said unto him, It is written again, Thou shalt not tempt the Lord thy God. Again, the devil taketh him up into an exceeding high mountain, and sheweth him all the kingdoms of the world, and the glory of them; And saith unto him, All these things will I give thee, if thou wilt fall down and worship me. Then saith Jesus unto him, Get thee hence, Satan: for it is written, Thou shalt worship the Lord thy God, and him only shalt thou serve. Then the devil leaveth him, and, behold, angels came and ministered unto him* (Matt. 4:4-11, KJV).

It is no sin to be tempted. The sin is in yielding. Christ resisted Satan's temptation, and Satan departed from Him for a season. "For we do not have a high priest who cannot sympathize with our weaknesses, but One who has been tempted in all things as *we* are, yet without sin" (Heb. 4:15). Only He is without sin, but He has faced temptations thrown at Him by the devil who tempts us.

Christ's Services on Earth

1. To be a sacrifice by dying on the cross to pay the penalty for man's sins.
2. To prepare His disciples to live for God's purposes. He helped them to know and love God and to establish His church.
3. To teach them to love one another (fellowship).
4. To give them the Word so they could grow to maturity (discipleship).
5. To show them how to serve (ministry).
6. To send them out to tell others (mission).

Jesus modeled a purpose-driven life, and He taught others how to live it. God wants us to introduce people to Christ and to bring them into His fellowship; help them to grow to maturity, to discover their place of service, and send them out to reach others.

Jesus' Ministry

As Jesus began His ministry, multitudes came out to hear His preaching. Many felt Jesus had come to set up the kingdom of God and to redeem Israel from Roman control. Jesus started with His plan projected, and never swerved from it. He constantly prayed to determine God's will. His plan was to establish the kingdom of God in the hearts of individuals and not to rely on the weapons of political and material strength, but only on the power of love and the force of truth. The public ministry of Jesus lasted three years, from age 30 to 33.

The Religious Leaders

The main religious men of the time were the Pharisees. They arose as champions of the separateness of the Jews from other nations. The Sadducees were another part of religious sects and belonged chiefly to the upper and wealthy classes. The Pharisees and scribes formed what we should call the middle class, although there were many members from the higher ranks of life. The lower classes, the country people, were separated by a huge chasm from their wealthy neighbors. Down below all these was a large class of those who had lost all connection with religion and well-ordered social life. Christ began His ministry in a society where the upper classes were devoting themselves to selfishness and scepticism.

The Year of Obscurity

Christ emerged from the wilderness after 40 days of temptation with a grasp on His future plan. He appeared once more on the bank of the Jordan river, and John the Baptist singled Him out as the great successor to himself of whom he had often spoken. Some of John's disciples became Jesus' disciples.

Christ Selected His Apostles and Began His Ministry

Jesus summoned His twelve disciples and gave them authority over unclean spirits, to cast them out, and to heal every kind of disease and every kind of sickness. Now the names of the twelve apostles are these: The first, Simon, who is called Peter, and Andrew his brother; and James the son of Zebedee, and John his brother; Philip and Bartholomew; Thomas and Matthew the tax collector; James the son of Alphaeus, and Thaddaeus; Simon the Zealot, and Judas Iscariot, the one who betrayed Him (Matt. 10:1-4). He first picked Andrew, Peter, Phillip, and Nathanael. The men who became the twelve apostles were from ordinary occupations, but . He called them to full-time service. They became mighty men who carried on His ministry and helped found His church on earth.

Jesus and "The Twelve" went to Cana in Galilee to attend a marriage celebration. There He performed His first miracle and displayed His powers (see John 2:1-10). That section closes with: "This beginning of His signs Jesus did in Cana of Galilee, and manifested His glory, and His disciples believed in Him" (v. 11). He returned to Judea to attend the Passover. While visiting the temple, He purged the temple of the sellers of animals and the money changers. He railed at them: "'Take these things away; stop making My Father's house a place of business.' His disciples remembered that it was written, 'Zeal for Your house will consume me'" (John 2:16b-17).

When Jesus followed John the Baptist, He baptized by the hands of His disciples. Jesus came first to the Jewish nation. He was the Messiah promised to their fathers, the Fulfiller of the nation's history. He had a far wider mission to the whole world, but He began with the Jews, and at Jerusalem. The leaders rejected Him so He expanded His worldwide community, accepting Jews and Gentiles alike.

His signs, wonders, and miracles excited the broadest attention. He first cured leprosy, and the amazement of the people knew no limits. The miracles of Jesus were of two kinds: those He wrought on man and He performed in the sphere of nature, such as turning water into wine, stilling the tempest, and multiplying the loaves. He healed the blind, crippled, and ill, and His human nature was endowed with the Holy Spirit without measure. His miracles were also symbols of His spiritual and saving work.

The Miracles of Jesus in the Gospel of John

Changing water into wine (2:1-11)
Healing of the official's son (4:46-54)
Healing the invalid at Bethesda (5:1-15)
Feeding of the 5,000 (6:1-15)
Walking on the Sea of Galilee (6:16-21)
Healing the blind (9:1-11)
Raising Lazarus from the dead (11:1-44)
The harvest of 153 large fish (21:1-14)

Why Did Jesus Do Miracles?

First, He performed miracles because His Father gave Him these signs as proof that He had sent Him, and He was in truth the Messiah prophesied in the Old Testament. Second, the miracles of Christ were the natural outflow of the divine fullness that dwelt in Him. He was and is God; God was in Him, and His human nature was fully endowed with the Holy Spirit. Third, His miracles were symbols of His spiritual and saving work.

Jesus Shared Two Favorite Stories:

Jesus and the Woman of Samaria

John 4:7-26

A Samaritan woman came to draw some water, and Jesus said to her, "Give me a drink of water." (His disciples had gone into town to buy food.) The Samaritan woman answered, "You are a Jew and I am a Samaritan—how can you ask me for a drink?" (For Jews will not use the same dishes that Samaritans use.) Jesus answered, "If you only knew what God gives, and who it is that is asking you for a drink, you would have asked him and he would have given you living water." "Sir," the woman said, "you don't have a bucket and the well is deep. Where would you get living water? Our ancestor Jacob gave us this well; he, his sons, and his flocks all drank from it. You don't claim to be greater than Jacob, do you?"

Jesus answered: "Whoever drinks this water will get thirsty again; but whoever drinks the water that I will give him will never be thirsty again. For the water that I will give him will become in him a spring which will provide him with living water, and give him eternal life." "Sir," the woman said, "give me this water! Then I will never be thirsty again, nor will I have to come here and draw water." "Go call your husband," Jesus told her, "and come back here." "I don't have a husband," the woman said. Jesus replied: "You are right when you say you don't have a husband. You have been married to five men, and the man you live with now is not really your husband. You have told me the truth."

"I see you are a prophet, sir," the woman said. "My Samaritan ancestors worshipped God on this mountain, but you Jews say that Jerusalem is the place where we should worship God." Jesus said to her: "Believe me, woman, the time will come when men will not worship the Father either on this mountain or in Jerusalem. You Samaritans do not really know whom you worship; we Jews know whom we worship, for salvation comes from the Jews. But the time is coming, and is already here, when the real worshipers will worship the Father in spirit and in truth. These are the worshipers the Father wants to worship him. God is Spirit, and those who worship him must worship in spirit and in truth."

The Lost (Prodigal) Son

Luke 15:11-24

Jesus went on to say: "There was a man who had two sons. The younger one said to his father, 'Father, give me now my share of property.' So the father divided the property between his two sons. After a few days the younger son sold his part of his inheritance, and he went to a country far away, where he wasted his money in reckless living. He spent everything he had. Then a severe famine spread over that country, and he was left without a thing. So he went to work for one of the citizens of that country, who sent him out to his farm to take care of the pigs. He wished he could fill himself with the bean pods the pigs ate, but no one gave him any.

"At last he came to his senses and said: 'All my father's hired workers have more than they can eat, and here I am, about to starve! I will get up and go to my father and say, Father, I have sinned against God and against you. I am no longer fit to be called your son; treat me as one of your hired workers.' So he got up and started back to his father. He was still a long way from home when his father saw him; his heart was filled with pity and he ran, threw his arms around his son, and kissed him.

"'Father,' the son said, 'I have sinned against God and against you. I am no longer worthy to be called your son.' But the father said to his servants, 'Quick! Bring the best robe and put it on him. Put a ring on his finger and sandals on his feel. Bring the fattened calf and kill it. Let's have a feast and celebrate. For this son of mine was dead and is alive again; he was lost and is found. So they began to celebrate.

"Meanwhile, the older son was in the field, he heard music and dancing. So he called one of the servants and asked him what was going on. 'Your brother has come,' he replied, 'and your father has killed the fattened calf because he has him back safe and sound.' The older brother became angry and refused to go in. So his father went out and pleaded with him. But he answered his father, 'Look! All these years I've been slaving for you and never disobeyed your orders. Yet you never gave me even a young goat so I could celebrate with my friends. But when this son of yours who has squandered your property with prostitutes comes home, you kill the fattened calf for him!'

"'My son,' the father said, 'you are always with me, and everything I have is yours. But we had to celebrate and be glad, because this brother of your was dead and is alive again, he was lost and is found'".

The Sinlessness of Jesus Christ

The Meaning of Sinlessness

To grasp the meaning of *sinlessness,* we must first understand the concept of sin. *Sin* could be defined as *any failure to conform perfectly to the holy character and will of God.* God requires people to be holy because He is holy (Lev. 11:44; 1 Pet. 1:15-16), but they fail to fulfill that requirement (Rom. 3:23).

Sin consists of four basic elements. First is a disposition of enmity against God, often called *the sin nature.* The Bible teaches that sin is inscribed indelibly upon the human heart—the inner control center of humans where all the decisions of life are made (Jer. 17:9) and the source of wrong thoughts and acts (Matt. 15:19). It further declares that "because the mind set on the flesh is hostile toward God; for it does not subject itself to the law of God, for it is not even able to do so" (Rom. 8:7). The *King James Version* says, "The carnal mind is enmity against God." Second, sin involves wrong acts. The Bible classifies such acts as murder, adultery, fornication, theft, false witness, blasphemy, and evil deeds (Matt. 15:19; John 3:19). Third, sin includes wrong thoughts, attitudes, intents, and impulses. For instance, the Bible signifies that lusting after forbidden things and certain kinds of anger are sin (Matt. 5:21-22, 27-28). Fourth, failure to do good deeds that should be done is sin (1 Sam. 12:23; Jas. 4:17).

So, according to these facts, we can conclude that a sinless person is one who always conforms perfectly to the holy character and will of God. Such a person does not possess a disposition of enmity against God (a sin nature), never commits a wrong act, never has a wrong thought, attitude, intent, or impulse, and never fails to do good deeds that should be done. Now, where does that leave us sinners? Some actually claim that they have reached sinless perfection, but what does John have to say about that?

> *If we say that we have no sin, we are deceiving ourselves and the truth is not in us. If we confess our sins, He is faithful and righteous to forgive us our sins and to cleanse us from all unrighteousness. If we say that we have not sinned, we make Him a liar and His word is not in us* (1 John 1:8-10).

Even as "God is light, and in him is no darkness at all" (John. 1:5, KJV), so Christ asserted that He was "the light of the world" in the midst of moral and spiritual darkness (John 8:12; 9:5; 12:35-36). He also indicated that because He radiated the light of sinless moral perfection, He would be hated and rejected by sinful human beings (John 3:19-20; 15:22-24). Hebrews 7:26 informs us that "it was fitting for us to have such a high priest, holy, innocent, undefiled, separated from sinners and exalted above the heavens." In mind and conduct He perfectly fulfills the divine requirements to be mankind's perfect High

Priest. Thus, as one who is completely free from sin, He did not have to bring an atoning offering for Himself, like the imperfect priests of the Old Testament.

Summation

The Bible lucidly teaches that Jesus Christ was totally sinless. In other words, He never failed to be conformed perfectly to the holy character and will of God. Therefore, He did not possess a sin nature, never committed a wrong act, never had a wrong thought, attitude, intent, or impulse, and never failed to do good deeds that should have been done!

The Human Character of Jesus

Purposefulness - He was possessed of purpose that drove Him.

Faith - Closely connected to this quality was faith, by which is meant His astonishing confidence in the accomplishment of His purpose.

Confidence in His success would appear only less remarkable than His success itself. One of Christ's successes was the institution of the church.

Graciousness - The people wondered at the gracious words that proceeded from His mouth.

Originality - He did not follow religious tradition. He was loyal to the truth.

Love of Mankind - Love to men/women was the passion which directed and inspired Him, and filled Him with boundless pity for humanity. It gave Him the most intense sympathy with every form of pain and misery.

Love for God - It is the supreme honor and attainment of man to be with God in feeling, thought, and purpose. Jesus had this in perspective.

Jesus the Teacher

He was the supreme Teacher. One of His favorite titles was "Teacher." His miracles drew in people to hear His words. He was and is the Living Word (John 1:1-3). Jesus was recognized as a prophet, and His preaching created widespread excitement. His words were heard with wonder and amazement. Jesus was successful in preaching and teaching because He spoke in parables. A parable is a short story or narrative drawn from life or nature by which a valuable lesson is taught or a moral precept is conveyed. His scenarios were from nature or everyday experiences. His parables are known for their clarity, purity, chasteness, intelligibility and simplicity. Young and old like to hear a story. Storytelling is one of the most eminent means of piquing interest, securing attention, and putting across vital truths. By connecting His teaching to the scenes of life, experience, or nature, He grabbed their attention and stirred their hearts. Each parable was designed to teach one overriding, pivotal truth.

His thoughts were God's thoughts, for He is the God-man. His desires were never in the least different from God the Father. His purpose was God's purpose for Him (prayer, Scripture, and study). His perfect manhood was in union with perfect Deity. God was manifest in the flesh.

The Cross and the Resurrection—Our Only Hope

(also see Chapter 5 of this book)

John 7: 37-39
In the last day, that great day of the feast, Jesus stood and cried, saying, If any man thirst, let him come unto me, and drink. He that believeth on me, as the scripture hath said, out of his belly shall flow rivers of living water. (By this spake he of the Spirit, which they that believe on him should receive: for the Holy Ghost was not yet given; because that Jesus was not yet glorified)

Four Accounts of Jesus' Life and Ministry: The Gospels

In a previous chapter, we referred to the four accounts of our Lord's life and ministry. Referred to as the Gospels, they are Matthew, Mark, Luke, and John. Let us recap:

Matthew

Matthew wrote his Gospel with the Jews in mind. It was written in a framework of Hebrew thought and diction, well acquainted with the Old Testament with frequent quotations from the Law and the Prophets. His aim was to prove that Jesus was The Messiah. Matthew's writing for the Jews traced the regal line of the house of David from Abraham to Jesus. He recognized Jesus as the "Son of Man." The implications of the miraculous conception and virgin birth are complete.

Mark

Mark beamed his account toward the Romans. Supposed to be the pupil of Peter, Mark wrote with Peter's spirit seeming to pervade this Gospel. It is believed Mark was the first-written of the four accounts. Mark wrote for the Roman people who liked men of action. Mark emphasized what Jesus did and taught. He, at the same time, assumed Christ's divine-human nature. He wrote nothing about the virgin birth because the Romans were not particularly interested in that subject. Mark's plan was to present Jesus as a man of action, who dealt with the masses of the common people. He recorded Jesus' Great Galilean ministry.

Luke

Luke wrote for the Greeks, representative of the Gentiles, for he was a non-Jew. He was a medical doctor (M.D.). His Gospel was historical. He was more of a trained historian than the other evangelists. The Greeks loved beauty and grandeur. Luke wrote of Jesus as a perfect man. He recognized that Christ was more than human—that He was the divine-human Savior of the world. Luke started with the birth narrative and the genealogy of Jesus, which he traced back to Adam.

John

John supplies what the other evangelists omitted. He dwells expressly on the work of Jesus in Judea. John includes some private interviews, His interior life, His most profound and mysterious sayings, and the fervor and sublimity of His farewell discourse. John discloses the fact that he laid emphasis upon Jesus as the God-man. John supposed on the part of his readers a knowledge of Jesus in general as He moved about Palestine engaged in His work among the masses.

Statements Regarding Christ's Human Nature and His Body

That Christ had an actual human body is seen from John's telling us that the Word which was in the beginning with God and which was God became flesh and *dwelt among us* (John 1:1-14). *Flesh*, in this passage, refers to His physical body consisting of flesh and bones—for, we are told, this *Word dwelt among us*. These words can mean nothing other than that Christ had a real, literal body. The same apostle informs us that he and his fellow-disciples had seen Christ with their own eyes, had heard Him with their own ears, and had handled Him (His body) with their own hands. Here is the essence of his testimony:

Our Lord was thoroughly human—in all that the word indicates—but apart from sin. At the same time He was God in the fullest sense of that term. There was a union between the divine nature and the human spirit in such a manner as to allow only one consciousness. In Him was the perfect union of divine and the human. He was the spiritual head of the new race, the company of born-again, saved people. This truth was declared in I Corinthians 15:45. "So also it is written, 'The first man, Adam, became a living soul.' The last Adam became a life-giving spirit."

Jesus' Praying

He was a man of deep prayer to the Father, offering us an example of what a prayer life ought to be. It was His delight and constant resource. When He was so tired with the labors of the day that He was ready to collapse from sheer exhaustion, He would escape away from the crowds and His disciples to the mountain-top, and spend the whole night in communion with His Father. He never undertook crucial steps without time with the Father. Jesus spoke frequently about forgiveness. Read Matthew 6:14-15 on how strongly He felt on this subject.

Verse 14 - For if you forgive men/women when they sin against you, your heavenly Father will forgive your sins.

Verse 15 - But if you do not forgive men/women their sins, your Father will not forgive you.

Chapter 7
God the Holy Spirit

I will ask the Father, and He will give you another Helper, that He may be with you forever; that is the Spirit of truth, whom the world cannot receive, because it does not see Him or know Him, but you know Him because He abides with you and will be in you (John 14:16-17).

The Holy Spirit: the Third Person of the Trinity

The Promise of the Spirit

The Lord Jesus Christ promised His apostles the coming of the Spirit as He was nearing the close of His earthly ministry. He actually explained why it would be better for Him to go away, to ascend to the Father in Heaven.

But now I am going to Him who sent Me; and none of you asks Me, "Where are You going?" But because I have said these things to you, sorrow has filled your heart. But I tell you the truth, it is to your advantage that I go away; for if I do not go away, the Helper will not come to you; but if I go, I will send Him to you (John 16:5-7).

The apostles must have sat there, nonplussed, asking themselves,

"How could it possibly be better for our Lord to go away?" But Jesus pointed out, "If I do not go away, the Helper will not come to you" (John 16:7). If you project that statement a bit, maybe you can better understand it, for Jesus could, in His incarnate body, be in only one place at a time. When He was with His disciples on a mountain, He couldn't be in the marketplace or the temple. But the Holy "Comforter" (KJV) or Helper the Father was sending would have the capacity to dwell in every believer any where in the world. That, Jesus indicated, would be to their advantage after His ascension to the Father.

The Three Aspects of the Holy Spirit:

- The baptism of the Holy Spirit
- The fulness of the Holy Spirit
- The manifestation of the Holy Spirit.

The Gift of the Holy Spirit and Baptism of the Holy Spirit

We don't have much of a problem confessing our sins and believing in Jesus Christ for our salvation. But when it comes to trusting God with day-to-day situations, that often changes. We often take things into our own hands and then complain when matters don't pan out. As a result we don't sense the closeness of the Holy Spirit.

At the time of conversion and being "born again," the Holy Spirit enters our lives to live. The Holy Spirit is more than a sensation or feeling. He is the Third Person of the Trinity. He is God in us.

Paul testified, "I have been crucified with Christ; and it is no longer I who live, but Christ lives in me; and the life which I now live in the flesh I live by faith in the Son of God, who loved me and gave Himself up for me" (Gal. 2:20). How can Christ, who has ascended into heaven, live in us? He does through the Holy Spirit. The same Spirit of God who abided with Jesus throughout His earthly ministry is the One who now has residence in the heart of each and every believer.

Paul in Ephesians warned against lying, stealing, wrong kinds of speech, and bad attitudes toward one another.

> *And do not give the devil an opportunity. He who steals must steal no longer; but rather he must labor, performing with his own hands what is good, so that he will have something to share with one who has need. Let no unwholesome word proceed from your*

> *mouth, but only such a word as is good for edification according to the need of the moment, so that it will give grace to those who hear* (Eph. 4:27-29).

Then he laid this on them. "Do not grieve the Holy Spirit of God, by whom you were sealed for the day of redemption" (Eph. 4:30). That word "grieve" means to make sad, cause grief and pain, burden down, and render sorrowful. How could a conscientious Christian do that to the Spirit? Probably the worst response is to ignore Him! He is God of very God living inside of believers. He is with us in all we face as our Helper, our Teacher, and our Friend to keep us from falling. And, if we ignore Him, living as though He were not within us, we are treating Him as an outsider. No wonder it grieves Him.

The Difference Between the Baptism and the Filling of the Holy Spirit

Since the Day of Pentecost (see Acts 2), the baptism of the Holy Spirit occurs at the split second one believes in and accepts Jesus Christ as Lord and Savior. "But now God has placed the members, each one of them, in the body, just as He desired" (1 Cor. 12:18). At conversion, when one is born again, one is baptized in or with the Spirit. The descent of the Holy Spirit on the Day of Pentecost signified His coming to indwell believers. In the Old Testament the Spirit would come and go within a person's life—for a particular empowerment and then leave. It is often explained that "there is one baptism and many fillings."

Being filled with the Holy Spirit is to surrender control of one's life to God's will without holding back. The key is obedience to God. Sanctification is the process of becoming more like Jesus Christ, our example and "model." Sanctification (becoming holy and pure in Christ) is a lifelong journey

> *Blessed be the God and Father of our Lord Jesus Christ, who according to His great mercy has caused us to be born again to a living hope through the resurrection of Jesus Christ from the dead, . . .* (1 Pet. 1:3). *But grow in the grace and knowledge of our Lord and Savior Jesus Christ. To Him be the glory, both now and to the day of eternity. Amen* (2 Pet. 3:18).

Too many professing Christians recoil from the words "holiness," "purity," "righteousness," and "sanctification." Yet, without these qualities a person evinces that he is not born again. Essentially, it means we are to become like our Savior—and, of course, more like His Father, who is also ours. The apostle John summed up the end result of our sanctification:

> *"Beloved, now we are children of God, and it has not appeared as yet what we will be. We know that when He appears, we will be like Him, because we will see Him just as He is* (1 John 3:2, author's underline).

There you have it. Even as our Lord Jesus is like the Father, so we will be like the Father, the Son, and the Holy Spirit! We will not be God, but we will have His traits. In sanctification the believer is guided to maturity by the Holy Spirit. "For you were called to freedom, brethren; only do not turn your freedom into an opportunity for the flesh, but through love serve one another" (Gal. 5:13).

The Living Bible paraphrase of Romans 12:12 goes: "Don't copy the behavior and customs of this world, but be a new and different person with a fresh newness in all you do and think. Then you will learn from your own experience how his ways will really satisfy you." Because of all Christ has done, believers are new persons, new "creatures" or "creations" in Him. Therefore if anyone is in Christ, he is a new creature; the old things passed away; behold, new things have come" (2 Cor. 5:17).

In this pilgrimage, join your heart and arms with multiplied millions of fellow believers from every race and background, because He has made you one in Him. The Scriptures explain that sanctification is progressive.

Walking Daily in Faith

We must yield ourselves to our Lord Jesus day by day. The Spirit-filled life truly sets in once we are totally persuaded that we can do nothing except through the strength of the Spirit. Paul counseled us to let Christ's teachings predominate in our hearts, causing us to become rich in wisdom and understanding. The Holy Spirit employs the Bible, the written Word of God, to teach, to scold, and train us in living for Christ.

All Scripture is inspired by God and profitable for teaching, for reproof, for correction, for training in righteousness; so that the man of God may be adequate, equipped for every good work (2 Tim. 3:16-17).

To the extent that we listen to the Word and heed it, we are filled with the Spirit. At conversion, the Spirit enters our inmost being. At our surrender to God, the Spirit, already entered, assumes full possession.

Outworkings of the Spirit

The same power of the Spirit that enabled the apostles to preach the Gospel is available to us today. Never before had the full impact of sin's repulsiveness been brought to bear on men's hearts and consciences as when the Spirit's power was on the apostles.

Not to believe in Jesus Christ, and to willfully reject Him, makes up the sinister core of sin. The sin of sins is to reject Him who is the Light of Life, God's only provision for our eternal salvation. The Holy Spirit convicts people with respect to sin. Many reject the truth of Jesus' Godhead and Saviorhood. They refuse to humble themselves and to admit they are sinners in desperate need of the Savior. Finally, to deny the Holy Spirit's work and power is to commit the unpardonable sin. Blasphemy against the Holy Ghost (Matt. 12:31, 32; Mark 3:28, 29; Luke 12:10) is a continued and obstinate rejection of the gospel—thus, the unpardonable sin—because as long as a sinner remains in unbelief he voluntarily shuts himself off from pardon. One evidence that a person has committed the unpardonable sin is his constant attributing to the power of Satan those miracles Christ performed, or generally those works that are the result of the Spirit's ministry. Jesus warned:

Therefore I say to you, any sin and blasphemy shall be forgiven people, but blasphemy against the Spirit shall not be forgiven. Whoever speaks a word against the Son of Man, it shall be forgiven him; but whoever speaks against the Holy Spirit, it shall not be forgiven him, either in this age or in the age to come (Matt. 12:31-32).

For this there is no provision for escape from judgment. The Son of God prays—intercedes—for us from his throne in heaven. The Holy Spirit prays for us from the throne of our heart.

The power of the Holy Spirit is exhibited in a believer's life through two outlets: the gifts of the spirit and the fruit of the Spirit. The gifts of the Spirit are for building up the Body of Christ —"for the equipping of the saints for the work of service, to the building up of the body of Christ" (Eph. 4:12).

The fruit of the Spirit comprise the fragrance that invites non-believers to become members of Christ's body. "But the fruit of the Spirit is love, joy, peace, patience, kindness, goodness, faithfulness, gentleness, self-control; against such things there is no law" (Gal. 5:22-23).

God Calls Us to Follow the Leading of His Spirit

Our sovereign Lord has a definite plan in mind of each of our lives. But the only means of ascertaining His plan is by knowing Him. To know God, to have an intimate spiritual relationship with Him, should be the "magnificent obsession" of every believer. Paul testified: "That I may know him, and the power of his resurrection, and the fellowship of his sufferings, being made conformable unto his death" (Phil. 3:10). The Holy Spirit is an agent of communication. Through Him God provides knowledge and wisdom for any eventuality that confronts us.

The Spirit gives us leadership in even the minutest details of daily life and service—as to where to go and not to go, what to do and what not to do. Jesus made this promise based on His Father's ability. While many people argue that believers must have a "second blessing" or a "second experience," God's Word makes this plain: **When we accept Christ as our Savior, His Spirit comes to indwell us.** The question is not how much of the Spirit we have, but how much of us does He have?

A Spirit-filled Life

A Spirit-filled life means that a person is under the control of the Spirit and in submission and surrender to Him. It implies that the person empowered by the Spirit has laid down his self-will and yielded to God's will. Paul wrote to the Christians at Rome:

> *Therefore I urge you, brethren, by the mercies of God, to present your bodies a living and holy sacrifice, acceptable to God, which is your spiritual service of worship. And do not be conformed to this world, but be transformed by the renewing of your mind, so that*

you may prove what the will of God is, that which is good and acceptable and perfect (Rom. 12:1-2).

How are we to do that? The Holy Spirit transforms us and renews our minds so we can not only know but also do the will of God. The more we allow God to work in us, the more we will experience the evidence of His Spirit working within us. "But when He, the Spirit of truth, comes, He will guide you into all the truth; for He will not speak on His own initiative, but whatever He hears, He will speak; and He will disclose to you what is to come" (John 16:13).

The Spirit cannot give us guidance as long as we insist on having our own way and doing our "own thing." The stubborn, self-willed believer gropes along in the dark, even though God offers a powerful flashlight to light his path. Yet, he refuses to accept the illumination, preferring to stagger and stumble along. That sort of believer is in a backslidden position.

First, we have to ask the Spirit to lead us; then by an act of will place our life situations and our future in Him. God's Spirit empowers us for ministry . . . but also restores us, comforts us, and heals us when we have fallen prey to sin or trials. God has not left us comfortless. He has provided a potent, unswerving Source of hope through His Holy Spirit—but it is our responsibility to ask for help and empowerment.

Day-by-Day Provisions

There is an old hymn with words by Mrs. M.A. Kidder that go: "Ere you left your room this morning, did you think to pray?" Did you? Do you spend time thinking through and praying for your day? Never "fret" or worry about it, but still anticipate possible problems and ask the Lord to give you guidance in handling each detail. Then claim His victory as you seek the leadership of His Holy Spirit.

While going through your day-to-day routine, ask yourself, "How much of myself am I making available to God? How much of my life is Spirit-inspired versus self-indulgent? Be honest, remembering that God has one major goal in mind—that is, to draw you into a close personal relationship with His Son.

We can praise God that through Jesus Christ our sins are forgiven and our relationship is restored to our Heavenly Father. A splendid means of increasing your awareness of the Spirit is to begin each day with a pledge to walk in the Spirit. Pray that the fruit of the Spirit will be in evidence to those around you—even though they may not at first understand why. Once again focus on Galatians 5:22-23. Remember that the fruit (plural) of the Spirit are implanted into the inward life of every born-again believer.

When irritations arise, and they will, remember that a mind centered on the things of the Spirit results in a life and of peace. If you mope and think negatively, brooding over life's problems, chances are you will undergo extra stress and lack genuine peace. The apostle Paul wrote that the mind of the flesh is fixed on the things of the flesh, but . . .

> *If ye then be risen with Christ, seek those things which are above, where Christ sitteth on the right hand of God. Set your affection on things above, not on things on the earth. For ye are dead [to the old life], and your life is hid with Christ in God. When Christ, who is our life, shall appear, then shall ye also appear with him in glory* (Col. 3:1-4. KJV).

About six years ago, while I served as a leader for Bible Study Fellowship, one of the men in my class, remarked, "I know about God and Jesus Christ His Son, but who is this fellow, the Holy Spirit." I attempted to explain but also promised myself I would do a special study of the Holy Spirit. Of course, I believed in the Holy Spirit, but I did not understand all the roles of the Spirit. I hope this is a help to you.

Walking in the Spirit

When I retired, I began to live a life of deeper faith. As I walked through the hours of the day, God guided me through the indwelling of the Holy Spirit. Being led by Him ushered into my life a new sense of contentment. When I began emptying myself of me, my selfish desires and habits, the Holy Spirit was free to live out His life through me. I no longer wanted to do things my way. Instead, I sought God's way. I then had a deepened awareness of God's Spirit living in and through me. This is the nature of life in Christ. Yes, the Holy Spirit is for us the presence of Jesus Christ since He ascended to the Heavenly Father. We are indwelt by the Spirit of God, and He is the living essence of Jesus in us.

The teachings of Peter and Paul correspond exactly on the plan of salvation—that people must repent and believe (have faith) in Jesus and His death on the cross and resurrection to pay the penalty for our sins.

> *That if thou shalt confess with thy mouth the Lord Jesus, and shalt believe in thine heart that God hath raised him from the dead, thou shalt be saved. For with the heart man believeth unto righteousness; and with the mouth confession is made unto salvation* (Rom. 10:9-10, KJV).

John the Baptist preached repentance and water baptism, calling out about Jesus, "Behold the lamb of God that takes away the sin of the world" (John 1:29). That lamb, Jesus, would come after him and would baptize with the Holy Spirit. The simple secret of being "born again" (receiving the Holy Spirit) is repentance and faith in Jesus Christ, asking Jesus to come live in our hearts through the Holy Spirit.

God provided the gift by His grace to enable us to receive the Holy Spirit. People must reach out to receive the gift by faith and opening up their hearts to receive Christ into their lives.

The Victory Is Yours

After the crucifixion the disciples hid themselves for fear they too would end up like Jesus. The place they chose, the upper room, to remain was, in fact, the last site where they had communed with the Lord. Being there helped them to recall His words of assurance. "Do not be afraid. I will come to you. I will not leave you comfortless; I will send another who will guide you into all wisdom and truth." Then suddenly came the words spoken aloud to them, "Peace be with you." They beheld their risen Lord standing before them. He had come to them in their darkest hour, as He had promised.

The Holy Spirit is God's agent of love and grace. He understands all about you—your joys, sorrows, fears, defeats, and victories. He perceives your desires and works ceaselessly to shape them after God's "good and acceptable and perfect will" (see Rom. 12:2).

> *"Now the Lord is the Spirit, and where the Spirit of the Lord is, there is freedom"* (2 Cor. 3:17, NIV).

> *"For the one who sows to his own flesh shall from the flesh reap corruption, but the one who sows to Spirit shall from the Spirit reap eternal life. And let us not lose heart in doing good, for in due time we shall reap"* (Gal. 6:8-9, NIV).

Roles of the Holy Spirit

- He reminds us of Jesus' teachings.

"The Helper, the Holy Spirit, whom the Father will send in my name, He will teach you all things, and bring to your remembrance all that I said to you. Peace I leave with you; not as the world gives, do I give to you. Let not your heart be troubled, nor let it be fearful" (John 14:26-27).

The more we turn to Jesus for guidance and insight, the more we are magnetized to Him in friendship. The desire for sin fades as we move closer to Him. We develop a hunger to learn more about Him, and the Spirit of God is then free to reveal Himself to us.

- He comes alongside us, helping us to understand the Word of God.
- He is a Source of communication with God, for He is God, the Third Person of the Trinity, the Godhead.
- He is an intercessor, aiding us in our prayers but also praying for us to the Heavenly Father. He literally intercedes for us in prayer. "And in the same way the Spirit also helps our weakness; for we do not know how to pray as we should, but the Spirit Himself intercedes with deep groanings too deep for words; and He searches the heart and knows what the mind of the Spirit is, because He intercedes for the saints according to the will of God" (Rom. 8:26-27).

Ask God to give you a heart that longs to know more about Him. Pray that you will become more sensitive and receptive to God's Spirit, His leading, and how He seeks to communicate with you. While God spoke primarily through His prophets in the Old Testament, today He speaks to the hearts and minds of those willing to seek Him.

Realize that Satan will do all within his diabolic power to mar your relationship with God.

Refuse to yield to thoughts of condemnation, defeat, and fear.

- More about the Spirit's role as intercessor. "The Spirit also helps our weakness; for we do not know how to pray as we should, but the Spirit Himself intercedes for us. . ." (Rom. 8:26). His role in prayer is to assist us in praying adequately to the Father. As Jesus intercedes for us as our High Priest, so the Holy Spirit joins in to intercede for us in prayer. When we hardly speak or even think, "... the Spirit helps us in our weakness. We do not know what we ought to pray for, but the Spirit himself intercedes for us with groans the words cannot express." So, God the Son and God the Holy Spirit help us carry our petitions "boldly to the throne of grace" (see Heb. 4:16).

Though the Scriptures themselves are light for us, there is still a necessity for additional illumination so we can lucidly perceive the light. The same Holy Spirit who inspired the Scriptures throws light on the Word for our benefit, so we can hear, receive, properly understand, and assimilate God's message.

- He is a Teacher.

> *I have yet many things to say unto you, but ye cannot bear them now. Howbeit when he, the Spirit of truth, is come, he will guide you into all truth: for he shall not speak of himself; but whatsoever he shall hear, that shall he speak: and he will shew you things to come. He shall glorify me: for he shall receive of mine, and shall shew it unto you. All things that the Father hath are mine: therefore said I, that he shall take of mine, and shall shew it unto you. A little while, and ye shall not see me: and again, a little while, and ye shall see me, because I go to the Father* (John 16:12-15).

Jesus promised about the Spirit: "He will teach you all things" (see John 14:26). Jesus Christ was the greatest teacher the world has ever known, but when He was ready to depart, He briefed His apostles about the soon coming of a teacher who would "guide you [them] into all truth"(John 16:13, KJV). Considering all that the incarnate Jesus taught, that is absolutely amazing. All truth!

- Christ dwells in the believer through the Spirit. I cannot overemphasize: for those who have accepted Christ as Lord of their lives, Christ dwells in them through the Holy Spirit. The King of Kings has received all authority, and the indwelling Spirit is infinitely more powerful than Satan and his demons.

"Dear young friends, you belong to God and have already won your fight with those who are against Christ, because there is someone in your hearts who is stronger than any evil teacher in this wicked world" (1 John 4:4). That someone is none other than the Holy Spirit.

- We are the temple of the Holy Spirit who is in us.

- The Holy Spirit convicts the world concerning sin, righteousness, and judgment of sin (see John 16:8-11).

Concerning sin—The Holy Spirit makes us aware that sin is our major problem and that Jesus has given us a marvelous gift. The Spirit is to convict us of sin and make us feel guilty enough that we will confess our sins and trust in Jesus.

- The Spirit reminds us of God's righteousness. He convicts mankind of the fact that God has already judged sin to the extent that whoever believes and has faith in Jesus Christ will never come into condemnation (see Rom. 5:1, 8:1).
- The Spirit understands the thoughts of God and imparts knowledge to believers (Rom. 8:9; 11:1; 2 Cor. 3:16; 2 Tim. 1:14).
- He encourages us, is our personal Friend, is our guide and counselor, peace for soul, illuminates, directs us, warns us.

The Second Aspect of the Holy Spirit

The fullness of the Holy Spirit involves sanctification. Our Lord Jesus declared, "I am come that they might have life and that they might have it more abundantly" (John 10:10). Among His promises was that of the Holy Spirit's coming: "But you will receive power when the Holy Spirit has come upon you; and you shall be My witnesses both in Jerusalem, and in all Judea and Samaria, and even to the remotest part of the earth" (Acts 1:8). And their lives immediately became an unending record of signs, wonders, and miracles done in the power of the Spirit. Stephen, the first martyr for his Lord, was stoned to death for preaching the gospel. He was "full of grace and power, was performing great wonders and signs among the people" (Acts 6:8).

The apostles and other disciples were filled with a burning desire to share the gospel of God's love to all the world—still every Christian's commission today. According to knowledgeable accounts all of the apostles, except John (who was exiled to the Isle of Patmos) suffered horrible death for their faith.

Saul of Tarsus, later called Paul, carried Christ's message all over the Mediterranean world and into Asia and Europe. He ended up writing 13 Books of the New Testament and was the greatest missionary ever. Yet, before his encounter with Jesus on the Road to Damascus, he was a fanatical persecutor of Jesus' disciples. He wrote the Galatians:

"For I neither received it [the gospel] of man, neither was I taught it, but by the revelation of Jesus Christ. For ye have heard of my conversation in time past in the Jews' religion, how that beyond measure I persecuted the church of God, and wasted it" (Gal. 1:12-13, KJV). After his conversion, he was consumed with an unquenchable love for unsaved mankind, and lost his head on a Roman chopping block because of his stand for Christ. He testified, "To the weak I became weak, that I might win the weak; I have become all things to all men, so that I may by all means save some" (1 Cor. 9:22).

Tradition has it that Peter the apostle was crucified upside down for his faith. He did not feel worthy of being slain in the same manner and position as his Lord and Savior. There is no doubt that next to Paul, he had more of an impact than any other Christian then or since. He wrote two Epistles, 1 and 2 Peter. He was transformed from a fearful and impetuous follower of Jesus to a flaming evangelist who preached on the Day of Pentecost, and 3,000 souls were saved (see Acts the second chapter). He became a prominent leader in the Jerusalem church. What accounted for the difference in these men's lives? The anointing and infilling of the Holy Spirit!

The Bible teaches there is a fullness of the Holy Spirit greater than usually received at conversion. Fullness occurs when we completely yield our lives to Christ, fully trusting and committing to Him. For instance, on the Day of Pentecost the disciples ". . . were all filled with the Holy Spirit and began to speak with other tongues, as the Spirit was giving them utterance" (Acts 2:4). They "were all filled with the Holy Spirit." The account goes:

> *But Peter, taking his stand with the eleven, raised his voice and declared to them: "Men of Judea and all you who live in Jerusalem, let this be known to you and give heed to my words. "For these men are not drunk, as you suppose, for it is only the third hour of the day; but this is what was spoken of through the prophet Joel: 'And it shall be in the last days,' God says, 'That I will pour forth of My Spirit on all mankind; And your sons and your daughters shall prophesy, And your young men shall see visions, And your old men shall dream dreams; . . .'"* (Acts 2:14-17).

Yet, only a few days later the disciples, under extreme persecution, prayed:

And now, Lord, take note of their threats, and grant that Your bond-servants may speak Your word with all confidence, while You extend Your hand to heal, and signs and wonders take place through the name of Your holy servant Jesus (Acts 4:28-29).

The Scripture then records: "And when they had prayed, the place where they had gathered together was shaken, and they were all filled with the Holy Spirit and began to speak the word of God with boldness" (Acts 4:31). The happenings on the Day of Pentecost clearly showed that the disciples were filled with the Spirit; then they were filled again several days later. What could that indicate? Precisely that there is one initial baptism with or in the Spirit but multiple fillings.

Indwelling Holiness

Since the Holy Spirit is indeed holy, He cultivates holiness and righteousness within us. When we allow the Spirit to control our lives— which means the surrender of our wills to God's will—we love every word from God. "But He [Jesus] answered and said, "It is written, 'Man shall not live on bread alone, but on every word that proceeds out of the mouth of God'" (Matt. 4:4).

We will then request, as did the Lord Jesus, "Not My will, but yours be done." We will trust God in trials and tribulations and also in triumphs; in darkness as well as in the light. We will walk by faith and not by sight (see 2nd Cor. 5:7), and we will rely on God with unswerving confidence, "leaning on the everlasting arms," as the old song goes—resting in His love. The Spirit curtails our excessive craving for the "bangles, baubles, and beads" of this wicked world system and causes us to set our "affections on things above, not on things on the earth" (see Col. 3:2, KJV). The Spirit thus will guide us into all truth (see John 16:13).

The Spirit Is the Commander in Our Spiritual Warfare

Spirit-filled Christians are not perfect, but they "press toward the mark for the prize of the high calling of God in Christ Jesus" (Phil. 3:14, KJV). They still have the flesh to contend with, for the old sin nature wants us to live for self, but the new spiritual nature wants us to live for God. The Holy Spirit is the competent agent of our cleansing, sanctification, and righteousness. The Holy Spirit "raises" or rears us in Christ, nurtures us as God's children, and helps us mature and become more like Christ. He fulfills the role of Sanctifier in the process that begins the moment we are saved and continues until death when the believer is made totally righteous and glorified in Christ.

The Holy Spirit is a gift from God by God, but the fullness of the Holy Spirit is up to us. This can be soon after being "born again" spiritually or be progressive over a lifetime.

Questions About Receiving the Spirit and the Spirit's Fullness

How do we receive the Holy Spirit? By repenting of our sins, asking God for forgiveness, and having belief and faith in Christ's crucifixion and resurrection.

How do we receive the fullness of the Spirit? By committing our lives to Christ and giving Him complete obedience and trust.

The apostles were again and again filled with the Holy Spirit, but they were baptized with the Holy Spirit only once. The receiving of the Holy Spirit depends on one set of conditions and the fullness of the Spirit on another.

If we don't have His fullness, we may think we have not received Him. The truth is we should accept forever the fact that we have received Him—then proceed to know the secret of His fullness.

How May We Experience His Fullness?

How, then, will our yearnings for the fullness of the Spirit be gratified? How are we going to experience His abundance of the fruit of the Spirit? What is the clue to this overflowing life in the Spirit, this fullness? If we are born again, we have definitely received the Holy Spirit. Without the Spirit we could not be saved in the first place. Neither could we have the assurance of salvation. It is a matter of *faith*, not *feelings*. Yet, we may jump to the conclusion that the Spirit does not indwell us because of a lack of power within our lives—else how explain the decrepit evidence of His presence and power?

Let me nail this down: we must plainly recognize that every child of God has received the gift of the Holy Spirit. It is of the utmost importance that this superb be vividly seen and accepted by the believer. Paul wrote: "But ye are not in the flesh, but in the Spirit, if so be that the Spirit of God dwell in you. Now if any man have not the Spirit of Christ, he is none of his" (Rom. 8:9).

If ever there was a time when the power of God filled a person and burned in his heart, it was when Peter preached his mighty sermon on the Day of Pentecost. He was caught up in the Spirit's anointing of power. The God of truth spoke through him and answered the pleading of the multitude, "What shall we do?" He answered with authority: "Repent, and each of you be baptized in the name of Jesus Christ for the forgiveness of your sins; and you will receive the gift of the Holy Spirit" (Acts 2:38). It is apparent from many passages in the Bible that baptism is an ordinance carried out after faith in Christ as a sin-bearer. God taught through Peter this tremendous truth: the two main conditions of receiving the Holy Spirit are repentance and faith in Christ for the forgiveness or remission of sins.

No other conditions are necessary. Repent (turn from, do an about face from one's sins) of your sins and believe in the Lord Jesus Christ for salvation, and you will receive the gift of the Holy Spirit. Baptism is essential for our obedience. Paul urged upon his hearers "repentance toward God and faith in our Lord Jesus Christ" (Acts 20:21b).

The Secret to Fullness

All right. You have received the gift of the Spirit. He has entered your life to live forever. What, then, is the secret of His fullness, of His superabundant life of peace, power, and love? It is absolute, through-and-through surrender of your life to God—to do His will instead of your own. So, when you (we) surrender your (our) sins and believe, the Holy Spirit immediately fills us.The receiving of the Holy Spirit is God's answer to repentance and faith. At conversion the Spirit enters. At surrender the Spirit, already entered, assumes full possession. The supreme, human condition of the fullness of the Spirit is a life wholly surrendered to God to do His will.

> *Therefore I urge you, brethren, by the mercies of God, to present your bodies a living and holy sacrifice, acceptable to God, which is your spiritual service of worship. And do not be conformed to this world, but be transformed by the renewing of your mind, so that you may prove what the will of God is, that which is good and acceptable and perfect* (Rom. 12:1-2).

The unbeliever has the self-life but not the God life within him. He walks in the flesh and in that only. The Spirit may and does strive with him—but not in him—for only "he who is Christ's" has the Spirit. But if that person without Christ then repents and has faith in Him, there is a marvelous change. What happens? He is born again, born from above, born of God, born of the Spirit.

And what do these phrases signify? That a new life, a divine life, the life of God has come into him. God Himself, in the person of the Holy Spirit, has stepped in to live in him. He has received the Holy Spirit and now has what he did not have, and what every unsaved person does not have—a new nature.

The Conflict

But when the new life through the Spirit came in, did the old life, the old nature, totally evacuate? If he had, then to receive the Spirit would be at once and forever to be filled with Him, for He would have full possession. However, this is not the case. The old life does not completely leave when the new comes in. About this God's Word and our own experience are painfully clear. The apostle Paul struggled with this ever-present reality:

> *For we know that the Law is spiritual, but I am of flesh, sold into bondage to sin. For what I am doing, I do not understand; for I am not practicing what I would like to do, but I am doing the very thing I hate. But if I do the very thing I do not want to do, I agree with the Law, confessing that the Law is good. So now, no longer am I the one doing it, but sin which dwells in me. For I know that nothing good dwells in me, that is, in my flesh; for the willing is present in me, but the doing of the good is not. For the good that I want, I do not do, but I practice the very evil that I do not want. But if I am doing the very thing I do not want, I am no longer the one doing it, but sin which dwells in me. I find then the principle that evil is present in me, the one who wants to do good. For I joyfully concur with the law of God in the inner man, but I see a different law in the members of my body, waging war against the law of my mind and making me a prisoner of the law of sin which is in my members* (Rom. 7:14-23).

But now, as a believer, the born-again person has a dual nature.

In him are both "the flesh" and "the Spirit"—the old life and the new. These two co-exist; both dwell in Him. But as extreme foes, they struggle for the mastery of his life. Paul also explained this warfare in his Epistle to the Galatians. "For the flesh sets its desire against the Spirit, and the Spirit against the flesh; for these are in opposition to one another, so that you may not do the things that you please" (Gal. 5:17).

For each not only wants to be in him but to have full possession. Each strives to fill him. The problem is changed. It is no longer: How shall he receive the Spirit? That is settled; he has received Him, but he discovers a joint-tenant with the flesh. Wherefore the question now is, having two natures within him, how will he be filled with one of them? How will he experience the fullness and abundant life of the Spirit, and be delivered from the life and power of the flesh?

The solution seems patently clear. How else could he be filled except by yielding himself unreservedly to the one he wants to control and fill him? He has the power of choice; he can surrender himself to either. At one time he had yielded himself as a servant to the flesh (see Rom. 6:19). Wasn't he then "filled with all unrighteousness"? (see Rom. 1:29). Now he should allow the Spirit to dominate and fill him with righteousness. Think of this analogy. It is as though the fresh air of springtime should waft through a huge house laden with putrid stenches. Suppose, though, you open up only one room to the invigorating air and leave all the other rooms shut tight and smothered with the nauseating odors. The refreshing, untainted air has entered, but how can it possibly fill the house until it is allowed to rush through and purify the entire dwelling?

There is only one attitude that the surrendered life should assume, and that is to experience the Spirit's fullness. How? To "trust and obey," as the old hymn by J.H. Sammis goes. The essence of surrender to God involves the absolute bending of our wills to obey His will. During the wedding feast at Cana of Galilee, Mary, the mother of Jesus, instructed the servants, "Whatsoever he [Jesus] saith unto you, do it" (John 2:5, KJV). There is the key to the filling of the Spirit. Do what Jesus desires and wants for one's life.

The disaster of the fall in the Garden of Eden is centered around man's doing *his own will*, but the divine blessedness of the new life is involved in doing *God's will*. In surrender is obedience and vice versa. That surrender—a supreme act of obedience—marks the onset of a life of obedience to God the Holy Spirit to whom we have yielded.

How far will you climb up this ladder toward the height of complete surrender? He will meet you where you meet Him. The only limit to His fullness is the limitation you impose on your surrender. The more consummately and unwaveringly you yield yourself—with your time, talents, possessions, plans, hopes, aspirations, and purpose—to Jesus Christ, the more you will enjoy the blessed fullness of His Spirit. You may have all the fullness you will accept, and provide for, in your life.

Dr. Charles Stanley noted "that being filled" with the Holy Spirit is like a believer having a seven-room house. Upon conviction the Holy Spirit enters his house and he is confined to one room. As the Holy Spirit begins to work with him (sanctification), he turns over two rooms, then three rooms—and as he fully surrenders his life to God's will, the Holy Spirit is allowed to occupy and run the whole house.

Do we want God to pour out the fullness of the Holy Spirit? He has done so in Christ. "For in Him all the fullness of Deity dwells in bodily form" (Col. 2:9). Do we want God to then put us "in Christ" where the fullness dwells? He has done so— "But by His doing you are in Christ Jesus, who became to us wisdom from God, and righteousness and sanctification, and redemption" (1 Cor. 1:30). The rest depends on our submission and availability. Put your complete trust in Christ and commit to do God's will. In surrender is obedience.

Indwelling and Manifestation

We must distinguish between the indwelling of the Holy Spirit and His manifestation, that is, His fullness. By indwelling is meant His presence in us. That occurs when one is born again by the Spirit, converted, saved, passed from spiritual death to spiritual life. By manifestation (or showing) is meant the consciousness of that presence.

One's being "born again" does not depend on oneself. If you are a believer, you were born of God, but your walk with Him does depend on you. Indwelling should be associated with sonship; manifestation with obedience and commitment with God. Sonship is the gift of God and cannot be rescinded; so is the indwelling of the Spirit. But obedience and communion are mainly in our heads and hearts. We should trust God to work through us. It is one matter to work for God, yet another to have God work through us. God, of course, desires the latter.

The Manifestation of the Holy Spirit

In John 14:21 our Lord lays down the general conditions of the manifestation of the Spirit: "He who has My commandments and keeps them is the one who loves Me; and he who loves Me will be loved by My Father, and I will love him and will disclose [manifest, KJV] Myself to him." He plainly refers here to the revealing of Himself through the Spirit, declaring as a irrevocable truth that the conditions of that manifestation are the keeping of His commandments, doing what He instructs us to do—meaning not the commandments of the Law but those of grace, faith, and love, which fulfill the Law.

The Lord Jesus plainly asserts that the manifestation of God comes to those who do the will of God. So, when the person in the case was a sinner, the will of God for him was to repent and believe in the Lord Jesus Christ for the salvation of his soul. He did that, and immediately there arose a manifestation of God at conversion. The Spirit was received and entered to live forever. As time marches on, he realizes there is within him a self-life that is enmity with the God-life, a self-will that opposes the divine will—and that God's will for him is giving up of all self-will and the yielding himself totally to God to do His will.

At conversion, there was a tremendous manifestation of God in the fullness of the Spirit, exactly as He promised. But now, instead of stopping, claiming "the blessing," and trying to live the rest of his life on his experience, the believer should press on to this related truth—since the Spirit manifests Himself to the person who does God's will, the constant manifestation of the Spirit can come only to him who continually does God's will.

In other words, though these times of Spirit power have sprung from these acts of doing God's will, a continual manifestation can arise only from an ongoing, daily living in the will of God. So, the surrender of one's life is simply the onset of a life of surrender. The act of consecration must be embedded into a life of consecration, if that blessing is to be continued. For by indwelling is meant, as we have seen the presence of the Spirit in us as believers; by manifestation is indicated the sensing of His presence; the inner revelation of the Spirit to our spirit. Now pay attention to this:

Its Certainty. Will there be such a manifestation of the Spirit's fullness when we yield our lives to Him? Will we be aware of a tremendous inner change in our lives? Will there be a conscious transformation, a sensed new condition of Christian experience? Absolutely! There will be a change; a realization of His presence to a degree never known before.

The flaming evangelist of a previous era, Charles G. Finney, testified that he emerged from the depths of the woods, after accepting Christ, and walked toward his law-office. As he did he found himself repeating out loud: "I must preach the gospel." Almost unconsciously he had, in the split second of his conversion, surrendered his entire life to God and so was filled with the Holy Spirit. Years later Finney entered a factory to preach, and was so full of the Holy Spirit that all the workers knelt down on their knees in reverence.

The Nature of Abiding. What does it mean to abide, to dwell, in Christ? Abiding in Him indicates that He is indwelling but is also constantly revealing Himself through the Spirit. Every genuine believer longs for that spiritual intimacy with Jesus. Jesus taught His disciples:

> *As the Father hath loved me, so have I loved you: continue ye in my love. If ye keep my commandments, ye shall abide in my love; even as I have kept my Father's commandments, and abide in his love. These things have I spoken unto you, that my joy might remain in you, and that your joy might be full. This is my commandment, That ye love one another, as I have loved you. Greater love hath no man than this, that a man lay down his life for his friends. Ye are my friends, if ye do whatsoever I command you* (John 15:9-14, KJV).

So, all of His commandments, which constitute the abiding life, are represented in the marvelous twofold commandment of faith and love. There is the faith side of the abiding life in the Spirit, the first half of the great commandment of I John 3:23 ("This is His commandment, that we believe in the name of His Son Jesus Christ, and love one another, just as He commanded us"), the continual keeping of which presents to us the final yearning of the heart. Abiding in Him constantly gives us continued assurance of His abiding in us.

So, what is this faith that makes up such an important segment of this abiding life in the Spirit? Is it different from the faith by which we are saved, through which we receive forgiveness of sins and the gift of the Holy Spirit? The answer is found in I John 3:24: 'The one who keeps His commandments abides in Him, and He in him. We know by this that He abides in us, by the Spirit whom He has given us." This is not a question of our salvation but of our communion (fellowship) with Christ through His Spirit. It impacts not our eternal security in Him but our pure walk in Him.

Not trusting in Christ will cost one his eternal soul. But failure to abide in Him, after accepting Him as Lord and Savior, costs one his conscious communion with Him. "He who has My commandments and keeps them is the one who loves Me; and he who loves Me will be loved by My Father, and I will love him and will disclose [manifest] Myself to him" (John 14:21).

Abiding is the consistent, constant keeping of His commandments; in response He manifests Himself to us in an ongoing communion with us. How can we possibly keep His commandments and do His will? Read 1 John 3:23 again. "This is His commandment, that we believe in the name of His Son Jesus Christ, and love one another, just as He commanded us." To us who are under grace, all the commandments are filled in faith working through love.

Jesus Christ is spiritual life (see John 14:6). The spiritual life in the believer is not his own; it is Christ dwelling in him. The believer never is the recipient of spiritual life which is in his own possession, independent of and separate from Christ. The believer receives Christ to indwell in the power of the Holy Spirit. The apostle Paul discovered that he was not only justified by faith, but that the just must live by faith. Not only that he received the Spirit, but that he had to walk in the Spirit. Faith in which we are born of God is also the faith of abiding. This faith is that regular attitude by which one who—in himself is spiritually dead—is constantly looking to and every moment is drawing upon the life of another—of Jesus Christ within him.

Only through our union with Christ have we received the gift of the Holy Spirit—only as we come closer to Him and as we daily draw strength from Him do we have a nearness to Him. We must by a life of prayer, communion, and trust continue moment by moment drawing on Him "in whom dwelleth all the fullness of the Godhead bodily" (Col. 2:9, KJV).

Abiding is keeping His commandments: To abide in love is to incarnate His magnificent law of love into everyday life. Self must be denounced. The habit of selflessness must be replaced by the habit of love. The believer is the temple of the Holy Spirit. Faith is the gateway of communion with God. Love is the gateway of ministry to mankind.

The person who keeps them both steadily open has learned to abide in Christ. Through faith the life of God flows into us. Through love it flows out to others.

There is the unsaved, dying world whom He loves even as He loved us. Unless they behold Christ through us; unless they hear of Him through us, they will die in darkness. Unless He touches them through us, they will never experience the thrill of His life and power.

Christ wants us to be like Him.

Gipsy Smith wrote:

Christ the transforming light
Touches this heart of mine
Piercing the darkest night
Making His glory shine
O to reflect His grace
Causing the world to see
Love that will grow
Til others may know
Jesus revealed in me!

Chapter 8
God's Salvation Plan

The Bible, God's written love letter to us, says: "For God so loved the world that he gave His only begotten Son, that whosoever believeth in Him should not perish; but have everlasting life" (John 3:16, KJV).

"Jesus saith unto him, I am the way, the truth, and the life: No man cometh unto the Father; but by ME" (John 14:6, KJV, author's caps)

"Therefore we are buried with him by baptism into death: that like as Christ was raised up from the dead by the glory of the Father, even so we also should walk in newness of life" (Rom. 6:4, KJV)

It is my prayer that you have accepted Christ as your Lord and Savior. If not, you can do that this very moment. "For whosoever shall call upon the name of the Lord shall be saved" (Rom. 10:13, KJV). Ask Christ to come into your heart and save you. He will forgive your sins, and you will be "born again" into God's family (John 3:3,5).

Salvation, or Being Saved, Is a Gift of God's Grace

Grace means that God has provided for our salvation. "For by grace you have been saved through faith; and that not of yourselves, it is the gift of God; not as a result of works, so that no one may boast" (Eph. 2:8-9).

There is nothing we can do to earn it. All we must do is reach out by faith and receive it as a present from Christ. I pray that, if not already, you will decide on giving yourself to Christ, and then you will have eternal life through Him.

> *That if you confess with your mouth Jesus as Lord, and believe in your heart that God raised Him from the dead, you will be saved; for with the heart a person believes, resulting in righteousness, and with the mouth he confesses, resulting in salvation* (Rom. 10:9-10).

Adam and Eve were in perfect fellowship and communication with the Creator until the day when they disobeyed the Lord (Gen. Chapters 1 and 3, also Chapter 5 of this book). On that ill-fated day man died spiritually, and his physical body became subject to death, as God had warned him. The warning involved physical, spiritual, and eventual eternal death unless succeeding generations would appropriate the means of salvation provided for through Christ's death on the cross and resurrection from the tomb (see 1 Cor. 15:1-8).

The forces of physical death began to prey on man's body the day he disobeyed God. He was then driven from God's presence and died spiritually. Men have been alienated from God from that day until now unless they receive God's gift of grace, believing in Christ's death and resurrection and accepting Him into their lives by faith.

God's Desire Is to Save All People

Since God wills that all men and women be saved and come to the knowledge of the truth, He has made ample provision for the salvation of every person

> *This is good and acceptable in the sight of God our Savior, who desires all men to be saved and to come to the knowledge of the truth. For there is one God, and one mediator also between God and men, the man Christ Jesus, who gave Himself as a ransom for all, the testimony given at the proper time. For this I was appointed a preacher and an apostle (I am telling the truth, I am not lying) as a teacher of the Gentiles in faith and truth* (1 Tim. 2:3-7).

God does not want anyone to be lost. "The Lord is not slow about His promise, as some count slowness, but is patient toward you, not wishing for any to perish but for all to come to repentance" (2 Pet. 3:9). The Holy Spirit regenerates and changes us. When we are willing to bend our wills and allow God's will to be done, the Holy Spirit does the rest: He gives us the essential elements for spiritual growth. It is marvelous to relax in Him and to realize that He keeps us saved. He grants to us genuine freedom from the bondage of sin. "So if the Son makes you free, you will be free indeed" (John 8:36).

Freedom from the Penalty of Sin

First, Christ frees us from the penalty of sin. We must understand that we have sinned against God. "For all have sinned and fall short of the glory of God" (Rom. 3:23). We have broken God's laws and have failed Him. We have fallen short of His requirements. The best person among us is a sinner, and this sin has cut us off from God. Our sin comes between God and us so He has to hide His face from us and will not hear us. We may laugh at this and alibi that our sins are small and don't amount to anything . . . but God is pure, righteous, and holy; in His sight we have caused offense. Until we turn to Christ and repent, we are separated from God. We can try to cover up our sins, but God declares that we cannot get away with hiding our sins.

But isn't this glorious? Christ assumed the penalty of our sin. He died that cruel death on the cross for people like you and me, sinners who had failed Him and broken His laws. "He [God] made Him [His Son, Jesus] who knew no sin to be sin on our behalf, so that we might become the righteousness of God in Him" (2 Cor. 5:21). He bore the payment, penalty, and punishment for our sins so, if we receive Him, we will not face condemnation for our sins. "Therefore, having been justified by faith, we have peace with God through our Lord Jesus Christ" . . . "Therefore there is now no condemnation for those who are in Christ Jesus" (Rom. 5:1, 8:1).

On that cross the Lord Jesus accepted accountability for us, shouldering the sin and judgment for us. We cannot fathom the grace and mercy of God. "O the depth of the riches both of the wisdom and knowledge of God! how unsearchable are his judgments, and his ways past finding out!" (Rom. 11:33, KJV). No wonder John Newton called God's grace amazing!

Maybe your past will try to haunt you, but you are free. The full penalty has been paid. The Judge of the universe will never intone, "You are guilty. I pronounce sentence on you"—because Christ accepted that sentence for you. Accept it by faith.

Through Justification we are saved from the Penalty of Sin. Through Sanctification we are being saved from the Power of Sin. Through Glorification we will be saved from the Presence of Sin.

The Work of the Holy Spirit in Conviction

The new birth occurs when the Holy Spirit convicts a person of his sins and leads him to repentance. With belief and faith that Jesus Christ paid the penalty for his sins by dying on the cross, he becomes a new creature. The Holy Spirit helps him overcome sin. At the moment of his regeneration (born again spiritually), he is introduced to God by the work of the Holy Spirit. When he comes to Him, He accepts him as he is. Billy Graham always uses "Just As I Am" by Charlotte Elliott as his invitation hymn in his Crusades.

Just as I am without one plea,

but that thy blood was shed for me,
and that Thou bidd'st me come to Thee,
O Lamb of God, I come.

That's exactly how we must approach Him—just as we are. From the moment of conversion, being born again into His family, God begins to rebuild our lives and our relationship with Him. That process of rebuilding is called *sanctification*. It is one of the major aims of the Holy Spirit in our lives, teaching us about Christ and helping us to become like Him. It requires a lifetime for most of us.

Through renewing of our minds by the Word of God and power of the Holy Spirit, God produces a growing and healthy believer who, as he matures, is transferred into the person God desires him/her to be. We become salt and light from Christ to brighten our path.

Jesus Has Purchased Your Passage

God has purchased your passage to heaven, and His Holy Spirit equips you for the journey. God loves you to the extent that he wants you to be with Him forever. God stands at the door and knocks with the ticket to heaven in hand, but the choice to travel with Christ is up to you. Jesus invites: "Behold, I stand at the door and knock; if anyone hears My voice and opens the door, I will come in to him and will dine with him, and he with Me" (Rev. 3:20). You must invite Him into your life. As the old song goes, "Trust and Obey." Becoming a Christian is climbing on board with Christ. He—the Way, the Truth, and the Life—stands at the door and invites,

> *Come to Me, all who are weary and heavy-laden, and I will give you rest. Take My yoke upon you and learn from Me, for I am gentle and humble in heart, and you will find rest for your souls. For My yoke is easy and My burden is light* (Matt. 11:28-30).

There are many vehicles in life's journey, each promising a passageway to happiness. God's conveyance travels to heaven. Others carry you to false happiness, which can never fill the vacuum in your heart. All the devil's buckets have holes in them. The word for boarding the wrong vehicle is sin. Sin is when we determine, "I'll go my way instead of God's way.

We are saved by our recognition of Jesus Christ as our God and worship Him as such. "Doubting Thomas" fell before his Lord and Savior and cried out, "My Lord and my God" (John 20:28).

On the Day of Pentecost, Peter declared to his hearers that they would have to recognize the Deity and Messiahship of Jesus in sincere worship in order for their sins to be forgiven. Submitting to baptism in the name of Christ is an open confession in the form of an overt act declaring one's faith in the death, burial, and resurrection of our Lord.

God's Salvation Plan

God can give your life purpose, meaning, and direction if you sincerely follow these steps:

Step 1
God Loves You and Has a Purpose for Your Life

In fact, He has five purposes for your life.

1. God made you to be a member of His family.
2. He wants you to be a model of Jesus' character.
3. He wants you to be a magnifier of His glory.
4. He wants you to be a minister of His grace.
5. He wants you to be a messenger of His Good News!

God's Love

The Bible says… "For God so loved the world, that He gave His only begotten Son, that whoever believes in Him shall not perish, but have eternal life" (John 3:16).

God's Plan—Peace and Life

He has a new life for you. Jesus declared, "The thief comes only to steal and kill and destroy; I came that they may have life, and have it abundantly" (John 10:10).

HE DIED IN OUR PLACE ON THE CROSS

"But God demonstrates His own love toward us, in that while we were yet sinners, Christ died for us" (Rom. 5:8).

Realize that God made you and keeps you. Without Him you would have nothing. He decides what is right and wrong because He is holy, perfect, and pure. He is God almighty. He made you in His image so you could worship, honor, relate to, and delight in Him. God has authority over your life, and you are responsible to reflect Him (Ps. 100:3; Acts 17:24-31). But as we've already seen, simply knowing that God loves you and has a wonderful plan for your life isn't enough. There are certain things that block us from Gods love.

Step 2
Our Sin Impedes God's Purpose

Man is Sinful

"For all have sinned and fall short of the glory of God" (Rom. 3:23).

People choose to disobey God and go their own way. This results in separation from God.

Man Is Separated from God

"For the wages of sin is death, but the free gift of God is eternal life in Jesus Christ our Lord" (Rom. 6:23).

Jesus Christ Is God's Only Provision for Sin

Through Him you can know and experience God's life and God's plan for your life.

Step 3
Jesus Christ Is the Only Way of Salvation.

Respond to God's Remedy—the Cross of Christ

God sent His Son to bridge the gap. Christ did this by paying the penalty for our sins when He died on the cross and rose from the grave. Through Him you can know and experience God's love and God's plan for your life.

HE DIED IN OUR PLACE ON THE CROSS

"But God demonstrates His own love toward us, in that while we were yet sinners, Christ died for us" (Rom. 5:8).

HE ROSE FROM THE DEAD

"For I delivered to you as of first importance what I also received, that Christ died for our sins according to the Scriptures, and that He was buried, and that He was raised on the third day according to the Scriptures, and that He appeared to Cephas [Peter], then to the twelve. After that He appeared to more than five hundred brethren at one time, most of whom remain until now, but some have fallen asleep" (1 Cor. 15:3-6).

HE IS THE ONLY WAY TO GOD

Jesus declared, "I am the way, and the truth, and the life; no one comes to the Father but through Me" (John 14:6).

Step 4
We Must Respond in Faith to Jesus.

You Must Repent and Ask God for Forgiveness. *Admit and confess your sins to God.* "He who conceals his sins does not prosper, but whoever confesses and renounces them finds mercy" (Prov. 28:13).

Repentance means:

To acknowledge your sins
To be sorry for your sins
To confess (to own up to) your sins
To be willing to forsake your sins
To have your life changed by Christ

You must believe and have faith that Jesus Christ, the Son of God, died on the cross to pay the penalty for your sins, and He was resurrected on the third day to assure believers' resurrection and being with Jesus in heaven. The Bible states, "Faith cometh by hearing and hearing by the Word of God" (Rom. 10:17, KJV).

Place your trust in Christ and receive Him as your Savior.

Christ is ready. "Here I am! I stand at the door and knock. If anyone hears my voice and opens the door, I will come in" (Rev. 3:20).

Receive Him now.

> *"But as many as received Him, to them He gave the right to become children of God, even to those who believe in His name"* (John 1:12).

Receive God's Son as Lord and Savior.

You cross the bridge into God's family when you ask Christ to come into your life.

It is not enough merely to know the facts about Jesus. We must turn from our rebellious ways and come to Him. We must receive Him in order to be saved. "But as many as received him, to them he gave the power to become the sons of God" (John 1:12, KJV).

How to receive Christ.

1 Admit your need (I am a sinner).
2 Be willing to turn from your sins (Repent).
3 Believe that Jesus Christ died for you on the cross and rose from the grave.
4 Through prayer, invite Jesus Christ to come in and control your life through the Holy Spirit. (Receive Him as your Lord and Savior.)

> **WOULD YOU LIKE TO RECEIVE JESUS CHRIST as your Savior from sin and Lord of your life?** If so, would you pray right now? Perhaps you would like to kneel and pray (Phil. 2:10). You can pray aloud to Him with words from your heart, or you might want to pray this prayer.

Model Prayer to Be "Born Again"

Dear God: I confess and repent of my sins and turn from them. I believe and have faith that Jesus Christ, the Son of God, was crucified (killed) on the cross and shed His blood to pay the penalty (pardon) for my sins and that He rose on the third day from the grave to conquer sin and death and assure us of salvation and our future resurrection to spend eternity in heaven. I ask Christ to baptize me with the Holy Spirit and invite Him to come live in me through the Holy Spirit. I open up my heart and inner life to You as my Savior and Lord. I surrender my life to your Spirit and from this day forward I trust you and commit my life to your service to carry out your will. I pray in the name of Jesus.

Amen.

____

Name

____

Date

> *Therefore being justified by faith, we have peace with God through our Lord Jesus Christ: By whom also we have access by faith into this grace wherein we stand, and rejoice in hope of the glory of God* (Rom. 5:1-2, KJV).

We are pardoned of our sins, and God will remember them no more. God has written believers' names in the Lamb's book of life in heaven, and your fellowship with God has been restored.

"In whom we have redemption, the forgiveness of sins . . . To them God has chosen to make known among the Gentiles the glorious riches of the mystery, which is Christ in you, the hope of glory (Col. 1:14, 27, KJV).

> *"For they shall know me, from the least of them unto the greatest of them, saith the Lord: for I will forgive their iniquity, and I will remember their sin no more"* (Jer. 31:34, KJV).

"Behold, for peace I had great bitterness: but thou hast in love to my soul delivered it from the pit of corruption: for thou hast cast all my sins behind thy back" (Isa. 38:17, KJV).

"He will turn again, he will have compassion upon us; he will subdue our iniquities; and thou wilt cast all their sins into the depths of the sea" (Mic. 7:19, KJV).

When We Accept Christ, We Are Baptized by the Holy Spirit

He comes to live in our hearts and becomes the Comforter, Teacher, Guide, Sanctifier, and Revealer of truth.

"For by one Spirit we were all baptized into one body, whether Jews or Greeks, whether slaves or free, and we were all made to drink of one Spirit" (1 Cor. 12:13, KJV).

We Are Adopted into the Family of God and Are Heirs to All His Promises, including His indwelling here and an eternal home with Him In heaven when He calls us away.

For you have not received the spirit of bondage and fear; but he has received the Spirit of adoption, whereby we cry, ABBA, Father. The Spirit itself beareth witness with our spirit, that we are the children of God: And if the children, then heirs; heirs of God, and joint-heirs with Christ; if so, be, we suffer with him, that we may also be glorified together (Rom. 8:15, KJV).

God accepts us as we are and, through the power of the Holy Spirit, works to help us grow spiritually in Christ. We are children of God through faith in Jesus Christ (see John 1:12). The gift of sonship and daughtership is ours not through being born physically, but through accepting Christ as our Savior (being born again spiritually).

"Being born again, not of corruptible seed, but of incorruptible, by the word of God, which liveth and abideth for ever" (1 Pet. 1:23, KJV).

We Are Heirs and Joint Heirs with Jesus (see Rom. 8:17).

"Because you are sons, God has sent forth the Spirit of His Son into our hearts, crying, 'Abba! Father!'" (Gal. 4:6).

We Are Eternally Sealed in Him.

The sins of God's born-again children grieve Him but do not destroy their justification or nullify their adoption. However, sins do affect our relationship with God. "Be ye holy; for I am holy" (1Pet. 1:16, KVJ). Knowing God involves faith, assent, consent, and commitment. Faith expresses itself in prayer and obedience.

Summary

One of the inherent truths about mankind is that we have been planned after and created in the image of God. God has chosen to fashion us in a manner that reflects several of His wonderful characteristics, and He has provided an avenue for man to enjoy personal fellowship with Himself. There is a picture of that fellowship in the Book of Genesis when Adam and Eve enjoyed a direct relationship with the Triune God. Tragically, sin entered the scene, and the result was separation from God. By His grace, He has enabled us to have that relationship reestablished through His Son.

At the moment of our regeneration (our new birth), we are introduced to God by the work of the Holy Spirit. We come to Him, and He accepts us just as we are. From that point, God begins to rebuild our lives and our relationship with Him. That process of rebuilding is called **sanctification**. It is one of the main works of the Holy Spirit in our lives. It is a slow process that may require a lifetime. It is possible for each one of us to respond and cooperate with the Holy Spirit in our sanctification, even as it is possible to miss out on opportunities given by God to grow and become like the Lord.

Renewal of Our Minds

The gateway God has dispensed to each of us is in the rebuilding process of our minds. It is through the renewing of our minds, by the Word of God and by the power of His Holy Spirit, that God produces a growing, vibrant believer who, as he is nurtured, is transformed into the person God desires him to be—into the image of His Son.

> *Therefore I urge you, brethren, by the mercies of God, to present your bodies a living and holy sacrifice, acceptable to God, which is your spiritual service of worship. And do not be conformed to this world, but be transformed by the renewing of your mind, so that you may prove what the will of God is, that which is good and acceptable and perfect* (Rom. 12:1-2).

Each day, if we submit to God's movement in our lives, our growth will express itself variously. Our relationship with God will deepen. In His Sermon on the Mount, Jesus referred to His followers:

> *Ye are the salt of the earth: but if the salt has lost his savour, wherewith shall it be salted? it is thenceforth good for nothing, but to be cast out, and to be trodden under foot of men. Ye are the light of the world. A city that is set on a hill cannot be hid. Neither do men light a candle, and put it under a bushel, but on a candlestick; and it giveth light unto all that are in the house. Let your light so shine before men, that they may see your good works, and glorify your Father which is in heaven* (Matt. 5:13-16, KJV).

> *We will become more of the salt and light of the world, which He intends us to be. We will yearningly apply and live out His commandments. The love of God will manifest itself in our lives to others. And each day, with God's help and if we are growing, our fellowship with our Lord will grow sweeter and sweeter, as it was meant to be. There is an old song "Every Day with Jesus Is Sweeter Than the Day Before, every day with Jesus, I love Him more and more. Jesus saves and keeps me, and He's the one I'm waiting for, every day with Jesus is sweeter than the day before."*

My favorite Bible Book is Paul's letter to the Romans. And this is the best summary I could leave with you:

> *And so, dear brother and sister, I plead with you to give your bodies to God. Let them be a living and holy sacrifice—the kind he will accept. When you think of what he has done for you, is this too much to ask? Don't copy the behavior and customs of this world, but let God transform you into a new person by changing the way you think. Then you will know what God wants you to do, and*

> *you will know how good and pleasing and perfect his will really is* (Rom. 12:1-2).

May God bless you, keep you, and guide you on your journey for Him.

MOVING ON FROM SPIRITUAL INFANCY

JUSTIFICATION is an event that happens only once. It is the experience of moving from darkness to life, from death to life. **SANCTIFICATION**, on the other hand, is a process. It begins at conversion and continues until you are fully transformed into the image of Jesus Christ.

Justification (Rom. 1:5)

Justification is God's judicial act by which the sinner is free from all guilt and sin because Jesus died in his place and because of the sinner's faith in Christ. God then looks upon the forgiven sinner as though he had never sinned. Justification by faith in Christ is only the initiation of God's purpose for us. The continuation of that purpose is a life sustained by Christ's power.

God's Word teaches that when we believe, we are placed in Christ (Eph. 1:6-7). On that basis we will stand justified and declared righteous by God simply because in Christ, we are righteous. The righteousness that belongs to Jesus has become our birthright.

Sanctification (Rom. 6:1—8:11)

Sanctification is defined as the work God does in believers to bring them increasingly into deeper conformity to Jesus Christ. Our justification is in the crucified Savior, and our sanctification is in our risen Savior. Justification by faith in Christ is only the beginning of God's purpose for us.

The process of sanctification (becoming holy and pure in Christ) is lifelong (see 1 Pet. 1:3; 2 Pet. 3:18). Too many professing Christians recoil from the words "holiness," "purity,“ "righteousness," and "sanctification." Yet, without those qualities, one gives evidence that one is not born again. Sanctification means we are to become like our Savior—and, of course, more like the Heavenly Father, who is also ours. The apostle John summed up the end result of our sanctification: "Dear friends, now we are children of God, and what we will be has not yet been made known. *But we know that when he appears, we shall be like Him, for we shall see Him as He is*" (1 John 3:2, my italics). Even as our Lord is like the Father, so we will be like the Father, the Son, and the Holy Spirit! We will not be God, but we will have His traits.

Glorification (Rom. 8:12-39)

Glorification is when we will be completely like Jesus, because sin will be forever removed from us in our glorified bodies we will receive at the resurrection and rapture. God's plan for our salvation does not end in this world. It reaches its consummation in the next world. What grace starts here, glory will complete there.

> *"For in it the righteousness of God is revealed from faith to faith; as it is written, 'But the righteous man [the just, KJV] shall live by faith'"* (Rom. 1:17). *We are called to live by faith, and in the present life we will not be disappointed. We will not be made ashamed of the faith and hope we have placed in Christ* (Rom. 5:5).
>
> *At last, when we are glorified—when God's glory is revealed in reference to us* (Rom. 8:18)*—we certainly will feel no shame for having lived a life of faith, as our salvation through Christ is carried to glorious completion. As a glorified person, we will be rid of the very presence of sin and will no longer suffer the consequences of sin.*

ONLY GRACE GUARANTEES SALVATION

> *For this reason it is by faith, in order that it may be in accordance with grace, so that the promise will be guaranteed to all the descendants, not only to those who are of the Law, but also to those who are of the faith of Abraham, who is the father of us all* (Rom. 4:16).

We could have no guarantee of eternal life if it depended on our efforts. Since salvation rests on grace, an unearned gift, it can be guaranteed. It is not practically free; it is **absolutely** free! It resides on God's grace and depends on God's character. Perhaps you were taught that salvation relies on strong faith, but it does not. It depends on the receiver of our faith—God Himself, the Giver of the gift!

The Holy Spirit Convicts Us

One of the most devastating effects of sin is that it blinds us to our own sin condition, and the Holy Spirit can open our eyes. Only He can convict us in the depths of our sin and can convince us of Gospel truth. I believe that this is what Jesus meant when He declared, "No one can come to Me unless the Father who sent Me draws him; and I will raise him up on the last day" (John 6:44).

The Word of God solemnly warns about frustrating the calling of the Holy Spirit: "Then the Lord said, 'My Spirit shall not strive with man forever, because he also is flesh'" (Gen. 6:3a). Without the "striving" of the Holy Spirit, no one could ever come to Christ.

WARNING!!!

There is a deadly danger that people's hearts will become so hardened by sin that they will no longer hear or heed the wooing of the Holy Spirit. We must not neglect God's warnings: "A man who hardens his neck after much reproof will suddenly be broken beyond remedy" (Prov. 29:1).

The Holy Spirit Can Be Resisted

The Holy Spirit does all He can to lead every sinner to salvation. But since man is a free-moral agent, he can resist the Spirit's call. The Spirit cannot regenerate the sinner until he believes; faith (which is man's contribution) precedes and makes possible the new birth. So, man's free will limits the Spirit in the operation of Christ's saving work. The Holy Spirit can draw to Christ only those who allow Him to move in their lives. Until the sinner responds, the Spirit cannot give life. God's grace, therefore, is not invincible or irresistible; it can be, and often is, resisted and thwarted by men.

The Holy Spirit Regenerates Us

Along with repentance and faith, a work of the Holy Spirit in man's heart is regeneration, another term for rebirth or being born again: "He saved us, not on the basis of deeds which we have done in righteousness, but according to His mercy, by the washing of regeneration and renewing by the Holy Spirit" (Titus 3:5).

This is a once-for-all change, though sin has continuing effects. The sinner in his natural state is spiritually dead. In regeneration that which is dead is made alive. "But a natural [unsaved, unconverted] man does not accept the things of the Spirit of God, for they are foolishness to him; and he cannot understand them, because they are spiritually appraised" (1 Cor. 2:14).

The sinner, justified by God from guilt of a broken law, is forgiven of every sin. Regeneration, like justification, is immediate and constitutes a one-time act of the Holy Spirit, through the person who is born again.

Free Will or Human Ability

Although human nature was tragically affected by the fall, man has not been abandoned in a state of complete spiritual powerlessness. God lovingly enables every sinner to repent and believe, but he does not interfere with a man's freedom. Each sinner possesses a free will, and his eternal destiny depends on how he uses it. Man's freedom lies in his ability to choose good over evil in spiritual matters. His will is not totally enslaved to his sinful nature. The sinner has the power either to cooperate with God's Spirit, and thus be born again, or to resist God's grace and then perish spiritually. The lost sinner must have the Spirit's assistance, but he does not have to be regenerated by the Spirit before he can believe, for faith is man's act and precedes the new birth. Faith is the sinner's gift to God; it is man's contribution to salvation. Yet, that same gift is first presented to the sinner by God. "For by grace you have been saved through faith; and that not of yourselves, it is the gift of God; not as a result of works, so that no one may boast" (Eph. 2:8-9). Both the grace and the faith are gifts from God—"not of yourselves." Augustus M. Toplady wrote:

Should my tears forever flow,
Could my zeal no languor know,
These for sin could not atone,
Thou must save and Thou alone,
In my hand no price I bring,
Simply to Thy cross I cling!

CHAPTER 9

What Does It Mean To Be "Born Again"?

A Christian is committed to Christ; she/he has a new character. But being finite, the Christian still makes mistakes. Yet, the primary fact is that the born-again person has supernatural powers that are employed in a new way, and his/her movements are elevated by a new direction.

The Christian is a wandering planet that becomes stable in its movement by entering a new orbit. The born-again person is not perfect. He/she will likely sin again but will not practice sin as a way of life (1 John 3:6-9). Many people are puzzled about what it means to be born again. Since the question is popular—and since being born twice is the greatest event in a person's life—let me attempt to explain the term "born again."

Being born again means:

THEY HAVE ACCEPTED JESUS CHRIST AS THEIR PERSONAL SAVIOR AND HAVE PUT THEIR FAITH AND TRUST IN HIM AFTER REPENTING OF THEIR SINS; BELIEVING JESUS DIED ON THE CROSS TO PAY FOR THEIR PARDON; AND ALSO BELIEVING HE WAS BURIED AND ON THE THIRD DAY WAS RESURRECTED FROM THE GRAVE TO CONQUER SIN AND DEATH AND ASSURE US OF OUR RESURRECTION AND ETERNAL LIFE IN HEAVEN.

Famous people like Evangelist Billy Graham, President Jimmy Carter, and President George W. Bush have claimed they have been "born again." So have athletes, astronauts, and scientists like Louis Pasteur, entertainers, educators, farmers, and people from every walk of life.

God is involved in this change in your life and enables you to change. The choice of what a person does with their life is up to them. Whether a person remains born once (physically) or becomes "born again" (spiritually) is up to them. Society often judges a person on one incident or one page in their life. This is dreadfully sad because, with God's help, they have the ability to change and become what God expects of them.

Saul, whose name was changed to Paul, was a murderer—yet he was called by Christ to be an apostle and missionary to both Gentiles and Jews. John Newton was a slave trader and later was converted to Christ and wrote hymns like "Amazing Grace."

Every person needs to re-examine himself/herself and realize they have this possibility of a changed life through being "born again." As a person in life faces frustration, sadness, disappointment, and despair, he would do well to pause and understand that every person's self is invaluable. What about the errors and weaknesses in life? We don't throw away a computer because it makes an error or a piano out of tune. We recognize the potential of the computer and the piano and help change them.

Where Did "Born Again" Come From?

The Christian source for the term born again is in the Gospel of John, the third chapter (John 3:1-10ff.) when Jesus encountered a Jewish leader named Nicodemus. Jesus informed Nicodemas that he had to be "born again" or he couldn't have eternal life. Nicodemus asked, "How can a man be born again when he is old?" Jesus answered "Truly, truly, I say to you, except a man/woman be born of water and the Spirit, they cannot enter the Kingdom of God. That which is born of the flesh is flesh; that which is born of the spirit is spirit."

A husband and a wife come together and produce a new creation. That's physical birth. The new birth has its beginning and completion in God, but each individual has chosen to be born again (spiritual birth).

The route to eternal life is to openly admit your sins, ask forgiveness, believe by faith that Jesus died on the cross as the penalty for your sins; believe Christ was resurrected on the third day to conquer sin and death and assure us of our resurrection and eternal life in heaven. Commit your life to God's will, and He will make you a new creation, giving you a new life. God has sent His Son, Jesus Christ, to give His life that we may have a new life if we trust Him as a gift of God to deliver us of our old life and believe God will give us a new life.

A Miracle and Mystery

Being born again is a mystery and a miracle that happens in a moment of commitment to Jesus Christ. The new creation is not born full grown, but he/she immediately begins to experience life in a new dominion. The new dimension is spiritual life.

It is one matter to rejoice that you can and will have life beyond physical death, but it is marvelous news to realize that quality of life changes at the instant of commitment to Christ. We become new creatures and begin to live life with a new perspective. "Therefore, if any man be in Christ, he is a new creature, old things are passed away: behold, all things are become new" (1 Cor. 5:17, KJV).

We're aware of a new design for our lives and a new source of power as we look to God for guidance. Life's supremely super moment is the instant we are born again through our acceptance of God's gift of Jesus Christ and our commitment to God through following Jesus and turning our lives over to Him.

Let's summarize these thoughts to keep in mind:

> God the Father sent Jesus, His Son, to live a perfect life on earth and die on the cross to deliver us from spiritual death and to grant us spiritual life.
>
> Jesus did what God sent Him to do, and God raised Jesus from death to live forever.
>
> Each person can make a personal commitment to turn his life over to God, be forgiven, and receive the gift of eternal life that Jesus provided.
>
> The newborn Christian has the presence and the power of God's Spirit to help him live the new life.

The experience of the new birth enables a person to remove his eyes from himself and turn them toward God and His will. God's plan for each individual's life is far better than she/he could dream up for herself/ himself. The Bible teaches that those who are born again have a fresh and purposeful life now, plus the assurance of an eternal life with God in the future.

No one born of God makes sin a practice, for God's nature abides in him. A believer can sin, but this is sure: he won't enjoy it and will ask God for forgiveness. In the seasons of life, a person is born once and experiences childhood, youth, adulthood, and death.

New birth comes by committing oneself individually to Jesus and receiving salvation as a gift. A person can be certain about his/her salvation. Baptism doesn't have saving power in itself. It is a symbol that pictures dying to the old life and thought and being raised to a new, dynamic way of thought and life (see Rom. 6:4). When a person makes a decision to trust Jesus Christ as Lord and Savior, the person begins a new life of a higher quality than he could have imagined before he had the experience.

The Bible teaches us that rebirth is an individual experience that occurs when a person turns from self-commitment and commits himself to trust and follow Christ as Master of his life. The gift of eternal life is God's gift of grace, which means that God has given mankind a gift man did not deserve. Accepting the gift is the means of receiving a new life and new hope (see John 3 and 1 Cor. 15).

In the new birth we do not quit being a human being, but we become a new spiritual being. One is a new person in commitment, thinking, direction, relationship, and from every standpoint of life. Everyone is born once, but not everyone is born twice (born again.) Good works never made anyone a Christian, but they do reflect plenty about a person's commitment to Christ (Eph. 2:8-9; Jas. 2:5).

How a person spends his time and money and expends his energy shows where his love is, Christ or self. In the new-birth experience, God forgives the offender, and the offender is reconciled to God.

Repentance is necessary for salvation (Matt. 3:2,8; 4:17). There is more to salvation than conviction and repentance. There is also . . .

Trust. The Bible declares, "Believe in the Lord Jesus, and you will be saved, you and your household" (Acts 16:31). This sort of belief is more than intellectual agreement that Jesus lived. When a person entrusts his life and destiny to Jesus, then he trusts with a kind of belief for salvation that includes conviction of sin, confession, trust, and surrender to Christ.

Confession alone is not salvation but connected with conviction, repentance, and trust, confession is a key concept in conversion.

That if you confess with your mouth Jesus as Lord, and believe in your heart that God raised Him from the dead, you will be saved; for with the heart a person believes, resulting in righteousness, and with the mouth he confesses, resulting in salvation. For the Scripture says, "Whoever believes in Him will not be disappointed" (Rom. 10:9-11).

Forgiveness. When a person responds to conviction with repentance, trust, and confession, God forgives the person of all his sins and gives him a new life, new in time and quality. The person is a new creature and is born again.

Meeting God is not an accident of life. God is searching for us. God sent the Holy Spirit who urges us to accept Christ. Spiritual birth does not end in death but in life that has no ending and that has a quality the physically born cannot conceive of until they are "born again." Believers in Christ are born again not only to a hope but also to an inheritance that is the substance of hope. The inheritance is eternal. "In whom also we have obtained an inheritance, being predestinated according to the purpose of him who worketh all things after the counsel of his own will" (Eph. 1:11, KJV).

Love For Others. The Bible teaches that love for others is another sign a person has been born again. "Beloved, let us love one another, for love is from God; and everyone who loves is born of God and knows God" (1 John 4:7).

The life that is devoid of this love lacks one of the evidences of spiritual life. Every person has the right to believe or not to believe; however, those who do not believe usually do not read the Bible, much less study it. People are busy, many with two or more jobs. This is the reason I spent 1,500 hours researching the Bible to help people understand God's Word.

The Bottom Line is you have to be "born again" to have fellowship with God and receive assurance of eternal life.

Point of Reference. Our point of reference should be Jesus. Keep the eyes of faith on Him. When people do not live right, do not speak right, and do not think right, you have to wonder about their "point of reference." If the morals and the changing beliefs of our generation are one's point of reference, then one has chosen to ignore the

Bible as that focal point. If Satan is not tempting you, you ought to examine yourself. Watch out. You and Satan may be walking side by side. If the Bible is your point of reference, you have the guidance about how God wants you to live. The Bible sets the standard for judging life and for knowing in which direction to go.

Conscience. God did give us a conscience to help us discern right from wrong. However; conscience is not a reliable guide unless the conscience is tuned in to the Word of God. You have to tie conscience and your senses to the Word of God and the leadership of the Holy Spirit. Paul wrote: "I am telling the truth in Christ, I am not lying, my conscience testifies with me in the Holy Spirit" (Eph. 1:11). A conscience outside of God may be weak, confused, or dead and not working at all. This same Paul noted that, sadly, some people's consciences would be "seared with a hot iron" (1 Tim. 4:2, KJV). "Seared with a hot iron" meant that their consciences were insensitive or totally dead. Most so-called "serial killers" have no regrets and absolutely no feelings of remorse.

Some of the Truths We Have Uncovered:

New spiritual birth comes by committing oneself to Jesus and receiving salvation as a gift from God

A person can be certain about their salvation.

God is open to us, and any believer can talk directly to God.

Christ serves as our advocate and high priest.

Whether a person is a Baptist, Methodist, Presbyterian, Pentecostal, or whatever, he has the experience of salvation the same way by trusting Jesus as Lord and Savior and committing to Him.

Teaching About Rebirth. The Bible teaches that rebirth is an individual experience which occurs when a person turns from self-commitment and commits himself to trust and follow Jesus Christ as the Master of his life.

Varied Answers

Christians who witness have often asked people "Are you saved?" or "Are you born again"? You can imagine the answers they have received. Surveys on this have produced many answers:

"I hope so."

"I used to be, but the church burned down."

"I don't think so."

"It doesn't matter what you believe as long as you are sincere."

"My mother and father were Christians."

"I went to church regularly with my parents."

"I give to the church regularly."

"I believe in keeping the Ten Commandments for salvation."

"I don't believe nobody is going to be lost.

"I believe everybody is going to heaven."

The answers have come from ordinary people. They have associated salvation with being good, getting better, and going to church. But salvation is through a personal experience with Jesus Christ. No one can save himself. God does the saving, but people must do the responding to the offer of salvation.

Sovereignty of God vs. Free Will of Man. God provided the gift for man to be reconciled to God by His Son Jesus Christ dying on the cross to pay the penalty for sin, and God raised Jesus from the dead on the third day to assure believers of being resurrected later. Man has to accept the gift from God by repenting of sin, confessing sin, believing by faith that Jesus died on the cross and was resurrected, and inviting Christ to come live in his heart. After a person confesses he has faith in Jesus, and asks Him to come live in him, what does God do?

He justifies us and grants us righteousness.

He makes us a member of His kingdom.

He baptizes believers in Christ with the Holy Spirit.

He sends the Holy Spirit to come live in us.

He forgives and forgets our sins, and there is no condemnation.

The Holy Spirit helps us to live an abundant life and become more like Jesus. This is called sanctification, a lifetime process.

The Spirit helps build our character and prepare us for heaven.

The Holy Spirit prays for us.

Jesus Christ prays to the Father for us and serves as our advocate and high priest.

No one is born full grown; but the Christian has God to help him grow and overcome the "self" that does wrong. We're saved from self (Rom. 7:2,4-8). We're saved from sin (Matt. 1:2). Because we are still human we don't quit sinning (John 1:18), but we quit *practicing* sin as a way of life (John 3:6-9). From the new birth onward, we have a new nature that points in a new direction, and we should continually focus on the Lord Jesus Christ.

God Sanctifies Us. Day by day He renews and refines our nature. The Holy Spirit works within us, purifying our nature, stimulating us to love and good works. We cannot sanctify ourselves, and the sooner we recognize our helplessness, the better. The Holy Spirit within sanctifies and challenges us to repentance, to faith, and to good works, to discipline, to effort, and to fight the good fight of faith. The life which God is sanctifying is not a life that is passive, but a life which is continually being stimulated to activity. Every advance we make in the life of holiness and every victory that by His grace we win is attributed to God and to God alone.

What is the extent of sanctification? God sanctifies us, and He will do it to completion when God calls us away in physical death or He returns in the second coming. Paul also employs another word: "And the very God of peace sanctify you wholly; and I pray God your whole spirit and soul and body be preserved blameless unto the coming of our Lord Jesus Christ" (1 Thess. 5:23, KJV). This word translated "whole" means "entire." The sanctifying purpose of God includes every part of a person. Sanctification not only involves victorious living but the inward, unseen purifying of the nature:

It isn't merely a matter of keeping the old nature suppressed within us; it is the transformation by the Spirit of God of our entire nature: spirit, soul, and body. Our sanctification is "blameless." The word means "without reproach." God's purpose is the final removal of all sin from the Christian's life, so we shall be like Christ.

Sanctification also includes the body, because one day the Holy Spirit will work on our bodies with all their limitations, with all their inclination to weakness and corruption. They will finally be rendered whole and well when the whole creation is redeemed at the final coming of Christ.

When will the sanctification process be completed? "Faithful is he that calleth you, who also will do it" (1 Thess. 5:24, KJV). When God begins a work in a person, He always completes it: "Being confident of this very thing, That he which hath begun a good work in you will perform it until the day of Jesus Christ" (Phil. 1:6, KJV). At His second coming (which will be a day of terror for those who have rejected God) we will be preserved blameless before Him. The work of salvation will then be complete. That day and the completion of our salvation is as sure as the faithfulness of God Himself. The work of sanctification is not a hopeless struggle; it is a process that God has guaranteed.

Babes in Christ

The heaviest baby ever born was 23 pounds, as far as we know. No woman ever gave birth to a six foot, 225-pound baby. So, Christians are not born full grown. One's condition and destiny are changed in a moment of commitment to Jesus Christ. Yet, the very fact of their new birth calls for a unending changing and growing in their thoughts and outlooks. Being born again transforms the inner person. Paul wrote, "Let this mind [attitude of life] be in you, which was also in Christ Jesus" (Phil. 2:5, KJV).

The Sermon on the Mount (Matt. 5-7) is a pattern to follow for an outline of the thoughts, attitudes, and actions Jesus had and that He wants His followers to have. Galatians 5:22-23 says, "But the fruit of the Spirit is love, joy, peace, patience, kindness, goodness, faithfulness, gentleness, self control; against such things there is no law."

The new-birth experience gives us a new nature, but we still have our human nature (old). When we receive spiritual life, we are new creatures, and we are able to begin to please God (Rom. 8:6-9). But this doesn't mean we will always please God. When a Christian falls short of his commitment he does not become unborn; rather he must turn again from that disobedience and sin and ask God for forgiveness. "If we confess our sins, He is faithful and righteous to forgive us our sins and to cleanse us from all unrighteousness" (1 John 1:9).

The true Christian is to turn his eyes upon Jesus: whenever he diverts his eyes off the real goal of Jesus, he must come back with a renewed commitment. Christians may sin and temporarily fall into the gutter, but they don't stay there. They ask God for forgiveness and move on if they are genuinely born-again believers.

Mature Christians love one another, believe in and do what is right. If they stumble in sin they don't enjoy it and turn back with a repentant heart. Spiritual salvation is permanent, but our level of commitment to Christ varies as we move toward being a mature Christian. Christians learn they have won the war, but the battle between our new spiritual nature and our old human nature for our minds continues on a day-by-day basis. The more we turn over to the Holy Spirit, the easier it is to live a Christian life. The Holy Spirit can help us overcome fear, self-centeredness, hostility, greed, prejudice, insecurity, jealousy, gossiping, lack of forgiveness, and other sinful emotions and attitudes.

Victory in Jesus!

Christ provides Christians (the born again) with a security that nothing and no one can snatch away (Rom. 8:32-39). The victory over death is life (eternal life) that death cannot conquer. After the Christian's physical death, there is life on an infinitely higher plane: HEAVEN!

> *And He will wipe away every tear from their eyes; and there will no longer be any death; there will no longer be any mourning, or crying, or pain; the first things have passed away. And He who sits on the throne said, "Behold, I am making all things new." And He said, "Write, for these words are faithful and true* (Rev. 21:4-5).

Tips for Living

When life becomes difficult we need to read Philippians 4:13 ("I can do all things through Christ which strengtheneth me," KJV) or 1 Peter 5:7: ("Casting all your care [anxiety] on Him, because He cares for you," KJV).

The Bible is God's value system for mankind. It shows us what is best for us. The Christian is one who has Bible-based convictions. Salvation is a gift from God; receiving that gift involves a voluntary commitment to Christ and His way of living.

The Christian life is the greatest life in the world. However, the Christian life is not a "snap." It is filled with temptations, problems, and sometimes illness. The Christian does not have all the answers to what happens in life. The Christian does have the assurance of eternal life in heaven and the power of the Holy Spirit to assist in living his daily lives.

Turning from self-will to God's will through accepting Jesus' death on the cross for us sounds too easy. Most people seem to feel that nothing is for free. Yet, salvation is free for us. Who paid? Our salvation cost God the death of His Son, Jesus Christ, on the cross. No wonder John Newton could call it "Amazing Grace"!

Review of God's Salvation Plan

Adam sinned and passed the sin nature to all mankind, resulting in the loss of our fellowship with God. God's righteousness hates sin, but God's love nature caused Him to develop a provision for paying the penalty (pardon) for man's sins and restoring relationship with God. God sent His Son Jesus Christ to give His life on the cross and shed His blood for our sins.

God the Holy Spirit deals with a person's soul to convict him of his sin and to bring him to God through repentance and faith (Acts 20:26).

How to Receive God's Gift and to Be Justified (Made Right) Before Him:

Confess and **Repent** of one's sin. **Ask** God for forgiveness.

Believe and Have Faith that Jesus died on the cross to pay the penalty for one's sin and that Jesus was resurrected on the third day to conquer death, Satan, and sin, assuring us (believers) we will be resurrected and join Jesus in heaven for eternal life with Him.

Invite Christ to come into our body.

God, because of man's faith, grants us righteousness and justifies us (looks upon us as though we had never sinned) if we commit to Him. Man trusts God and commits his life to Him. Man asks the Holy Spirit to come live in his body and empowers him to become like Christ. When God in the Bible speaks of "man" . . . He is referring to mankind, men and women.

Friend, if you feel led by the Spirit to accept Christ, I invite you to pray this prayer now:

> **Father God, I confess and repent of my sins and turn from them. I believe Jesus Christ died on the cross to pay the penalty for my sins and that He rose on the third day from the grave to assure us of our resurrection and assure us we will join Him in heaven. I ask you to baptize me with the Holy Spirit and come live in my body, to guide me in the ways of Christ and empower me to be like Him. I give my life to you. Amen!**

If you prayed this prayer and meant it, you have been "born again" into the family of God. If you are already a Christian, you might pray this prayer and rededicate your life to Christ. May God bless each of you.

CHAPTER 10
Living a Christian Life

Peace I leave with you, my peace I give unto you;
Not as the world giveth, give I unto you. Let not
Your heart be troubled, neither let it be afraid . . . .
In the world ye shall have tribulation: but be of
Good cheer; I have overcome the world (John 14:27; 16:33, KJV).

All but the mentally deranged are searching for peace and satisfaction. They are frantically striving for fulfillment in their lives (Eccl. 12.1). Have you been seeking pleasure and wealth to fill the emptiness in your heart? Only by surrendering your life to Jesus Christ will you find eternal satisfaction and joy.

I have found that exercising faith in God often involves doing the opposite of what the world suggests. The world advises, "Take care of number one." God replies, "Make Me number one, and I'll take care of you." The world contends, "You are captain of your ship." God answers, "Let Me be the captain of your ship, and I'll steer you straight forever."

The world insists, "Trust in yourself and plan your life." God says, "Trust in Me, put your life in My hands, and I'll make it count for all eternity."

The Bible promises, "My God shall supply all your needs according to his riches in glory by Christ Jesus." (Phil. 4:19, KJV)

As we live our lives with maturity and skill, we must possess three things:

1. Faith in God, for it enables us to find our true self, the self God created us to be.
2. Moral knowledge, for it helps us to understand what destroys our humanity and what enhances it
3. The power of God's Spirit, for it is through the Spirit's power (and our obedience) that we are able to walk victoriously.

We live in a day when satanic manifestations and agents of evil run rampant as never before. If we are to function effectively in the last days, we must return to Bible study. Nothing repels Satan better than quoting God's Scriptures.

Are you happy with how God is shaping your life? God often makes something out of us that we do not have in mind. We have disappointments in love; diseases in our bodies; discouragement in our work; desperation in our families. For one reason or another, we are often unhappy with how life is shaping up.

You are not the Potter. You are only clay. What you must do is trust the Potter and yield to His hands. Are you willing to trust the Potter? Do you believe that He knows best, shapes best, fashions best? If you have given your heart to God, you can trust Him to transform you into something useful and beautiful. If that seems hard to believe, it is because He is not even close to being finished yet. He is taking the time to work on the parts of your life that are still lumpy and off-center. Some parts He may need to smash down and raise up all over again. Will you trust Him—really trust Him—to do what is best?

Solomon (Son of David) King of Israel

Solomon gave himself to pleasure. He testified, "I thought in my heart, 'I'll just test myself with pleasure, and I'll try everything there is in the world that gives me pleasure'" (Cf. Eccl. 2:1, 3).

He tried alcohol, women, and music. He had 700 wives. He had 300 concubines or mistresses. He ate the best food. He drank the finest wines. Just about everything that you're working for and dreaming about or thinking about, he had. Solomon said, "I denied myself nothing my eyes desired; I refused my heart no pleasure" (Eccl. 2:10, NIV). He gained all the pleasure that he could. But one day he sighed, "Everything is meaningless. I'm chasing after the wind. It's vanity" (Eccl.

1:14). A person can have all the riches in the world, and it won't fill the emptiness of his heart.

Solomon, too, finally came to a conclusion about how to have peace, fulfillment, and a life purpose: "Fear God and keep his commandments, for this is the whole duty of man. For God will bring every deed into judgment, including every hidden thing, whether it is good or evil" (Eccl. 12:13-14, NIV).

If your computer is locked up and is going nowhere, you can press a few buttons and start all over again. You can do that now. You may want to recommit your life to Christ. You may want to receive Him for the first time. You can open a "new document" and have a new beginning.

Solomon developed a love for the arts, for music, for culture, for beautiful gardens, and for concerts. He loved it all. He had it all. But it didn't bring him any peace of mind. And Solomon tried religion. He built a massive, gorgeous temple. But religion without a personal encounter with Jesus Christ does not save the soul. People are searching for a religion that satisfies, that gives peace. And millions of people are searching for God through religion.

Jesus warned, "Be on your guard against all kinds of greed; a man's life does not consist in the abundance of his possessions" (Luke 12:15, NIV). And the Bible also cautions, "The love of money is the root of all evil" (1 Tim. 6:10, KJV). Money is not the root of all evil; the *love* of it is the root of all evil. And how many of us are trying desperately to formulate our education and our careers in order to make money and to make more?

You may be living for pleasure—but that's like going to a theme park and standing in line for two or three hours to get on a merry-go-round. The ride lasts only a few minutes, and many people live their lives like that. They can hardly wait until the weekend to go out drinking and partying, yet the pleasures they experience are short-lived.

How Does God Guide His People?

God guides His people in many different ways. But it will always be 100 percent consistent with God's Word, because God does not contradict Himself. God's moment-by-moment leading comes through a variety of means. Sometimes it will be through the advice of good

Christian friends. Sometimes through prayer. Sometimes by listening to a sermon. Sometimes by an inner conviction that God has spoken to us. Sometimes by a deep sense of inner peace. Sometimes God will guide us through a particular passage of Scripture. Sometimes all of the circumstances of life clearly point in one direction. Sometimes He simply gives us the wisdom to make the right decision. Sometimes He "speaks" to us. Sometimes He guides us by His silence. Often it is a combination of all these factors put together.

God is committed to guiding His children on their journey from earth to heaven. And though His methods may change, and though sometimes they may be difficult to understand, God is committed to seeing that you ultimately reach your final destination.

God is personal and therefore knowable. He is a spirit, but He has all the characteristics of personality. He thinks, feels, acts, relates to persons, and speaks to His creatures through Scripture. God wants to communicate with men and women.

God is a Person, and He feels, as well as thinks and acts. He is our Father, when we have come to be His children, and we ought to tell our Father how much we love Him, as well as tell other people what a wonderful Father He is! God really does love **people**, and He really is love.

Include God in All You Do

Include God in your everyday life. How can you do that? If you know Jesus Christ as your Savior, God can now plug you into His will, into His plan. If you are going to find meaning in your work, you will only find it when you are in right relationship with God.

Otherwise, you can have the best job in the world and still be empty inside, because work in and of itself can't give you meaning (See James 4:13-17). The degree to which you allow God into your work is the degree to which you will discover meaning in what you do every day.

If you don't go to work tomorrow thinking, *I'm going to work for the Lord*, then you've missed the meaning of work. The fastest way to transform a bad job is with a new attitude. And the quickest means of getting a new attitude is to change bosses. What do I mean?

Paul teaches if you work for the Lord, you receive your reward from Him (Col. 3:22-24). If you're merely working for "the man," the man can give you whatever reward he wants. But if you're working for the Lord, the man has to give you what the Lord tells him to give you.

This is a subtle, yet significant, reorientation to work. God wants you to find meaning in your work, but what makes it meaningful is not the task itself, but your relationship with God in the task. Tasks can change. But even if you get a project you're not excited about, if your attitude is that you are participating with God in the project, He can change the *meaninglessness* of work into the *meaningfulness* of work.

Our Goal

I want this chapter to be a practical day-by-day guide to Christian living. That's why I have chosen topics that include daily living.

Loneliness and Hurting

Loneliness is the disease of our time, as one commentator put it. It seems as if the entire world goes on, and nobody cares. Loneliness lingers in the hospital bed and sits with the wife whose husband spends more time at work than at home. Loneliness strikes the divorced husband or wife and the children who are left behind. Loneliness isolates the aged and impersonalizes the poor. Cities are often the loneliest places in the world.

David asked, "What is loneliness?" Some describe it in physical terms. It's an empty feeling in the pit of the stomach, almost to the point of nausea. It's an underlying anxiety, a big black abyss. It's a sharp ache in moments of grief or separation. It's a long period of stress that wears you down until you're discouraged and defeated.

Lonely people need someone to help them up, to encourage them, to support them, to let them know they're not alone. Who is our Helper, our Comforter, for the times when we need encouragement?

God is our Comforter: In fact, Jesus referred to the Holy Spirit as the Comforter (KJV). There is considerable comfort and consolation in Christ. Paul extolled the Father and Son:

> *Blessed be God, even the Father of our Lord Jesus Christ, the Father of mercies, and the God of all comfort; Who comforteth us in all our tribulation, that we may be able to comfort them which are in any trouble, by the comfort wherewith we ourselves are comforted of God. For as the sufferings of Christ abound in us, so our consolation also aboundeth by Christ. And whether we be afflicted, it is for your consolation and salvation, which is effectual in the endur-*

ing of the same sufferings which we also suffer: or whether we be comforted, it is for your consolation and salvation" (1 Cor. 3:3-8).

God has given us a special assignment. We don't have to be accomplished counselors or ministers to be comforters. At some time we are all called to be comforters.

Are we approachable?

Do those who are hurting feel free to tell us their problems, to cry on our shoulders, to ask for help? Or do we tell a joke or quote a Bible verse and change the subject? If people feel safe talking about their problems with us, most likely we are approachable. Remember that confidentiality is the essence of being trusted.

Are we available?

A woman described her sense of isolation: "When I lost my husband, people I had known for years pretended not to see me in the marketplace, or walked on the other side of the street if they saw me coming. I felt like a leper." When we don't know what to say, we may deliberately avoid someone. But it is an insensitive attitude toward those who hurt. Don't be afraid to approach those in pain. If they don't want to talk, they'll tell you, but they may want someone to listen. They may feel like the psalmist who lamented, "Turn to me and be gracious to me, for I am lonely and afflicted."

Christian Fellowship

We are to love one another.

We are to set an example to one another: "Set the believers an example in speech, in conduct, in love, in faith, in purity."

We are to forgive one another: "Be ye kind one to another, tenderhearted, forgiving one another, even as God for Christ's sake hath forgiven you." Why should we be willing to forgive? Because God forgave us.

We are to edify one another: "Edify" means to enlighten, instruct, and improve. When we come in contact with others, do we seek to encourage them and build them up in the faith?

We are to be subject one to another: "In honor preferring one another . . ."

We are to be patient with one another: "The servant of the Lord must not strive; but be gentle unto all men."

We are to be courteous to one another: If we feel a brother or sister are wrong, and need rebuke, we must do it with gentleness, love, and patience.

We are not to judge one another: "Judge not, that ye not be judged. For with what judgment ye judge, ye shall be judged."

We are to serve one another.

We are to pray for one another: "God forbid that I should sin against the Lord in ceasing to pray for you." We may comment, "We'll remember you in our prayers," and sometimes that's the last of it. Let's pledge to pray for one another.

Is God speaking to you about your relationship with Him? Then you must make it right with Him. You need to make things right in your life. You need to pray and make this a moment of rededication to Jesus Christ.

Gossiping

If someone starts gossiping about another person, walk away. Have no part in idle gossip.

Make Christ King

Notice that the fruit of the Spirit is not what you do but what you are. When you became a Christian, God promised that if you asked Him to forgive you all your sins, He would do so. He kept His word. He will also do His work in your life if you submit to Him.

Remember to Forgive Others

If someone did you wrong, and you have carried hate and/or bitterness on your shoulders for years, you have a burden equal to carrying around a fifty-pound sack of potatoes on your shoulders 24/7. You are only hurting yourself. Forgive the person and ask God to forgive him. You will gain a good night's sleep that night and God will bless you. If you refuse to forgive others, God will not forgive you (Matt. 6:14-15).

Don't Flirt with Temptation

Don't go near a wasp's nest or bee hive, or you will be stung. A young man became an alcoholic in his teens but was able to overcome it and entered college. One night when he was a senior, some friends were going to a bar. He was invited and decided to go along. Late in the evening, one of his so-called friends suggested, "Man, come on and have one drink with us It's not gonna hurt anything." One drink led to many and he was back off the wagon.

A young couple and another couple went to a hotel restaurant for dinner. The restaurant also had a dance floor. She and her husband had been happy together. Going to the restroom, she met an old high-school boyfriend. He asked her to dance and she accepted. He pulled her up close, and her husband became angry and jealous. She would have done better to invite the friend to her table and introduce him and ask him to sit down and bring her up to date on the news.

God Gives Us Self-Determination

You choose to obey the sinful self or you choose to obey Christ and your new nature. Allow the Holy Spirit to reveal to you the areas of your life where you need to make Christ king.

Old and New Nature

From the time you were born, you had an old sin nature which began with Adam. From the time you were "born again," you have a new Christ nature. Your old nature seeks to exalt self; your new nature seeks to cause the love of God to flow through you. Your new nature functions in love, for the desires of the flesh are against the Spirit, and the desires of the Spirit are against the flesh.

Your Choice

Your choice decides which nature will control your life and which nature will be prevented from controlling your life. Before you became a Christian, the spirit of the old nature directed your life. Your thoughts, motivations, impulses, desires, and actions expressed that nature. The sinful nature wants what is contrary to the Spirit and the Spirit contrary to the sinful nature. Acts of the sinful nature include sexual immorality, impurity, adultery, witchcraft, hatred, discord, jealousy, fits of rage, selfish ambition, dissension, factions, extreme pride, envy, drunkenness, orgies, gossip, and the like. Not a pretty picture. Those who live like this will not inherit the Kingdom of God.

New Nature: Galatians 2:20

"I have been crucified with Christ; and it is no longer I who live, but Christ lives in me; and the life which I now live in the flesh I live by faith in the Son of God, who loved me and gave Himself up for me." The new nature has ushered in love, joy, peace, patience, goodness, kindness, and self-control, the fruit of the Spirit.

The Conflict of the Believer's Two Natures

To Christians, one of the most reassuring promises of the Bible is in 2 Corinthians 5:17, where we are informed that a newness and transformation has occurred within our lives through the new birth, "regeneration" (also called "being born again"; see John 3:5, 7; Titus 3:5).

Two natures beat within my breast,
One is foul, the other blest.
The one I love; the one I hate
The one I feed will dominate.

The conflict of the two natures, of course causes the Christian life to be unpleasant at times. The old nature continually vexes the new by seeking an egotistical approach to life. The old nature is sometimes referred to by Paul as "the old man." "Knowing this, that our old man is crucified with him, that the body of sin might be destroyed, that henceforth we should not serve sin" (Rom. 6:6, KJV; see also Eph. 4:22; Col. 3:9). That old rascal has an affinity with the world. Since the believer lives in the world, the old nature digs up plenty of carnality to feed upon.

Scripture candidly records that even the greatest believers, at times, became victims of their old natures. Adam and Eve walked personally with God and yet disobeyed Him; Noah, Abraham, Isaac, Jacob, Moses, the patriarchs who wore heavenly mantles, are reported as having lied, deceived, cheated, and even murdered. David had a warm, cordial relationship with God, yet he ultimately committed adultery, had his paramour's husband murdered, lied, cheated, and woefully backslid.

Paul wrote in Galatians 5:17; "For the sinful nature desires what is contrary to the Spirit, and the Spirit what is contrary to the sinful nature. They are in conflict with each other, so that you do not do what you want." Read Romans 8:3 and 1 Peter 2:11. The warfare within self is the severest battle we fight. Yielding of oneself, surrendering all to the will of God, requires a struggle, but it is priceless when one submits to God in holiness. In presenting ourselves to Christ, we must deliberately cast away all that would separate us from Him. The conscientious believer, then, will recognize his status and place total dependence on Christ for deliverance, allowing the Holy Spirit to examine, rebuke, guide, and bless.

> *So then, brethren, we are under obligation, not to the flesh, to live according to the flesh—for if you are living according to the flesh, you must die; but if by the Spirit you are putting to death the deeds of the body, you will live* (Rom. 8:12-13).

The Commencement of the Victorious Christian Life

Mastery over the old nature begins with salvation. It is further nurtured through the consumption of God's Word and kept up by walking in the Spirit (2 Cor. 5:17; 2 Tim. 2:15; Gal. 5:16). A consistent lifestyle for Christ speaks volumes to those outside of Christ. We are to put our motivation where our mouth is. We are to walk the walk and talk the talk, keeping in mind that the two natures reveal themselves, each wishing to have supremacy.

So, we must decide which one to submit to, which to feed, and which is to dominate. "The old man" has dynamics as in "the lust of the flesh, and the lust of the eyes, and the pride of life," which are "not of the Father, but . . . of the world" (1 John 2:16, KJV). We are at home in the world in the flesh. Our roots are physical, mental, emotional, environmental, and cultural.

When a person becomes a Christian, that old nature remains. It is true that we are immediately spiritually united with Jesus Christ at the moment of salvation, but internal changes occur through spiritual growth—through the inner workings of God as the Holy Spirit puts the Word of God into action.

You Have to Choose!

You are either a slave of one master or of another. Jesus clearly drew the line of demarcation: "No one can serve two masters. Either he will hate the one and love the other, or he will be devoted to the one and despise the other. You cannot serve both God and Money" (Matt. 6:24). The *King James Version* renders "Money" as "Mammon." Some translations refer to "materialism."

No neutral zone

There is no middle ground between heaven and hell. You are on the road to one or the other. The power of choice, the exercise of free-moral agency, is a daunting responsibility. The stakes are high. The consequences are eternal, and you can choose either to have your life controlled by the carnal self or by the Holy Spirit. You can opt for your own "selfish way" or you can choose God's pathway.

> *And a main road will go through that once-deserted land;*
> *Will be named "The Holy Highway." No evil-hearted men*
> *May walk upon it. God will walk there with you, even the*
> *Most stupid cannot miss the way* (Isa. 35:8, TLB).

Christ living within our body through the Holy Spirit is an awesome experience, and you live by faith in the Son of God. The indwelling Christ can control your life only when you choose to let Him do so. Jesus Christ is your new nature. He resides in you, and He has given the full presence of the Holy Spirit to live within you all. The power of God is in you because Christ is that power.

Self or Christ?

When you turn your life over to Christ, He does not snatch away your dignity, nor do you become a puppet. His life within you reveals the very nature of God to you. You are a vessel for Christ, and He is the light that is the very nature of God. Many people have tried to understand God but could not because they are not willing to become vessels for Christ. Lend your voice, hands, feet, and mind to God, asking Him to work through you. Only those who have received the new nature have the capacity to know God.

There is a simple decision you make as a Christian, hour by hour, day by day. It is to crown Jesus Christ as Lord of your life. When you do, His Nature is in control of you, producing the fruit of the Spirit in you.

God Must Test Our Belief

It is easy to worship God when all is copacetic in your life, when He has provided food, friends, family, health, and happy situations. But how do you worship God when stuff is tough? To mature your friendship, God will test it with periods of seeming separation. God has promised repeatedly, "I will never leave you or forsake you." This testing is essential for the development of your faith. Let me remind you that sin does disconnect us from intimate fellowship until we have repented and asked for forgiveness. We can grieve God's Holy Spirit and hinder our fellowship with God by our disobedience, conflicts with others, unsavory businesses, friendship with the world, and other sins. However, this feeling of being cut off from God often has nothing to do with sin. It is a test of faith.

When this happens, talk with the Lord about how you feel. Pour out your heart to Him. Our inexhaustible God can handle our doubts, anger, fear, grief, confusion, and questions. Center on who God is, praising Him for all your past experiences with Him. God's grace is always operative; He is still there for you, even if you may not always feel it. **The key is faith, not feelings.**

Through Christ, You Are a Member of God's Family

> *You were formed for God's family. God wants a family, and He created you to be a part of it. This is God's purpose for your life. He planned it before you were born. The entire Bible is the revelation of God building a family who will love Him, honor Him, and reign with Him forever. Paul wrote: "He predestined us to adoption as sons through Jesus Christ to Himself, according to the kind intention of His will"* (Eph. 1:5).

Because God is love, He cherishes relationships. His very nature is relational, else why would He have created human beings? And He identifies Himself in familial terms: Father, Son, and Spirit. The Trinity is God's relationship to Himself: a perfect pattern for relational harmony, and we should consider its connections.

When we have faith in Christ, God becomes our Father; we become His children; other believers become our brothers and sisters; and the church becomes our spiritual family. The family of God includes all believers in the past, the present, and the future.

Note an Important Distinction

Every human being was *created* by God, but not everyone is a *child* of God. The only means of truly joining God's family is by being born again into it. You become a member of God's family by your second birth. The invitation to be part of God's family is universal, but there is one condition: **faith in Jesus**. The Bible declares: "You are all children of God through faith in Christ Jesus."

Love

Life is all about love. Because God is love, the most pivotal lesson He wants you to learn is how to love. It is in loving that we are most like Him, so love is the foundation of every command He has given us. Jesus put it plainly:

> *"You shall love the Lord your God with all your heart, and with all your soul, and with all your mind." This is the great and foremost commandment. The second is like it, "You shall love your neighbor as yourself." On these two commandments depend the whole Law and the Prophets* (Matt. 22:37-40).

Stubborn pride

Stubborn pride, self-importance, and smugness can destroy fellowship faster than all else. As a result of pride, Satan lost his choice position in heaven. "Pride goes before destruction, And a haughty spirit before stumbling" ["a fall," KJV] (Prov. 16:18). Paul advised, "For I say, through the grace given unto me, to every man that is among you, not to think of himself more highly than he ought to think; but to think soberly, according as God hath dealt to every man the measure of faith" (Rom. 12:3, KJV).

Humility

We can develop humility practically by admitting our weakness, by being patient with others, and by being open to correction. Jesus promised: "Blessed are the meek: for they shall inherit the earth" (Matt. 5:5, KJV), meaning the humble.

Restoring broken fellowship

Believers in Christ must learn to be peacemakers. "Blessed are the peacemakers, for they shall be called sons of God" (Matt. 5:9, KJV).

How do we restore relationships?

1. Talk to God before talking to the person.
2. Always take the initiative.
3. Confess our part in the conflict.
4. Cooperate as much as possible.
5. Emphasize reconciliation.

Our Value

We generally assume that our value is determined by what we *do*. If I carry out my task well, maybe I may be promoted. If I do it poorly, I may be fired or demoted. The same mindset is true with human relationships. If I'm agreeable, "a nice guy," people will probably want to be around me. When I am a pain in the *gluteus maximus*, I'll undoubtedly be devoid of willing lunch partners. The earthly system is easily understood by all of us. Our performance is crucial to success as well as social acceptability.

However, no matter our disposition, God places infinite value on us. He looks at our heart and not at our possessions or achievements.

Strive for Excellence

If you claim allegiance to Jesus Christ as your Lord, you ought to strive for all the excellence you can in every endeavor. If you're a Sunday-school teacher, be the best you can be. If you're a Bible-study leader, lead your group with all your energy and heart. If you're a homemaker, make your home as superlative as it can be. When you're at your job, do the most excellent work you can. That's how to live the Christian life and let your light shine for Christ. It calls for discipline, but we must demand the best of ourselves and run the race to win. "Whatever you do in word or deed, do all in the name of the Lord Jesus, giving thanks through Him to God the Father" (Col. 3:17). As followers of the Lord Jesus Christ, we are to do everything "as unto the Lord," as Paul expressed it.

Jesus never promised us a rose garden . . . without thorns. Living for Jesus involves a certain amount of sweat and toil, for Satan (the devil) opposes us constantly. Jesus called us as His lifelong learners and followers. Our discipleship never ends. When we accept Him, He removes one set of problems—the burdens of sin, guilt, isolation, hopelessness, and separation from God. As that occurs He calls for us to become yoked (tied to) Him spiritually. "My Yoke is easy and by burden is light." (Matt. 11:30, KJV). In comparison with the awful burdens of a life without God, the load we bear for Him is light as a feather.

Yet, living a consistent Christian life—contrary to certain so-called preaching and teaching—is not all sweetness and light. We are to follow Him regardless of the costs, and He never promises that we will always have good sailing. Paul made it plain: "Suffer hardship with me, as a good soldier of Christ Jesus" (2 Tim. 2:3).

There is nothing on earth to compare with life in Christ, but our walk will be strewn with problems, suffering, tests, trials, and temptations. Amid all of our ups and downs, Jesus will provide love, joy, peace, and all the other fruit of the Spirit.

What Do Our Troubles Mean?

No doubt all of us have asked God, "Why has this happened to me? Why is there so much trouble? Why? Why? Why?" Although it is not easy for us to understand, it is simply that God in His wisdom wants to make something of us which we aren't yet, and have not reached. All that happens to us is for a purpose. The believer in Christ has this precious promise: "And we know that God causes all things to work together for good to those who love God, to those who are called according to His purpose" (Rom. 8:28).

He means to strengthen us in patience, good humor, compassion, humility, or meekness by giving us extra practice in exercising these qualities under sometimes difficult situations. Maybe He has lessons in self-denial and self-distrust to teach us. He may want to break us of complacency; unreality, or forms of pride and conceit. Or it could be His purpose is to draw us closer to Him in conscious communion. The fellowship with the Father and the Son is best and sweetest when the cross is the heaviest.

Conscience

A good conscience is one that is tender. The consciences of the godless may be so calloused that they scarcely ever act at all. In some unbelievers, their consciences are obliterated, destroyed. "By means of the hypocrisy of liars seared in their own conscience as with a branding iron" (1 Tim. 4:2). This means cauterized, dead, without feeling. Persons like serial killers, Ivan the Terrible, Hitler, and Mao Tse Tung have fallen into that category.

But the healthy Christian conscience is constantly in operation, listening for God's voice in His Word, seeking to discern His will in everything, active in self-watch and self-judgment. The healthy Christian recognizes his weakness and always suspects and distrusts himself, lest sin and Satan should be ensnaring him unawares. So, he constantly grills himself before God, scrutinizing his deeds and motives and ruthlessly condemning himself when he discovers in himself moral deficiency and dishonesty. The healthy Christian has a sense of God's presence stamped deep on his soul, trembles at it, and tests and reforms his life daily in response to it. We can begin to assess our real state in God's sight by asking ourselves how much exercise of conscience along these lines goes into our own daily living.

The Good News

God is never late, He is always right on time. Bill Bright, the founder of Campus Crusade for Christ, was called by God to do a Jesus film. Forty years later this was accomplished and has been shown to billions around the world, and millions have received Christ through this ministry. The timing was exactly right. In spite of unprecedented persecution of Christians, the Gospel is being spread all over the globe, especially in Third World countries.

Forgiveness

> *For if you forgive others for their transgressions, your heavenly Father will also forgive you. But if you do not forgive others, then your Father will not forgive your transgressions* (Matt. 6:14-15).

The genuine Christian will forgive and forgive and forgive, not to be saved but because he is already saved.

A Prayer for Courage (Being one in purpose)

Heavenly Father, I praise You for Your faithfulness. I believe that You are faithful to all who surrender their lives to Your will, submit to You in obedience, and stand firm by the power of Your Holy Spirit. Thank you for the promise of Your Word. Thank You for the promise of Your strength, authority, presence, and provision. Please help me to remember that You have called me to be the light of the world, to share Your love, forgiveness, and eternal life in Christ. Give me a hunger for Your truth, that I may be a doer of the Word and not a hearer only. I also ask that You would grant me the wisdom and courage to daily do what is right in Your sight. In the name of Jesus I pray. Amen.

All Things Work Together For Good?

Romans 8:28

One of the most assuring verses in the Bible is: "And we know that God causes all things to work together for good to those who love God, to those who are called according to His purpose" (Rom. 8:28). Through the cross, God uses things that, in and of themselves, are bad. Yet, He combines them, even as a chemist would use chemicals that, in and of themselves, might be injurious and mixes them to make a medicine that delivers healing.

Most of us eat a bit of salt with our food. Table salt is composed of both sodium and chloride. By themselves sodium and chloride are poison—but put them together and you have table salt. Salt flavors food, and a certain amount of salt is essential to health and life. God can use elements that are bad, yet put them in the crucible of His wisdom and love—and work them out for good. He gives us this glorious promise that He will do so.

Yes, we can have victory over sin and Satan. Yet, this verse teaches that we can also have victory over our circumstances. "All things" work together for good—to love the Lord.

The Best Resources on Family Life

Mothers and fathers, come to Jesus with your concerns about your children and your family. God affords you the best counseling there is through His Holy Spirit. It never was easy to rear children. Today it is far more difficult with all the distractions around our kids—so-called "peer pressure' and every kind of temptation. Peer pressure existed when I was a kid, but then it was called "running with the crowd." Children and young people in this generation are confronted with the grossest of evils all around them—cursing, dirty jokes, pornography on TV, in the movies, in publications, in CDs, and on the Internet, and a thousand-and-one other temptations to sin through premarital sex, alcohol, smoking, or other drugs. It's enough to drive a concerned parent up the wall!

Fathers and mothers should consider their children as younger members of the Lord's family. Conscientious parents should commit themselves to this divine calling: spiritually educating them for the here and now and for heaven later. So, the Christian home becomes a school where the parents serve as "under teacher," while Christ Himself is the Head Master.

Being a Christian parent is a dreadfully serious responsibility. No matter how you interpret it, the Bible teaches, "Train up a child in the way he should go, Even when he is old he will not depart from it" (Prov. 22:6). Dr. Spock's permissive book on child-rearing has sold more than 20 million copies around the world. **But the most effective book on the subject is The Book, The Bible.** It is a treasure trove of practical and workable principles about love, marriage, the family, and children.

God's Meaning of Marriage and Family

The written Word of God teaches the sanctity of marriage and that a family is a man and woman joined together under God's aegis. Jesus declared, "For this cause shall a man leave father and mother, and shall cleave to his wife: and they twain shall be one flesh" (Matt. 19:5, KJV; see also Matt. 19:11; Lev. 18:22; 20:13; Judg. 19:22-30; Jer. 23:14; Ezek. 16:49-50; Rom. 1:26-27; 1 Cor. 6: 9-11; 1 Tim. 1:10; 2 Pet. 2:6-10; Jude 7). The Hebrews often punished forbidden practices by stoning.

Of course, Jesus would not stone a person, but He will ultimately judge all sin, including sexual transgressions, whether heterosexual (fornication and adultery) and homosexual (men with men or women with women).

The Bible further teaches that children should obey and respect their parents. "Honor thy father and thy mother: that thy days may be long upon the land which the Lord thy God giveth thee" (Ex. 20:12, KJV). Paul gave a hearty "amen" to that commandment when he wrote: "Children, obey your parents in the Lord, for this is right. Honor your father and mother (which is the first commandment with a promise), so that it may be well with you, and that you may live long on the earth" (Eph. 6:1-3).

Temptation

Four Biblical Keys to Defeating Temptation

1 Refocus your attention on something else.
2 To avoid being stung, stay away from bees.
3 Reveal your struggle to a Godly friend or support group.
4 Resist the devil. James advised, "Submit yourselves therefore to God. Resist the devil, and he will flee from you" (James 4:7).

Put on salvation as your helmet and pick up the sword of the Spirit which is the Word of God as your weapon against Satan.

Rebuke the devil as the Lord Jesus did: "Get thee hence, Satan: for it is written, Thou shalt worship the Lord thy God, and him only shalt thou serve" (Matt. 4:10, KJV).

We must never let down our guard and think we are beyond temptation. God is faithful, so He will keep the temptation from becoming so strong that you can't stand against it. When you are tempted, He will provide an avenue of escape. "No temptation has overtaken you but such as is common to man; and God is faithful, who will not allow you to be tempted beyond what you are able, but with the temptation will provide the way of escape also, so that you will be able to endure it" (1 Cor. 10:13). Endurance develops every time you reject the temptation to give up. Every time you defeat a temptation, you become more like Jesus.

Satan identifies a desire inside, maybe a desire to have revenge or to control others or even a normal desire to be loved or to feel pleasure. Temptation begins when Satan suggests, by a small whisper or thought, that you yield to an evil desire. Always be aware of shortcuts. They are often temptations. Satan whispers, "You deserve it. It will be exciting, it will make you feel better."

We think temptation lurks nearby, but God teaches that it begins within us. If you don't have the internal desire, the temptation could not attract you. Christ had fasted for 40 days and was hungry. Satan suggested, "Turn the stones into bread." But Christ's character answered, "No".

Jesus expressed it, "For out of the heart come evil thoughts, murders, adulteries, fornications, thefts, false witness, slanders" (Matt. 15:19).

Satan's Steps to Temptation

Identifies a weakness within you.

Doubt - Satan wants you to doubt what God teaches about sin. He whispers, Don't you want to be happy?" Don't let evil thoughts or doubts turn you from the living God.

Deception - Satan is incapable of telling the truth and is the father of lies (John 8:44). Whatever he tells you will be untrue or simply half-truth. Satan croons, "It is only a little sin; you will feel better." But a little sin is like being "a little pregnant." One sin leads to another.

Disobedience - You finally act on the thought you've toyed with in your mind. What began as an idea is born into behavior. We are tempted when we are drawn away and trapped by our own evil desires. Then our evil desires conceive and give birth to sin. Do not be deceived by the devil; ask God for grace to overcome. When you sin, ask God for forgiveness.

Do not feel guilty for being tempted. You will never outgrow temptation on earth, but keep your eyes on Jesus. Temptation is a sign Satan hates you. Resisting temptation is a sign of your trust in Christ that He will give you the grace to resist temptation. Temptation becomes a sin only when you give in to it.

Attraction is the natural, God-given response to physical beauty, while lust is a deliberate act of the will. Actually, the closer you grow to God, the more Satan will try to tempt you. Sometimes while you are praying, Satan will suggest a bizarre or evil thought merely to distract or shame you. When this happens lash out, "Get away from me, Satan!" Focus on the Lord Jesus.

Request God's Help

Heaven's phones are free and you will never receive a busy signal. God is available to you and will provide you more than sufficient grace to handle temptation.

God blesses the people who patiently endure testing. Afterward, they will receive the crown of life that God has promised to those who love Him (James 1:12)

Golden Rules for Living

1. If you open it, close it.
2. If you turn it on, turn it off.
3. If you unlock it, lock it up.
4. If you break it, admit it.
5. If you can't fix it, call in someone who can.
6. If you borrow it, return it.
7. If you value it, take care of it.
8. If you make a mess, clean it up.
9. If you move it, put it back.
10. If it belongs to someone else, request permission to use it.
11. If you don't know how to operate it, leave it alone.
12. If it's none of your business, don't ask questions.

Christian Commitment

Without commitment, faith becomes only a creed that carries neither conviction or impact. Without commitment, work is devoid of its high calling of service and becomes only a means to achieve personal gain. Without commitment, people put together dangling relationships, touching on another for convenience's sake, using one another—then are disconnected again. Without commitment, life itself is suspended on quicksand and is sinking fast.

Commitment is a contract that is followed up by actions. It is the cement that glues relationships together. It is a stick-to-itiveness that lets no environmental factors or personal failures set back the original pledge, a marriage vow, or any other kind of promise. It is the stubborn root that plows deep into the soil. It is a prioritized involvement that is willing to take the risk and the time to understand the other person. It is a growing interest in cultivating long-lasting values and is not satisfied with immediate, instant results or gratification.

Commitment, most importantly of all, means giving the best—in fact, all one has. When we commit ourselves to God, it means offering ourselves as "living sacrifices," as Paul indicated in Romans 12:1. It is not only a once-for-all sacrifice, but a daily, continuous giving up of one's' "self-interest". It is a voluntary act that radiates from a deep surrender to God, an offering that gives God all our soul, our heart, our mind, and our strength.

Chapter 11

Seeking to Become More Like Christ

Therefore, if anyone is in Christ, he is a new creation; the old has gone, the new has come! God made him who had no sin to be sin for us, so that in him we might become the righteousness of God (1 Cor. 5:17, 21).

Jesus Christ launched a new movement in the world which is now called Christianity. He has turned the whole course of history in a different direction by it. He has transformed the lives of billions. Myriads today will testify to the saving power of Jesus Christ. It is true there are many hypocrites among so-called believers as there are in other groups. But the lives of and the testimonies of innumerable people prove absolutely that miracles do exist. Thousands of volumes have presented the unimpeachable testimonies of outstanding men and women who have had a miracle wrought in their lives when they accepted Jesus of Nazareth as their personal Lord and Savior.

God-shaped Vacuum

Human beings are born into this world with an empty place at the center of their being. One may have physical life but be without a spiritual dimension through which one can know God personally. All kinds of false cults and isms are searching for God. The fact is, though, He is actually searching for us.

Knowing God is possible only by accepting Christ as one's Savior. Men called apostles—whom Jesus selected to help start His church—preached and wrote that God loves everybody.

> *For God so loved the world [everyone] that he gave his only begotten son, that whosoever believeth in Him should not perish; but have everlasting life* (John 3:16, KJV).

Who Will Christ Listen To?

Jesus answered and said to him, "If anyone loves Me, he will keep My word; and My Father will love him, and We will come to him and make Our abode with him. He who does not love Me does not keep My words; and the word which you hear is not Mine, but the Father's who sent Me" (John 14:23-24, KJV).

Adopted into God's Family!

When we put our trust in Jesus Christ and ask Him to save us, God adopts us as His heirs to view and share in the glory into which God's Son, Jesus Christ, has come.

> *For ye have not received the spirit of bondage again to fear; but ye have received the Spirit of adoption, whereby we cry, Abba [daddy, papa] Father. The Spirit itself beareth witness with our spirit, that we are the children of God: And if children, then heirs; heirs of God, and joint-heirs with Christ; if so be that we suffer with him, that we may be also glorified together* (Rom. 8:15-17, KJV).

God sent His one and only begotten Son to save us from being found guilty and sentenced for breaking God's laws, which is sinning against Him and going against the moral laws He has set up. So, God sacrificed Jesus to save us from being condemned by the law, that we might receive the full rights of His daughters and sons.

> *But when the fullness of the time came, God sent forth His Son, born of a woman, born under the Law, so that He might redeem those who were under the Law, that we might receive the adoption as sons (Gal. 4:4-5).*

Adoption is a family idea, conceived in terms of love and viewing God as Father. In adoption, God receives us into His family and fellowship. He establishes us as His children and heirs. Ephesians 1:4-6 says:

> *According as he hath chosen us in him before the foundation of the world, that we should be holy and without blame before him in love: Having predestinated us unto the adoption of children by Jesus Christ to himself, according to the good pleasure of his will, To the praise of the glory of his grace, wherein he hath made us accepted in the beloved* (Eph. 1:4-6, KJV).

When we are facing the impossible, we can count on the God of the impossible (see Luke 1:37). Our lives may be out of control, but they are ultimately under His control. Christ alone can set us free from the bondage and slavery of sin. He is the only one who can give meaning, definition, and purpose to our lives. Closeness, affection, and generosity are the heart of the relationship. You and I have tremendous worth apart from looks, intelligence, and performance because Christ gave His life for us and attaches incalculable value to us. The greatest human experience is knowing God in an intimate spiritual relationship. It is mind-boggling. We may have a closeness with Christ, who is all-powerful, fully in charge. No one is mightier than He. One day every knee shall bow before Him and admit that He is King of Kings and Lord of Lords (see Phil. 2:5-11; Isa. 9:6).

God Is Not Only Holy and Just, He is Loving and Merciful!

But God is love. *"He that loveth not knoweth not God; for God is love"* (1 John 4:8, KJV).

God, though, satisfied His desire to show mercy and love to the unsaved by providing another Person to pay the debt they owe for sin.

The Gospels tell us that Jesus assumed the sinner's place in death. Instead of our getting the punishment we deserve, Jesus took our punishment. As a result, a gift is offered. Paul expressed this marvelous offer from God in Ephesians 1:7: "In Him we have redemption through His blood, the forgiveness of our trespasses, according to the riches of His grace."

How Can I Bring Glory to God?

Jesus told the Father, "I brought glory to You here on earth by doing everything You told me to do." All of us can honor God by attempting to carry out His will as revealed in scripture. The glory of God is a human being fully alive for Christ. The heart of man was God-centered when he was created. By disobeying the one prohibition placed on him, he wrecked his nature and, figuratively speaking, threw himself off center. His one act of disobedience, however, was sufficient to seriously mar his nature and to break the communion and fellowship with his Maker (Gen. 3:1ff.).

The day he transgressed, sin began to prey upon his body, and as a result physical and spiritual death began. Man is now in a sinful condition. He is born in sin. "Behold, I was brought forth in iniquity, And in sin my mother conceived me" (Ps. 51:5). Jeremiah gave us an X-ray picture of the human heart: "The heart is deceitful above all things, and desperately wicked: who can know it?" (Jer. 17:9, KJV). From the depths of man's being there arise evil thoughts and desires that result in corrupt and lawless actions.

"For out of the heart come forth evil thoughts, murders, adulteries, fornications, thefts, false witness, railings" (Matt. 15:19, KJV). In Hebrews 3:12 the writer spoke of the heart as being evil, for out of it unbelief arises. The Lord Jesus Christ, in talking to His disciples, said, "If ye then, being evil, know how to give good gifts unto your children, how much more shall *your* heavenly Father give the Holy Spirit to them that ask him?" (Luke 11:13). In this utterance we see reflected the conviction that man's heart is evil—not as it was originally.

Many times in our dreams, or even in prayer, evil thoughts enter our minds. This is Satan trying to distract your from Jesus. If we want to know what God is like, all we have to do is gather from the four Gospels how Jesus revealed Him by His teaching and works. It is the Holy Spirit's ministry in turn to produce in us . . .

A Journey with Purpose

The purpose of your life is far greater than your own personal fulfillment. You cannot determine your life's purpose by focusing on self. You must begin with God, your Creator. Being successful and fulfilling life's purpose are not the same issue. Since God intends to make you like Jesus, He will carry you through loneliness, temptation, stress, criticism, rejection, and many other problems. Keep your eyes on Jesus. Your focus will determine your feelings. The secret of endurance is to remember that your pain is temporary, but the reward will be eternal. God will never leave us on our own.

The Golden Gate Bridge in San Francisco has two towers that are solidly anchored, yet the suspended bridge can move by a sway of 20 feet. The towers maintain the strength of the bridge. Our towers should be Christ and His Word. We may sway, but we should constantly keep our eyes on Jesus and the Word of God.

Life on earth is merely the dress rehearsal before the real production in heaven. This life is preparation for the life to follow in eternity. Almost all of us will live less than 100 years, but we will live in eternity forever. One day your heart will stop beating. That will be the end of your time on earth but will not be the end of you. Your earthly body is a temporary residence for your spirit. The Bible says when this tent we live in, in our body, here on earth is over, God has prepared for us a house in heaven to live in, a home He Himself has made which will last forever. "For we know that if the earthly tent which is our house is torn down, we have a building from God, a house not made with hands, eternal in the heavens" (2 Cor. 5:1).

While life on earth provides numerous options, eternity offers only two: heaven or hell. The choice is up to us evidenced by our beliefs and how we live. Your relationship to God on Earth will determine your relationship to Him in eternity. If you love and trust God's Son, Jesus Christ, you will be invited to spend eternity with Him. On the other hand, if you reject His love and fail to accept His forgiveness and salvation, you will spend your life apart from God forever.

For the believer heaven will be indescribably glorious. "But just as it is written, 'Things which eye has not seen and ear has not heard, And which have not entered the heart of man, All that God has prepared for those who love Him'" (1 Cor. 2:9).

Steps Leading to Maturity

Believers are to grow in grace and in the knowledge of the Lord (see 2 Pet. 3:18). As we have seen, the growth is progressive. The Christian life does not begin with our physical birth but rather with our spiritual birth through a personal relationship with Jesus Christ. Only by constant contact with Him, through His grace and knowledge, can Christian character and steadfastness develop. As we seek to become like Jesus, we look at what our Lord requested or made available to us. The first step in finding the will of God is to do the right thing now. This attitude may appear overly simplistic but is not. When we practice doing the right thing, day in and day out, everything else seems to fall into place in the natural course of events.

God wants us to be ambassadors for Christ. God planned the scheme of redemption. Christ carried it out, and the Holy Spirit is beseeching lost sinners to accept the Christ and become reconciled to God.

God's Master Plan

Jeremiah 29:11 states, "For I know the plans that I have for you, declares the Lord, plans for welfare and not for calamity to give you a future and a hope." This verse makes it clear that God has a plan for each of us. The verse also plainly declares that the plan is designed to give us a future and a hope and not terrible, horrible experiences. God created the plan to show His love for us, not His judgment for our mistakes. His plan offers forgiveness when we need it, encouragement when we feel weak, and clarity when we don't see clearly.

Here is an example of a plan designed to give you a future and a hope. Paul explains in Ephesians 4:22-24 our three responsibilities in becoming like Christ.

That, in reference to your former manner of life, you lay aside the old self, which is being corrupted in accordance with the lusts of deceit, and that you be renewed in the spirit of your mind, and put on the new self, which in the likeness of God has been created in righteousness and holiness of the truth.

First: We must get rid of old ways of acting.

Second: We must change the way we think. Let the Holy Spirit change your way of thinking. Romans 12:2 says we are "transformed" by the renewing of our minds.

Third: We must "put on the character of Christ" by developing new, godly habits. Your character is essentially the sum of your habits; it is how you habitually act. The Bible urges us to put on, or wear, the new self—created to be like God in true righteousness and holiness. "As the Spirit of the Lord works within us, we become more and more like him and reflect his glory even more" (2 Cor. 3:18b (NLT).

The first step in spiritual growth is changing the way you think. The Christian life is far more than creeds and convictions—it includes conduct and character. Our deeds must be consistent with our creeds, and our beliefs must be backed up with Christ-like behavior. Christianity is not a religion or a philosophy but a relationship and lifestyle. The core of that lifestyle is thinking of others as Jesus did instead of ourselves.

Becoming like Christ is a long, slow process of growth. It is a gradual, progressive development that will occupy the rest of your life. Considerable confusion in the Christian life comes from ignoring the simple fact that God is more interested in building your character than all else.

Grow Up!

Your Heavenly Father's goal is for you to mature and develop the characteristics of Jesus Christ. Sadly, millions of Christians *grow older* but never *grow up*. They are stuck in perpetual spiritual infancy, remaining in diapers and booties. The reason is that they never *intended* to grow.

Spiritual growth is not automatic. It calls for an intentional commitment. You must *want* to grow, *decide* to grow, *make an effort* to grow, and *persist* in growing. Discipleship—the process of becoming like Christ—always begins with a decision. Jesus calls us, and we respond: "'Come, be My disciple,' Jesus said to him. So Matthew got up and followed him."

God as Our Potter

As the fruit of the spirit are applied to our life and submitted to God, we become like him. One of God's goals is to share our character, so we will manifest this kindness, mercy, love, purity, and wisdom in a manner that is reflected through our personalities. In other words, God is making us holy. Homer Rodeheaver wrote:

Christ the transforming light
Touches this heart of mine
Piercing the darkest night
Making His glory shine
O to reflect His grace
Causing the world to see
Love that will grow
'Til others may know
Jesus revealed in me.

Who Are the Elect?

The elect are those who accept God's invitation and into whose heart He comes. The non-elect are those who reject Christ' to come in to their body. The doom of the non-elect is set forth in Revelation 11:15 and chapters 21—22. Without genuine repentance involving a deep consciousness of sin, and the confession of it, there cannot be saving faith (Acts 20:21). Paul wrote: "For the sorrow that is according to the will of God produces a repentance without regret, leading to salvation, but the sorrow of the world produces death" (2 Cor. 7:10).

God's grace plus man's faith, also given by Him, confession, and repentance enable God's justification resulting in salvation.

Humility

"He that humbleth himself shall be exalted" (Luke 14:11, KJV). Micah reminds us of three things the Lord requires of us:

To do justly
To love mercy
To walk humbly with God (Mic. 6:8)

"Therefore he saith, God resisteth the proud, but giveth grace to the humble (James 4:6).

In all creation, only human beings are made in God's image. Like God we are spiritual beings. Our spirits are immortal and will outlast our bodies. We can think, reason, and solve problems.

Following Christ's Great Commission

Each of us must do our part in the Great Commission. We may not go to Africa as a missionary or to Mexico to help build a house for a poor family, but we can contribute funds enabling others to go. We can also pray for the missionaries' safety. When Jesus commands us to go out into the world and make disciples, we should adopt our family, neighbors, uncles, aunts, nephews, nieces, cousins, fellow office workers, shut-ins and hospital patients, and inmates in jails and prisons as our world and evangelize them as well as donate to missions.

My previous book was The *Gospel* . I sent copies to all 67 of my family as well as to prison ministries, the Salvation Army, rescue-mission ministries, neighbors, church members, and other friends. This was my world to evangelize. The book, praise the Lord, touched over 5,000 families. I also give regularly to my church, to the Billy Graham Evangelistic Association, and to the late Bill Bright's Campus Crusade. Campus Crusade developed the *Jesus* film that has been shown to perhaps a billion or more people around the world with results of millions of converts.

You might join the "Honey,-let's-do- this club." The story is that Dr. Bright called together a group of wealthy business people to explain his call by God to produce the *Jesus* film." A wealthy businessman from Dallas and his wife were there. After the presentation, the wife turned to her husband and suggested, "Honey, let's do this." The development of the film required millions of dollars because it called for quality and was translated into many languages.

You might turn to your husband (or wife) and indicate, "Honey, let's . . ." contribute to the distribution of the film, or hand out religious material to jails, nursing homes, college freshmen, sponsor a Bible-study group, and more. Let's all become a part of the Great Commission.

The light of God's Word shining in dark places touches an extremely important issue in the lives and ministries of believers. When people trust Christ as their personal Savior, they become children of the light. Every child of God is placed in his or her sphere of influence as a light to the lost. When we commission missionaries and send them into remote areas of the world, we are placing lights in dark places, places where we are unable to go ourselves.

As believers, we must exercise vigilance regarding the type of preaching and teaching we expose ourselves to. Unfortunately, many people in both the pulpit and the media—who make spectacular, dogmatic, and often-entertaining claims to have received a direct revelation from God—plague us. In many instances, they preach dramatically and influentially to huge throngs of people. But the fact remains that God has spoken definitively and in finality in the Scriptures. They, along with the leading of the Holy Spirit, are our source of divine revelation. Before ascending to Heaven, Christ issued His marching order to His disciples and to us.

The Great Commission Matthew 28:18-20 (KJV)

> *And Jesus came and spake unto them, saying, All power is given unto me in heaven and in earth. Go ye therefore, and teach all nations, baptizing them in the name of the Father, and of the Son, and of the Holy Ghost: Teaching them to observe all things whatsoever I have commanded you: and, lo, I am with you always, even unto the end of the world. Amen.*

Prayer and Evangelism

Another important part of evangelism is prayer. Neighbors might reject our message about Christ, but they cannot reject prayer. God hears it, and the Holy Spirit works to bring conviction.

I would like to share a story with you. A lady in the Midwest saw her son ride off with a motorcycle gang, and she didn't see him for 21 years. He would call her about once a year. She would pray daily for his safety and for his soul. On his 39th birthday he called her. "Mom, I just gave my heart to Christ." Her persistence in prayer paid off.

During the showing of the *Jesus* film in Africa a young man approached the group leader and asked for him to visit his house and pray for his father who was dying. The leader asked his father's name. The leader became concerned because his father was a tribal leader who had killed a number of Christians. After prayer, the leader and his staff went to the home and through an interpreter witnessed to and prayed for the father. The man accepted Christ into his life. As the leader turned to go, the Holy Spirit engulfed him, and he announced to the group, "You will now really see God's power in action." So, he returned to the bed of the father and pronounced, "In the name of Jesus Christ, God heals you." While holding the arm of the man, the father stood up and danced around the floor praising Jesus. He later escorted the team to other towns as they praised Jesus, and many people were saved.

God Gave Us Two Great Commandments:

Teacher, which is the great commandment in the Law? And He said to him, "You shall love the Lord your God with all your heart, and with all your soul, and with all your mind. This is the great and foremost commandment. The second is like it, 'You shall love your neighbor as yourself.' On these two commandments depend the whole Law and the Prophets" (Matt. 22:36-40).

"Love the Lord your God [Worship]
with all your heart, and with all your soul,
and with all your mind."

"This is the first and great and foremost commandment. The second is like it . . .

Love your neighbor as yourself [Ministry/Service]

On these two commandments depend the whole Law and the Prophets"

Christ After the Resurrection

Then the eleven disciples went to Galilee,
to the mountain where Jesus had told them to go.
*When they saw Him, **they worshiped Him**;*
but some doubted.
Then Jesus came to them and said,
"All authority in heaven and on earth has been given to Me.
Therefore go and make disciples of all nations (Evangelism),
Baptizing them in the name of the Father, Son,
and Holy Spirit (Fellowship),
and teaching them to obey everything
I have commanded you (Discipleship).
And surely I am with you always, to the very end of the age.
(Matt. 28:18-20)

We Serve God by Serving Others

The world defines greatness in terms of power, possessions, prestige, and position. Jesus, however, measures greatness according to service, not status. God determines greatness by the number of people you serve, not by the number that serves you.

I would like to share a story with you. A lady had two children, a boy 16 and a girl 15, who wanted to attend a school dance. The mother was opposed but wanted her children to be happy, so she agreed. As they prepared to leave, she told them she would be praying until they returned. She then went and kneeled at her bed.

The children left for the dance and returned at 1 a.m. They had danced, drank some, listened to dirty jokes, and by worldly standards had a good time. When they came into the den they could see their mother praying. This impressed them to the extent that they were ashamed. They knelt on each side of their mother and prayed to accept Christ into their lives.

Jesus reminds us:

> *If you love Me, you will keep My commandments. . . . He who has My commandments and keeps them is the one who loves Me; and he who loves Me will be loved by My Father, and I will love him and will disclose Myself to him* (John 14:15, 21).

The Holy Spirit

The Holy Spirit as a teacher through the Word of God encourages us to learn and pray. He assumes the role as guide, pointing us toward Christ and His kingdom. The Holy Spirit plays a major part in your seeking to become like Christ. He encourages, keeps, and comforts us. It is the Holy Spirit's work to carry out the process of sanctification as believers become more Godly and less worldly.

The Holy Spirit's goal is to conform us to the image of Christ and to make us holy, even as He is holy. His role is to abide in us and convict us of sin, moving us to continued repentance. One cannot have sanctification without being regenerated and justified before God. The Holy Spirit provides nine fruit of the Spirit for us to measure our growth in the Christian life.

God's Word indicates that Jesus was filled with the Holy Spirit without measure. It also confirms that when we obey God and are fully committed to carry out His will, we will be filled with the Spirit.

Review these nine fruit of the Spirit and measure how you live up to them. Pray for and seek the filling of the Spirit.

A soul-searching question: Is there any unconfessed sin in your life that keeps you from a close walk with Christ? Do you have any broken relationships that require mending? Whatever it is, leave it with Christ as you confess and repent.

The Fruit of the Spirit

First Cluster - speaks of Godward relationships (love, joy, and peace).

Love. "By this all men will know that you are my disciples, if you have love for one another" (John 13:35, KJV). True love is active, not passive. God showed His love for us by taking the initiate in providing for our salvation (2 Cor 5:19). Jesus' love knows no bounds—from the lowest to the highest, from the lowest sinner to the purest saint. Only the Holy Spirit can produce such fruit.

Joy. Jesus said, "These things I have spoken to you, that my joy might remain in you, and that your joy might be full" (John 15:11, KJV). Even as all the water in the world cannot quench the Spirit's fire, neither can all the troubles and tragedies of the world overwhelm the joy the Spirit kindles in human hearts.

Peace. Peace carries with it the idea of unity, completeness, rest, ease, and security, "Thou will keep him in perfect peace whose mind stayed on thee, because he trusteth in thee" (Isa. 26:3, KJV) When one is wholly committed to do God's bidding, all enemies of peace are overcome.

Second Cluster - speaks of interpersonal relationships (patience, kindness, and goodness)

If we are short-tempered, unkind, and rude, we lack the second cluster of the fruit of the Spirit. When the Spirit controls us, He works to transform us so the buds of patience, kindness, and goodness begin to blossom—and then become fruitful.

Patience. Patience is steadfast ("hanging in there," "not losing one's cool") under provocation. If we are irritable, vengeful, or resentful, the Holy Spirit is not in charge. Patience is a trait of true Christ-likeness, a quality we often like in others without demanding it of ourselves.

Kindness. Kindness and gentleness grow outward. Gentleness is love that endures. Jesus dealt tenderly and kindly with everyone, except self-righteous hypocrites like the scribes and Pharisees. He was justified in severely rebuking them. Even small children sensed His gentleness and approached Him eagerly without fear.

Goodness. Seek to be like God because He alone is perfectly good. Goodness is love in action and is always accompanied by patience and kindness by the power of the Holy Spirit. This trait of character becomes part of our lives that we might remind others of Him. "Let your light so shine before men, that they might see you good works, and glorify your Father which is in heaven" (Matt. 5:16, KJV)

Third Cluster - speaks of inward attitudes of one's self (faithfulness, gentleness, and self-control)

All of these mean putting God first, others second, and self third.

Faithfulness. In the New Testament "faithfulness" is closely akin to "faith," since faith telescopes into faithfulness or steadfastness. The Spirit works in us that He might work through us. " It is God who is at work in you, both to will and to work for His good pleasure" (Phil. 2:13). "For I am confident of this very thing, that He who began a good work in you will perfect it until the day of Christ Jesus" (Phil. 1:6). "You were faithful with a few things, I will put you in charge of many things" (Matt.25:21). Lack of faithfulness is a mark of spiritual immaturity. One sign of emotional immaturity is the refusal to accept responsibility.

Someday all Christians will stand before Christ to give account of the works we have done since our conversion. He will judge us, not on the basis of how successful we were in the eyes of the world, but how faithful we were where He put us. Sometimes the greatest test of our faithfulness is how much time we spend reading the Word, praying, and living in accord with the principles of righteousness.

Paul wrote to Timothy, "I have fought a good fight, I have kept the faith: henceforth there is laid up for me a crown of righteousness, which the Lord, the righteous judge, shall give me at that day" (2 Tim. 4:7, KJV) The ultimate reward for faithfulness is highlighted in Revelation 2:16, "Be thou faithful unto death, and I will give thee a crown of life" (KJV)

Gentleness (Meekness). Jesus said, "Blessed are the gentle ["meek," KJV] for they shall inherit the earth" (Matt. 5:5). Meekness is actually power and wildness under control. We might refer to this quality as love under discipline. How can we be gentle and humble in heart as Jesus was? (See Matt. 11:29).

First, we do not rise up defensively when our feelings are ruffled as Peter did when he cut off the high priest's servant's ear at the arrest of Jesus in Gethsemane (Matt. 26:53).

Second, we do not crave to have the preeminence (first place), as Diotrephes, "who loveth to have the preeminence," did (see 3 John 1:9, KJV). We must make sure that Christ is Numero Uno in all we think, say, or do.

Third, we do not seek to be recognized and highly regarded or to be considered the voice of authority. God is not pleased with "church bosses" who must have the say so about every minute detail in church. "Honor one another above yourselves" (Romans 12:10b).

Self-control (Temperance). John Wesley's mother once wrote him while he was a student at Oxford that "anything which increases the authority of the body over the mind is an evil thing." Modern examples are alcohol, other drugs, and illicit sex. The highest mark of nobility is self-control. We usually think of temperance in terms of alcohol or illicit drugs, but we should also include overeating, use of tobacco, unkindness, gossip, pride, and jealously.

The Holy Spirit wants to cultivate in us the nine fruit of the Spirit (love, joy, peace, patience, kindness, goodness, faithfulness, gentleness, and self-control). The Holy Spirit is already in every Christian's heart, and His intention is to produce the fruit in our spirits if we will let Him. It is essential that we allow the Spirit to eliminate the works of the flesh from our inner lives, so our "crop" of fruit is not stunted.

Above all else, to receive the fullness of the Holy Spirit is to be Christ-like. Christ is The Light, but we are His little lights. We are also the salt of the earth that should season society for the Gospel (see Matt. 5:13-14).

Measurement of How Well the Fruit Is (actually Are) Growing in You

Do you exhibit . . .

Love - even for those who are unlovely or those who do not love us in return?

Joy - in the middle of painful circumstances?

Peace - when a blessing or goal you were counting on doesn't come through?

Patience - when things are not going fast enough for you?

Kindness - to those who treat you unkindly?

Goodness - toward those who have been intentionally insensitive toward you?

Faithfulness - when friends have proved unfaithful?

Gentleness - toward those who have handled you roughly?

Self-Control - amid intense temptation?

Gifts of the Spirit from God

God gives every believer one or more spiritual gifts to be used in ministry and to help other believers. They are special God-empowered abilities for serving that are given only to believers.

You cannot earn your spiritual gifts or deserve them. That's why they are called gifts! They are an expression of God's grace to you. Christ has generously divided out His gifts to us. Neither do you get to choose which gifts you'd like to have. God determines which gift is your gift.

The spiritual gifts are given to you when you are "born again" to enable you to begin work immediately as a member of Christ's body, Some truths:

1st truth- Every Christian is given at least one gift.

2nd truth- God adds gifts as you mature spiritually.

3rd truth- A Spirit of obedience to Christ is the key to receiving additional gifts.

Spiritual gifts are the insignia of the Holy Spirit. The primary purpose of spiritual gifts is the building up of Christ's Body, the Church—not the personal gratification of the individual member. When we serve others through the use of our gifts, we are channels through which the grace and power of God are manifested.

> *Each one should use whatever gift he has received to serve others, faithfully administering God's grace in its various forms. If anyone speaks, he should do it as one speaking the very words of God. If anyone serves, he should do it with the strength God provides, so that in all things God may be praised through Jesus Christ. To him be the glory and the power forever and ever. Amen*" (1 Pet. 4:10-11).

The Holy Spirit distributes the gifts*:* "But one individually just as

He wills" (1 Cor. 12:11). Gifts are bestowed to edify one another, enabling us to serve and glorify Christ together. Each part of our human body (eyes, ears, feet, hands) is necessary to serve the whole. The Body of Christ requires members using their gifts for the upbuilding of the church. "As every man [woman] has received the gift, even so minister the same one to another, as good shepherds of the manifold grace of God" (1 Pet. 4:18). The Holy Spirit has supplied sufficient gifts to meet every need of the church. Our Divine Master wants all of the members to exercise all their gifts so His body may function smoothly and effectively.

The Bible lists approximately 21 gifts. I will touch on several.

Prophecy

The gift of prophecy is the Spirit-given ability to proclaim the Word of God with clarity and to apply it to a particular situation with a view toward correction and edification.

Evangelism (Ephesians 4:11)

Persons gifted in the area of evangelism have a strong desire to share the Gospel with non-believers in every situation and by all possible means. All believers are to witness; yet some have received special gifts for this ministry. "'Come, follow me,' Jesus said, 'and I will make you fishers of men'" (Mark 1:17).

Shepherding (Pastoring)

This entails watching out for the needs of the flock, counseling with members, guarding, guiding, and spiritually feeding with knowledge and understanding. Mature Christians being assigned to new Christians is another aspect of shepherding (1 Cor. 12:29-30; 2 Cor. 12:28; Rom. 12:6-8).

Preaching/ teaching (Romans 4:11)

The gift of preaching/teaching is the supernatural ability to explain clearly and apply effectively the truth of God's Word.

Exhortation (Encouragement, Romans 2:6-8)

The gift of exhortation involves the supernatural ability to come alongside to help, to strengthen the weak, reassure the wavering, steady the faltering, console the troubled, and to encourage the believers.

Knowledge and Wisdom (1 Corinthians 12:8-10)

It is not enough to be able to grasp and systematize the deep truths of God's Word. Also called for is the ability to relate those truths to the needs and problems of life. Wisdom involves the gift of putting knowledge to work in daily experience.

Helps (1 Corinthians 12:28; 1 Peter 4:11)

The gift of helps carries the meaning of assistance or lending a hand. The gift of helps is the Spirit-endowed ability to serve the church in any supporting role, usually temporal, though sometimes spiritual. The gift enables one to serve joyfully and diligently wherever and whenever required. The ultimate end of helps is the building up of others. Christian workers like ministers, released from temporal tasks, can concentrate more on spiritual priorities. Although they ended up preaching and teaching the Word, The Seven in Acts 6 were originally set apart for their gifts of helps.

Hospitality (Romans 12:6-8)

Peter urged the believers to use hospitality one to another without grudging (see 1 Pet. 4:9). "Do not neglect to show hospitality to strangers, for by this some have entertained angels without knowing it" [for instance, Abraham and Sarah] (Heb. 13:2). Open your home to help further God's work. "I was a stranger, and ye took me in" (Matt. 25:35, KJV).

Giving (2 Corinthians 8:1-5)

This gift involves giving without pretense, without drudgery, and with love. Persons gifted in the area of giving have the ability to give material goods and financial resources with joy so the needs of the Lord's work are met. They have the capacity to recognize financial needs. "Each one must do just as he has purposed in his heart, not grudgingly or under compulsion, for God loves a cheerful [actually "hilarious" in the Greek] giver" (2 Cor 9:7).

Administration/Government (1 Corinthians 12:28)

The gift of government is the Spirit-given expertise to preside, govern, plan, organize, and administer with wisdom, fairness, humility, service, confidence, ease, and efficiency. Persons gifted in areas of administrations are goal- and objective-oriented.

Mercy (Romans 12:6-8)

The gift of mercy means expressing compassion, especially in aiding the needy, whether physically and/or spiritually and emotionally. Persons gifted in the area of mercy model the emotions of our Lord as He "was moved with compassion on them" (Matt. 9:36). Their hearts immediately go out to those who are suffering and burdened with cares. These persons usually desire friendships in which there is deep communication and mutual commitment. They have a tendency to avoid confrontation and firmness and often close their spirits to those they feel are overly harsh or critical.

Faith (1 Corinthians 12:8-10)

The gift of faith is the Spirit-granted insight to single out what God wants done—then to sustain unwavering confidence that God will do it, regardless of seemingly insurmountable obstacles.

Discernment (1 Corinthians 12:8-9)

To discern, one has the ability to determine the real from the unreal; the genuine from the spurious. Discernment is the gift to distinguish between the spirit of truth and the spirit of error.

A person with this gift discriminates between that which is raised up by God and that which pretends to be. They have the Spirit-endowed ability to unmask Satan's trickery, to detect unbiblical teachings, and to ferret out false teachers. They have the enablement to spot a phony before others see through such Satan-led phoniness.

Miracles (1 Corinthians 12:8-10, 28-30)

A miracle is an event of supernatural power. God chooses certain persons to communicate, and at times to serve as instruments of, His miracle-working power.

Healing (1 Corinthians 12:8-10, 28-30)

Certain Bible scholars feel there are four basic kinds of healing:

Healing of Sin

Bitterness, resentment, and hatred are serious sins. One of the worst sins is lack of forgiveness. Christ pointed out:

> *Therefore if you are presenting your offering at the altar, and there remember that your brother has something against you, leave your offering there before the altar and go; first be reconciled to your brother, and then come and present your offering* (Matt. 5:23-24).

Often when Jesus would heal a person physically, He would add, "Your sins are forgiven." Though physical illness goes back to sin in the Garden of Eden, it is certainly not always directly linked to a person's sin. Yet, sometimes it is, as in the case of the Corinthians Who defiled the Lord's Supper (see 1 Cor. 11:30).

Inner Healing

If a child has a drunken father who is angry when he comes home, or has a mother who doesn't really want the child, that child is going to suffer in the soul. When we are loved, we begin to blossom like lovely flowers. When we ask the Lord to heal those things that have hurt us in the past, and continue to pull us down, He will do it. This type of suffering prevents us from receiving the freedom that Jesus Christ wants us to give back. Psychologists have had a field day with phobias. Many fret and strain over things that will never happen. So many are afraid they will never have enough money. Others fear the loss of a mate, either through divorce or death. One of the deepest fears is that we won't be loved and accepted. Many people feel that God can't possibly love them, but they have failed to become acquainted with the truth of John 3:16.

Physical Healing

Jesus came to people to re-create fellowship between God and mankind. If a man were a leper, then Jesus would cure his leprosy. Whatever the ailment, He would reach out to heal. "Jesus Christ is the same yesterday and today and forever" (Heb. 13:8). He does not change. If we call upon the Lord with faith, and if it is God's will, He will still heal us today.

The Healing of Demonic Illness

Though our secular age discounts Satan and his demons, the truth is that he and his devils or demons will continue their malfeasance until they are cast into the lake of fire for eternity. As during Bible days, today some illnesses are caused by demonic spirits. People with special experience in healing those illnesses should be called in, and the healing should be done in private. If you have a Bible-believing, Gospel-preaching pastor, talk with him. If not, find one! We must remember God is all-powerful and all loving, so he desires our healing.

All healing is from God. Only He can heal, and we should ask for healing in the "Name above every name," that of Jesus Christ (see Phil. 2:9).

The Gift of Leadership (Romans 12:6-8)

Persons gifted in this area are enabled to lead others toward spiritual growth. They often are considered visionary and have the knack of setting goals and motivating others toward accomplishing their goals. They usually can communicate effectively to large groups of people.

The Gift of Tongues (1 Corinthians 12:10)

According to Paul tongues was a lesser gift. "However, in the church I desire to speak five words with my mind so that I may instruct others also, rather than ten thousand words in a tongue" (1 Cor. 14:19). There is no doubt that this gift has continued through the centuries, yet Paul felt that the gifts of teaching and prophecy were far more vital. It is definitely one of God's gifts but should never become divisive. On the Day of Pentecost the gift of speaking in foreign languages was given to spread the Gospel. Those tongues were known. It appears that in Corinth some spoke in tongues that were unknown, except to the Holy Spirit. Perhaps those were "prayer" tongues basically to edify the tongues speaker. Tongues are neither the initial evidence of the Holy Spirit, as some contend, nor essential to salvation nor spiritual power.

Living in Christ

> *I am the true vine, and My Father is the vinedresser. Every branch in Me that does not bear fruit, He takes away; and every branch that bears fruit, He prunes it so that it may bear more fruit. You are already clean because of the word which I have spoken to you. Abide in Me, and I in you. As the branch cannot bear fruit of itself unless it abides in the vine, so neither can you unless you abide in Me. I am the vine, you are the branches; he who abides in Me and I in him, he bears much fruit, for apart from Me you can do nothing. If anyone does not abide in Me, he is thrown away as a branch and dries up; and they gather them, and cast them into the fire and they are burned* (John 15:1-6).

The Vine is Christ. We are the branches. As it were, the Holy Spirit is the life-giving juice that runs through the vine into the branch. The branch lives, grows, and bears fruit, not by struggles and effort, but by simply abiding (being there). By faith I have accepted the relationship of abiding. I am abiding Christ, and His Spirit is filling my heart with the fruit of the Spirit. All of these are living in me. I understood that upon receiving the Holy Spirit, I was endowed with a source of power that will align my character with God's righteous standard.

Characteristics of the Holy Spirit

Comforter; Counselor; Teacher; Spirit of Jesus Christ; Spirit of Power; Spirit of the Living God; Spirit of Truth; Spirit of Sonship (adoption); Spirit of Wisdom and Understanding; Giver of Gifts; Giver of the Fruit of Spirit; The Promised Holy Spirit; Voice of the Almighty; Voice of the Lord; The Sealer of Faith.

Pray with me.

> Dear Father, in the name of the Lord Jesus Christ, I come abiding in You, asking for the forgiveness of every sin and praying for the Holy Spirit to manifest His fruit in my life. Through the Spirit, may my life, without question, reflect Jesus Christ. In the Name of that is above every name. Amen.

Chapter 12

God's Plan for Our Abundant Life

Our faith in Christ ushers in blessings, not merely in the past and future but in the present as well. Our justification was on the basis of Christ's finished work, and we are to live day by day on the same basis. We have every right to appropriate what God gives us because of Christ's work on Calvary. We can do that with overwhelming confidence in a living Savior. Through Him life is no longer a tragic dead end but an open thoroughfare for glorifying God and reaping God's best in spite of life's struggles. Through Christ we can have strength through rough and tumble, uncertain times.

God's Spirit Working in You

The Holy Spirit produces a Christ-like character in the believer. From the moment a person receives Christ into his life, she/he is to grow spiritually and to become more and more like Him. As already pointed out, that process is referred to as sanctification. Let's review three important truths and examine how they relate to salvation present and also your continuing process of salvation. Salvation is in three tenses: the Christian was saved and has been saved, is being saved, and shall be saved! God does nothing slipshod or halfway.

Satan will stop at nothing to defeat your efforts to grow and serve your new Master. When you became a Christian, your old nature did not cease to exist. That "old man," as Paul called it, was struck a death blow, but he continues to kick until the Lord calls you home and returns in His second coming. Rather, Satan continues to work on your old nature to struggle against your new nature. That struggle is his attempt to finagle crippling sins into your life and defeat you. The key is your surrender to the Indwelling Christ. As He controls your life, He gives you daily victory over Satan's attempts to use your old nature to defeat you. This daily victory is salvation present.

You will never cease being amazed at what Christ did for you in that single moment when you prayed and asked Him to enter your life! He called you out of a world in which self ruled over all your decisions. He instantly forgave all the sin and wrong deeds you had ever done. He placed His own life inside yours and began to claim your existence as another perk of His kingdom. In a moment of time, you were forever set free from the worry that at the end of life you would be separated from God. Those matters are forever settled. Nothing can snatch away your new life in Christ. You are His forever!

Jesus assured:

> *My sheep [His followers] hear my voice, and I know them, and they follow me: And I give unto them eternal life; and they shall never perish, neither shall any man pluck them out of my hand. My Father, which gave them me, is greater than all; and no man is able to pluck them out of my Father's hand* (Matt. 10:27-29, KJV).

And the apostle Paul made it plain:

> *Who shall separate us from the love of Christ? shall tribulation, or distress, or persecution, or famine, or nakedness, or peril, or sword? As it is written, For thy sake we are killed all the day long; we are accounted as sheep for the slaughter. Nay, in all these things we are more than conquerors through him that loved us. For I am persuaded, that neither death, nor life, nor angels, nor principalities, nor powers, nor things present, nor things to come, Nor height, nor depth, nor any other creature, shall be able to separate us from the love of God, which is in Christ Jesus our Lord* (Rom. 8:35-38).

God's Plan for Your Life Here

God's ultimate goal for your life on earth is not comfort but character development. He wants you to grow up spiritually and become like Christ. God created your uniqueness, and He doesn't want to obliterate it. God wants you to exemplify the characteristics of the nine fruits of the Spirit. (love, joy, peace, patience, kindness, goodness, faithfulness, meekness, and self-control).

Having thanked God for what you have, you have a yearning for more? Hope, faith, assurance, enjoyment, glory. Ask Him for it. Climb the steps. Follow the example of Moses. Enter boldly in faith and ask God, "Show me Your glory." And you have the assurance that if you do so sincerely from your heart, in His own good season He will answer you. You have higher and greater assurance, from the Word of God itself, of the promise from the living God. "Draw near to God and He will draw near to you. Cleanse your hands, you sinners; and purify your hearts, you double-minded (Jas. 4:8). There James was addressing Christians who were struggling with the wiles of the world.

Every day dwell on this: God's purpose is for you to develop, character—to become more like Jesus—and to prepare for life in heaven. Why would God prepare heaven on earth, when He has planned the real thing for you in eternity? God gives us our time on earth for Him to build and strengthen our character for heaven. God is working in you, giving you the desire to obey Him and the power to do what pleases Him. The Holy Spirit often nudges us with a "gentle whisper." We allow Christ to live through us, For this is the secret: "Christ in you, the hope of glory" (see Col. 1:27).

We must choose to do the right in situations and then trust God's Spirit to give us His power, love, faith, and wisdom to do it. Since God's Spirit lives inside of us, this is always available for the asking. It is a fatal mistake to assume that God's goal for your life is material prosperity or popular success as the world defines it. The abundant life has nothing to do with material abundance. And faithfulness to God does not guarantee success in a career, or even ministry, but God does answer prayer according to His will. In God's eyes, the greatest heroes of faith are not those to achieve prosperity, success, and power in this life—but rather those who treat this life as temporary, preparing for eternity and assisting others to serve God.

God's Five Purposes for Your Life

Worship

We bring glory to God by worshipping Him. Worship is our first responsibility to God. In inviting us to glorify Him, God is calling us to enjoy Him. God wants our worship to be motivated by love, thanksgiving, and delight, not duty. Worship is a lifestyle of enjoying God, loving Him, and giving ourselves to be used for His purposes.

Love Others

We bring glory to God by loving other believers as members of God's redeemed family; we should love one another. Jesus taught us also to love even our enemies. "You have heard that it was said, 'You shall love your neighbor and hate your enemy.' But I say to you, love your enemies and pray for those who persecute you" (Matt. 5:43-44).

Have a Burden for the Lost

If you are a Christian, remember when you were without Christ, "dead in trespasses and sins" (Eph. 2:1, KJV). One of the first impulses when a person accepts Christ is: "I want other people to have what I have. I want them to be saved." You want to shout it from the rooftops, even if you are bashful. The old spiritual goes, "Go tell it on the mountain, over the hills and everywhere." God promises the soul-winner: "Those who have insight will shine brightly like the brightness of the expanse of heaven, and those who lead the many to righteousness, like the stars forever and ever" (Dan. 12:3). The writer of Proverbs explained, "The fruit of the righteous is a tree of life; and he that winneth souls is wise" (Prov. 11:30, KJV).

Become Christ-like

We also glorify God by becoming like Christ. When a person is first born again, they need help. Those who are already believers should help them to grow in maturity, not criticize them. "Even so ye, forasmuch as ye are zealous of spiritual gifts, seek that ye may excel to the edifying of the church" (1 Cor. 14:12, KJV; also see Eph. 4:12; I Thess. 5:11). "Edify" means to build up and strengthen.

Use Our Gifts

We bring glory to God by serving others with our gifts. Gifts were given to benefit others, even as others were given gifts to benefit us. As we do, God calls on us to share **"God's Good News."** Introducing others to Jesus and helping them to grow in Him is a marvelous privilege, thus helping them to discover their purpose and preparing them for eternity.

Enjoy the Abundant Life

Living the rest of your life in the glory of God will help you have and enjoy an abundant life (see John 10:10). One of the tremendous gifts God has given us is to enjoy life. He wired us with the five senses and emotions so you can experience it. He wants you to enjoy life, not merely endure it. The reason you are able to enjoy wholesome pleasure is that God made you in His image.

Cleaning house, cooking, caring for children, and working on a job are all ways we can glorify God. Begin each task with prayer. We should gradually turn all our life over to God and let Him work through us. A couple of years ago I began a prayer each time I climbed behind the steering wheel of my car. "Lord, I turn over this trip to You. Please make the trip safe and may I do everything I should do." I have noticed three results: more peace, driving under the speed limit, and I have been amazed how many green lights I catch." I am seeking to do this in all my endeavors, seeking God's guidance in all I do. Paul advised us: "Whatever you do in word or deed, do all in the name of the Lord Jesus, giving thanks through Him to God the Father" (Col. 3:17). Work becomes worship when you dedicate it to God and perform it with an awareness of His presence.

What makes God Smile? . . .

Our loving, serving, praising, and worshipping Him. Pleasing God should be the first purpose in His people. "For the Lord takes pleasure in His people; He will beautify the afflicted ones with salvation" (Ps. 149:4).

Giving Your Life to Jesus

If you have not given your life to Jesus, then do it right now.

- Believe God loves you and has a purpose for you and trust that He has chosen you to have a relationship with Jesus.
- Believe that no matter what you have done, God wants to forgive you.

- Ask Jesus to forgive your sins. Receive Him into your life as your Lord and Savior and accept His forgiveness, recognizing that there is no longer any condemnation for those sins. With your faith in Christ, your confession of sins, and your inviting Christ into your life, God sends the Holy Spirit into your body to live forever, and He will give you the power to fulfill your life's purpose. "For from Him and through Him and to Him are all things. To Him be the glory forever. Amen" (Rom. 11:36).

What Authority?

Is there an authority to tell us right and wrong, what is good and what is bad? Is there an ultimate authority we can depend on as a guide to living our lives? The answer is yes. That authority is God's Holy Word (the Bible), God's instruction book.

This inspired, infallible Book is called the Book (Ps. 40:7; Rev. 22:19); the Book of the Lord (Is. 34:16); the Book of the Law (Neh. 8:3; Gal. 3:10); the good Word of God (Heb. 6:5); Holy Scriptures, (Rom. 1:2; 2 Tim. 3:15); the Law of the Lord (Ps. 1:2; Isa. 30:9); the oracles of God (Rom. 3:2; 1 Pet. 4:11); the Scriptures (1 Cor. 15:3); the Scriptures of truth (Dan. 10:21); the sword of the Spirit (Eph. 6:17); the Word (Jas. 1:21–23; 1 Pet. 2:2); the Word of God (Luke 11:28; Heb. 4:12); Word of Christ (Col. 3:16); Word of life (Phil. 2:16); and the Word of truth (2 Tim. 2:15; Jas. 1:18). Under the leading of the Holy Spirit, rely on the Bible, God's Word, as your guide and compass along the twisting pathway of life. It will never lead you astray.

The Body of Christ—The Church

The Bible teaches that all believers make up the body of Christ, the universal church. The writer of Hebrews spoke of "the general assembly and church of the firstborn, which are written in heaven, and to God the Judge of all, and to the spirits of just men made perfect" (Heb. 12:23). There he was referring to universal church, to which every true, born-again believer belongs.

When a person is saved, he/she then should belong to a church that is a local expression of His body. Our spiritual growth is aided by our being baptized and joining a Bible-believing, Gospel preaching church. Christ founded the church and died for it with His blood (Eph. 5:25). The church is the only institution He started. The writer of Hebrews further encouraged believers about coming together for worship and fellowship. "Not forsaking our own assembling together, as is the habit of some, but encouraging one another; and all the more as you see the day drawing near" (Heb. 10:25).

Life Is Not a Rose Garden

Every Christian soon learns that life is not smooth. Then you come face to face with the fact that—even though Christ gave you a new nature at conversion—you found out the old sin nature still resides in our body. The one we feed will grow the most. The old nature is the means Satan uses in an attempt to defeat you and to mar your fellowship with the Father God. Satan sometimes causes us to have bad dreams to embarrass us. He even intercepts our prayers with bad thoughts. We must rebuke the devil through the power of the Holy Spirit, even as the Lord Jesus did.

Total obedience, trust, and commitment to Jesus will grant us fulfillment in the Spirit, and God's grace wills us the power to overshadow the old nature and make us holy as God is Holy.

Prayer

I strongly recommend a quiet time with God. For me between 7 and 8 a.m. and 9:30 to 10:30 p.m. are excellent times. It all depends on the person. Yet, in the morning is a splendid time for me; my mind is clear. A regular time provides needed spiritual nourishment. You must find time each day to be alone with God. End each prayer in the name of Jesus Christ. Christ is the source of spiritual life. God is a personal God, and you can talk directly to Him. He knows you inside and out. Nothing is hid from Him. Remember that He loves you with an everlasting love. "I have loved you with an everlasting love; Therefore I have drawn you with lovingkindness" (Jer. 33:3b).

Many people excuse themselves with, "But I don't know how to pray." That's why Jesus left us His "Model Prayer."

> *After this manner therefore pray ye: Our Father which art in heaven, Hallowed be thy name. Thy kingdom come. Thy will be done in earth, as it is in heaven. Give us this day our daily bread. And forgive us our debts, as we forgive our debtors. And lead us not into temptation, but deliver us from evil: For thine is the kingdom, and the power, and the glory, for ever. Amen*" (Matt. 6:9-13, KJV).

To jog your memory and keep your requests before you, make a prayer list: kids' safety, husband's soul, drive safely, neighbors, church, friends. Mention them one by one. Name names. Pray specifically. Too many prayers are, "God bless the whole world and all the missionaries on the home and foreign fields." Pray for the unsaved. Pray for people's healing.

If possible set up a specific time and place for prayer. Christ will be waiting. Keep your Bible and a notepad with you. Commune with God. Praise Him. Adore Him. Worship Him. Pray for your family and friends and also yourself. Years ago there was a book on prayer entitled *Prayer: Asking and Receiving*. It was an excellent book with the wrong title. Prayer is far more than merely asking and receiving.

"Something Happened, and Now I Know" . . .

Bill Gaither wrote those words in "He Touched Me." What a difference it did make when Jesus touched you! Since you became a Christian much of the "stuff" you enjoyed before you were saved isn't fun anymore. Now that Christ is your Lord, that junk seems flat and tasteless. Paul expressed that feeling well: "More than that, I count all things to be loss in view of the surpassing value of knowing Christ Jesus my Lord, for whom I have suffered the loss of all things, and count them but rubbish [KJV, "dung," excrement] so that I may gain Christ" (Phil. 3:8). Second Corinthians 5:15 sums up what has happened since you became a Christian: "And He died for all, so that they who live might no longer live for themselves, but for Him who died and rose again on their behalf."

The old life is passing away;
The new life is coming into being;
All this happened because you are in Christ;
Christ makes the difference between your old sin nature and your new life (Col 1:21-27)

And although you were formerly alienated and hostile in mind, engaged in evil deeds, yet He has now reconciled you in His fleshly body through death, in order to present you before Him holy and blameless and beyond reproach—if indeed you continue in the faith firmly established and steadfast, and not moved away from the hope of the gospel that you have heard, which was proclaimed in

> *all creation under heaven, and of which I, Paul, was made a minister. Now I rejoice in my sufferings for your sake, and in my flesh I do my share on behalf of His body, which is the church, in filling up what is lacking in Christ's afflictions. Of this church I was made a minister according to the stewardship from God bestowed on me for your benefit, so that I might fully carry out the preaching of the word of God, that is, the mystery which has been hidden from the past ages and generations, but has now been manifested to His saints, to whom God willed to make known what is the riches of the glory of this mystery among the Gentiles, which is Christ in you, the hope of glory* (Col. 1:21-27).

God is working in you, empowering you to do what fully pleases him. However, you must work out what God is working into you. You must choose to let the indwelling Christ control you. You must be committed to being an open vessel (channel) through which He can flow His love to others.

Our loving Shepherd (see Psalm 23) desires to lead us to green pastures beside still waters, so He can cleanse our diseased thoughts, heal our damaged lives, and restore our souls. He longs to guide us through the valley of the shadow of death, to free us from the fear of evil, and to comfort us with His rod and staff. He yearns to lead us along the paths of righteousness for His name's sake.

God Is Watching You Enjoy Creation

He gave you eyes to enjoy beauty,
Ears to enjoy sound,
Your nose to enjoy smells,
Taste buds to enjoy tastes,
Nerves under your skin to enjoy feeling.

Every act of enjoyment becomes an act of worship when you thank God for it. God smiles when we use our abilities. The Lord is pleased with those who worship Him and trust His love (Psalms 147:11).

A friend of mine was dreadfully sick and his system almost shut down. He was not able to eliminate for a while. When his system was restored and began to function, he praised God for it. Now, every time he goes to the bathroom, He praises the Lord! Have you thought of thanking God for all of your bodily functions?

The Heart of Worship

> *We have come to know and have believed the love which God has for us. God is love, and the one who abides in love abides in God, and God abides in him. By this, love is perfected with us, so that we may have confidence in the day of judgment; because as He is, so also are we in this world. There is no fear in love; but perfect love casts out fear, because fear involves punishment, and the one who fears is not perfected in love. We love, because He first loved us* (1 John 4:16-19).

The heart of genuine worship is to yield completely to God. It is a natural response to God's amazing love and mercy. We give ourselves to Him not out of fear and duty, but out of love, because He first loved us. The three barriers that block our surrender to God are fear, pride, and confusion. Trust is an essential ingredient to surrender. Fear keeps us from surrendering, but love casts out all fear. The more you realize how much God loves you, the easier surrender comes.

"But God demonstrates His own love toward us, in that while we were yet sinners, Christ died for us" (Rom. 5:8). God loves us so much that while we were still sinners, He gave His life for us. The second barrier is our own pride. We want to be in charge of everything. God wants us to look to Him, not ourselves. Our power is limited, but God's power is unlimited. "For nothing will be impossible with God" (Luke 1:37), the angel told Mary.

> *Paul admonished the Romans: "And do not go on presenting the members of your body to sin as instruments of unrighteousness; but present yourselves to God as those alive from the dead, and your members as instruments of righteousness to God* " (Rom. 6:13)

Surrendering is not giving up your personality. God does not want robots. He wants to use your unique personality to accomplish and carry out His plan. There is an old chorus that goes: "Let go and let God have His way. " We need to let go and let God use us as he did Abraham, Mary, Paul, Peter, and others. God never asks us to do anything without the Holy Spirit empowering us to do it.

Sometimes we may have confusion about surrendering to Jesus . You might think, *If I surrender, God may send me to a Third World coun-*

try. There's no telling what He might ask of me. God will never send you anywhere He has not prepared your heart to go.

The indwelling Christ will give you victory in every area of your life. He was tested in every way you might be and did not sin. Paul assured us: "No temptation has overtaken you but such as is common to man; and God is faithful, who will not allow you to be tempted beyond what you are able, but with the temptation will provide the way of escape also, so that you will be able to endure it" (1 Cor. 10:13). God will always give you a way to escape. He not only protects you, but He also provides all the resources necessary for you to triumph over trials and temptations.

How Should Christians Live?

You should live with a humble frame of mind.
You always should be aware of your own weaknesses.
You must try constantly to trust Christ more and serve Him better.
The fear of being unfaithful to God is a healthy fear.
You should always have a sense of awe at how God provides for your needs.
You should be genuinely fearful of not allowing Christ to give you what He alone can provide.

Freedom from the Influence of Sin

Will you ever be rid of that old nature, the nature of sin? Will the time ever come when your new nature does not have a daily struggle with the old nature? Yes! When Christ comes again, you will be set free from the presence and the influence of the old nature.

When God Seems Distant

When God seems distant, you may feel God is angry with you or disciplining you. In fact, sin does disconnect us from intimate fellowship with God. We grieve God's Spirit, and we hamper our fellowship with Him by disobedience. However, this feeling of abandonment from God often has nothing to do with sin. It may be a test of faith, one all must face. Will you continue to love, trust, obey, and worship God, even when you have no sense of His presence or visible evidence of His work in your life?

Faith, not feelings, pleases God. During times of spiritual dryness, you must patiently rely on the promises of God, not your emotions, realizing He is leading you to a deeper level of maturity. Don't be troubled by trouble. God's grace is still in full force for you, for God has promised, "I will never desert you, nor will I ever forsake you" (Heb. 13:5).

When we place our faith in Christ, God becomes our Heavenly Father, we become His children, other believers become our brothers and sisters, and the church becomes our spiritual family. Every human being was created by God, but not everyone is a child of God. The only means of becoming a part of God's spiritual family is to be "born again" (see Chapter 9, "What It Means to Be Born Again"). You become part of the human family by your physical birth, but you become a part of God's family by spiritual birth, being born again.

The invitation to be a part of God's family is universal, but men and women must have faith in Jesus Christ to be saved and adopted into His family. Here on Earth, we are given the riches of God's grace, but in eternity we will be given infinitely more. "But just as it is written, 'Things which eye has not seen and ear has not heard, And which have not entered the heart of man, All that God has prepared for those who love Him'" (1 Cor. 2:9).

First, we will be with Jesus forever.

Second, we will be completely changed to be like Christ.

Third, we will be free of the presence of sin, free from pain, death and suffering.

Fourth, we will be rewarded for our earthly service and re-assigned positions of service.

Fifth, we will share in God's glory.

Your inheritance is permanent, priceless, pure, and protected, waiting for your arrival.

See you in Heaven!

Chapter 13
Basic Beliefs to Know

Pray that God will make you sensitive to His Spirit, His leading, and how He seeks to communicate with you. Realize that Satan, the enemy, will do all within his diabolical power to harm your fellowship with the Lord. Never yield to thoughts of condemnation, defeat, and fear. Satan, his angels, and those he influences will always attempt to compromise truths. As believers, we should always question statements and doctrines unless they are backed up by God's Holy Word, the Bible.

Never Compromise the Following Basic Truths:

1. The inspiration and infallibility of the Bible. God led holy men to write the Bible, His written Word. It is inspired, which means that God "breathed on" it and kept it from errors. It is a perfect treasure of God's teachings and His history of redeeming people through His Son, Jesus Christ.

For the prophecy came not in old time by the will of man: but holy men of God spake as they were moved by the Holy Ghost [Spirit] (2 Pet. 1:21, KJV).

All Scripture is inspired by God and profitable for teaching, for reproof, for correction, for training in righteousness; so that the man of God may be adequate, equipped for every good work (2 Tim. 3:16-17).

2. Christ's Substitutionary Atonement. That means Jesus Christ died in our place on the cross so we would not have to suffer punishment for our sins if we ask Him to enter our lives and forgive our sins. If we sincerely call on Him, He will save us for eternity and give us a home in heaven.

But God demonstrates his own love for us in this: While we were still sinners, Christ died for us (Rom. 5:8). *In Christ we are set free by the blood of his death. And so we have forgiveness of sins because of God's rich grace* (Eph. 1:7, ICB). . . . *God made him who had no sin to be sin for us, so that in him we might become the righteousness of God* (2 Cor. 5:21).

3. The Deity of Jesus Christ. He is not only man who did no sin, but He is, first of all, God who had no beginning and will have no ending.

In the beginning was the Word [Christ], and the Word was with God, and the Word was God (John 1:1).

Jesus said to them, "Truly, truly, I say to you, before Abraham was born, I am" (John 8:58).

Christ endured the wrath of God for the sins of His people and was willing to lay down his life for all of us. Only God could solve the problem of sin. God proved His love for all mankind, Christ paid the price (pardon) for our sins, and the Holy Spirit draws people to Christ to receive this magnanimous gift. God wants to have fellowship with all mankind and desires for all to be saved (2 Pet. 3:9). However, people must decide to accept this gift in faith and invite Christ into their lives.

The Lord's incarnation and claim to Deity are the bedrocks of true faith. "Therefore I [Jesus] said to you that you will die in your sins; for unless you believe that I am He, you will die in your sins" (John 8:24).

Without the shedding of blood, there is no forgiveness of sin. "For the life of the flesh is in the blood, and I have given it to you on the altar to make atonement for your souls; for it is the blood by reason of the life that makes atonement" (Lev. 17:11). Shedding of blood designates human death. Flesh denotes human life. "And according to the Law, one may almost say, all things are cleansed with blood, and without shedding of blood there is no forgiveness" (Heb. 9:22). To receive God's pardon through Christ's death, one by faith must believe that one's personal sins are cleansed or removed through His precious life's blood shed on the cross.

The bread of life (everlasting life) is actually the flesh of Jesus that He gave for the life of the world at the cross (John 6:51). Believers spiritually eat the flesh of Jesus when they open their entire beings to receive and live by the fact that Jesus died to give them a "new humanity."

4. The Incarnation. Incarnation is the term conveying this essential Christian doctrine, which has at its core the fact that God so loved us that He condescended to become one of us so He could do for us what we could not do for ourselves. God, through the power of the Holy Spirit, by way of a virgin, became a man, and yet remained God. Jesus Christ, the Son, the second person of the Holy Trinity, became the God-man, fully God and fully man. The Bible reports that He was sent by His Heavenly Father, conceived by the Holy Spirit, and born of the Virgin Mary. God became an infant and grew up as other children. The Bible records that at age twelve he was "about my Father's business" (Luke 2:49). At age 30, He began His earthly ministry and was crucified at age 33.

Christ lived a perfect life, without sin, even though He was tested by Satan as humans are tested. The first Adam sinned and brought a curse; the second Adam, Jesus, lived a blameless life so He could be the spotless lamb to be sacrificed for our sins. Scripture teaches that God purposed and planned the Incarnation before the Foundation of the World (1 Pet. 1:20; Heb. 10:5; Isa. 9:6).

Adam's sin passed down the sin nature to all descendants, so Jesus had to have a Heavenly Father and earthly mother. It was essential that Christ be without sin in order to be a sacrifice for man's sins. Since God incarnate, the Lord Jesus, assumed the initiative to redeem us back to Himself, to purchase us out of Satan's clutches, He also had the right to bestow His holy nature on those who believe and are saved. To be born again means a new life (2 Cor. 5:17), one that reflects God's image and holy nature. God, having become flesh, made it possible for sinful people to live "abundant" lives (John 10:10), unfettered by sin and its awful consequences.

The Major Purposes of Christ's Incarnation

1. To Redeem Sinners (John 6:38-40). Redemption was the divine reason for the Incarnation. Adam's sin doomed mankind with an active sin nature (Eph. 2:1-3). It also severed man's personal relationship with God. The world desperately needed a Savior. God became flesh so He could die a physical death as the final sacrifice for our sins. God became a man to redeem lost sinners (1 Tim. 1:15).

2. To Regenerate Sinners (John 10:10). The God of revelation made Himself known through Jesus Christ (Heb. 1:1-2). Christ came to regenerate sinners and destroy Satan's influence on mankind (1 John 3:2). Christ snatched the power of death away from Satan. God became flesh to install a godly nature into sinful man and crush the devil's authority over humanity.

3. To Reveal the True and Personal God (John 14:9). When a disciple of Jesus requested, "show us the father," Jesus responded, "He that has seen me hath seen the Father" (John 14:8-9, KJV). The Incarnation was to disperse light into those who abide in the darkness of their own notions about God (John 12:46).

4. The Virgin Birth of Jesus. The virgin birth is central to the Christian faith. It attests to the identity of Jesus in that He is God in the flesh. The Hebrew prophets pointed to the divinity of the Messiah. Isaiah prophesied He would be "Immanuel," meaning "God with us" (Isa. 7:14). Isaiah also predicted the Messiah would be called "Wonderful Counselor, Mighty God, Eternal Father, Prince of Peace" (Isa. 9:6). Micah stated that the Messiah would be one who had existed "from the days of eternity" (Mic. 5:2).

If Jesus were the Messiah, as He claimed to be (Mark 14:61-64 and John 4:25-26), then He had to be God in the flesh. That requires a miraculous conception, because all people born of human parents are born with a fallen sin nature (Ps. 51:5 and Eph. 2:3). To deny the virgin birth is to deny the deity of Jesus.

If Jesus Christ were not God, His sacrifice was meaningless. No imperfect man could have died for our sins because his death would not have appeased our creator's demand for justice. Our sin bearer had to be and was a perfect man and thus, He had to be Deity. Satan hates the doctrine of the virgin birth because it explicitly points to the Deity of Jesus. That old deceiver has done all he can do to undermine the doctrine's validity. The Lord anticipated attacks on His Word, for the Holy Spirit directed an appointed man to give us most of the details regarding the virgin birth. That man was Luke, a medical doctor (Col. 4:14).

The Bible's leading champion of the virgin birth was a highly educated man who must have understood the biological aspects of conception and birth. He was one who would have been most leery regarding any "legend" of a virgin birth. Vital, too, is the fact that the virgin birth of the Messiah was prophesied by the Hebrew prophets. This fact discounts the idea that the virgin birth was a notion concocted by a band of ignorant shepherds.

Jesus was the prophetic "son of David," the victorious King Messiah, and He had to be a true blood descendent in order to redeem human beings. The angel Gabriel announced to the Virgin Mary that she would become the mother of the Messiah. To him the Virgin Mary replied, "How can that be, seeing I know not a man?" Gabriel replied, "The Holy Spirit shall come upon thee, and the power of the most high shall overshadow thee; wherefore the Holy being which is begotten shall be called the Son of God" (Luke 1:35, KJV). This passage attests that Mary would be overshadowed by the Holy Spirit and become the mother of Jesus, the Messiah.

God needed to create seed—pure, perfect, and holy in the womb of a woman whom He would appoint. This baby would grow into manhood and would be more than a man. He would be God/man.

That which was begotten was holy—thus free from any sin. Messiah Jesus looms on the historic horizon as the guiltless, sinless, perfect man—the God/man—the Lamb of God who would remove the sins of the world (John 1:29). He is the mediator (link, go-between) between God and man (1 Tim. 2:5). He is the way, the truth, and the life, and no one comes to God except by Him (John 14:6). The living Word of God, the second person of the Trinity—the Son of God—entered by miraculous conception and virgin birth.

God's love sent Jesus into the world (John 3:16; Rom. 5:8). The Word (John 1:14) in the person of Jesus of Nazareth was the only one who was begotten by the Father in the human venue. From this supernatural viewpoint He is referred to as the "one and only" begotten Son of the Father.

Thoughts on Christ's Kingdom

The angel Gabriel, in the "Annunciation" of Jesus' birth, announced to Mary that "He will be great, and will be called the Son of the Highest; and the Lord God will give Him the throne of His father David. And He will reign over the house of Jacob forever, and of His kingdom there will be no end" (Luke 1:32-33). Jesus has not yet received the promised throne of David (in Jerusalem) nor has He ruled over Israel. Gabriel's words reinforced Isaiah's prophecy of the Messiah's endless reign:

> *For a child will be born to us, a son will be given to us; And the government will rest on His shoulders; And His name will be called Wonderful Counselor, Mighty God, Eternal Father, Prince of Peace. There will be no end to the increase of His government or of peace, On the throne of David and over his kingdom, To establish it and to uphold it with justice and righteousness From then on and forevermore. The zeal of the Lord of hosts will accomplish this* (Isa. 9:6-7).

He who left heaven's glory to assume human form, out of His love for mankind gave Himself as a sacrifice for our redemption. The substitution of Himself as the payment for our sins was the only acceptable means by which divine justice could be satisfied. Jesus Christ, therefore, "is the propitiation [satisfaction] for our sins, and not for ours only but also for the sins of the whole world" (I John 2:2).

This book was written to convince readers of the urgent importance of believing the Word of God. Jesus warned of Satan's cunning. Of course, he does not want us to believe God or His Word. Jesus articulated this through a parable. "A sower went out to sow his seed. And as he sowed, some fell by the wayside; and it was trampled down, and the birds of the air devoured it . . . he who has ears to hear, let him hear" (see Luke 8:5-8).

His disciples failed to comprehend it, so Jesus explained the parable warning them of the devil's strivings among men: "Now the parable is this: The seed is the word of God. Those by the wayside are the ones who hear; then the devil comes and takes away the word out of their hearts, lest they should *believe* and be saved" (see Luke 8:11-12, author's italics).

The first mention of the concept of virgin birth in prophecy is found in Genesis 3:15 when God cursed the serpent, Satan, the devil:

> *And I will put enmity*
> *Between you and the woman,*
> *And between your seed and her seed;*
> *He shall bruise you on the head,*
> *And you shall bruise him on the heel.*

In this verse, God informs Satan that the Savior of mankind will be born as the seed of woman. Isaiah emphasizes that in Isaiah 7:14, where he prophesies the Messiah will be born of a "virgin." The angel Gabriel declared to Mary:

> *Fear not, you have found favor with God and behold you shall conceive in your womb and bring forth a son, and shall call his name Jesus. He shall be great and shall be called the son of the Most High, and the Lord shall give unto Him the throne of his father David, and He shall reign over the House of Jacob [Israel] forever; and of His Kingdom there shall be no end. The Holy Spirit shall come upon thee, and the power of the Most High shall overshadow you. Wherefore also the holy thing begotten shall be called the Son of God* (Luke 1:3 and 3:5).

5. The Necessity for Virgin Birth. If Jesus were to be the sin bearer, He could not possibly have an earthly father because Jesus would have been a sinner like you and I—and an unfit sacrifice. Jesus had to be God because only God is perfect, without sin. The sacrifice had to be perfect. However, God cannot die. That is why He had to have a body that could taste death and rise from the dead—and why He will someday come again to restore the Davidic kingdom and reign on the throne of King David of Israel forever.

Animal blood never was intended to remove the sin of man, merely to cover it temporarily. That was transitory until the time was right for a perfect sacrifice to be offered once and for all. That spotless, blameless sacrifice was the Messiah of Israel who died to remove, not only the sins of the Jewish people but of people all over the world—Jew and Gentile alike. But I emphasize that each individual must receive salvation. "So then each one of us will give an account of himself to God" (Rom. 14:12).

6. The Crucifixion of Christ. God performed four miracles in the process of salvation for sinners: The Incarnation—God became the God-man, fully God and fully man; the Virgin Birth; the Crucifixion of Christ; and the Resurrection. The Bible reveals from the beginning the necessity for the shedding of blood in order to atone for and make right for the sins of those forgiven as a result of Christ's giving His life. God's power was shown in the fact that His Son procured salvation for all who believe in Him, the crucifixion, and resurrection, and who accept Him into their hearts.

Not only does the crucifixion herald the grace, love, and mercy of God, it also reveals the wisdom and power of God. God's wisdom is exhibited in the Cross, for this plan of salvation was formed before the foundation of the world. God realized that man would be powerless to save himself after the fall. He comprehended what would be necessary to restore man to fellowship with Him. God's power was exhibited in the fact that His Son's death secured salvation for all who believe, and it humbles all who come to faith in Him via the Cross. The crucifixion defeated the devil and all the powers at his disposal. The dominion of sin in the life of the redeemed was broken, and the ability to live a victorious life in Christ was restored.

Only God could resolve the problem of sin. Salvation is all of God. The marvel of the Son of God dying to reconcile sinful people to Himself is remarkable. No wonder the songwriters penned, "Oh, the wonder of it all" and "How great Thou art" and "I stand amazed in the presence of Jesus the Nazarene." The more we come to comprehend the magnitude of what was accomplished by Jesus Christ on the cross at Calvary, the more sacred and solemn this remembrance becomes. As we mature in our understanding of all it cost God in Christ for our salvation, the more Good Friday will become one of the most significant days of the year.

7. The Resurrection

> *Jesus said to her, "I am the resurrection and the life; he who believes in Me will live even if he dies* (John 11:25).

If our Lord's body had remained in the tomb, there would be no resurrection for Jesus or for those who have accepted Him. "He . . . was delivered over because of our transgressions, and was raised because of our justification" (Rom. 4:25). In the great resurrection chapter, 1 Corinthians 15, the apostle Paul lucidly declares that the basis of Christianity is the resurrection of our Lord Jesus Christ. Christ while in *sheol* (the place of departed spirits) conquered Satan, abolished death, and delivered life and immortality to life through the gospel. Because of that all believers' souls, when their bodies die, go directly into the presence of God in heaven.

Animal blood was intended only to temporarily remove man's sin. It was only for a short period until the time was right for a perfect sacrifice made once and for all. "But when the fulness of the time was come, God sent forth his Son, made of a woman, made under the law, To redeem them that were under the law, that we might receive the adoption of sons" (Gal. 4:4-5, KJV). That perfect sacrifice was Jesus Christ our Savior.

Christ's resurrection is a certification and a promise of our resurrection and fellowship with Him and with all of the saved throughout eternity. When Jesus returned from *sheol*, and His spirit re-entered and immortalized His physical body, He emerged from the tomb as the Glorified Redeemer. Paul exclaimed in Ephesians 4:8-10:

> *Wherefore he saith, When he ascended up on high, he led captivity captive, and gave gifts unto men. (Now that he ascended, what is it but that he also descended first into the lower parts of the earth [sheol]? He that descended is the same also that ascended up far above all heavens, that he might fill all things.)*

He ascended on high; He led away those believers who were in a pre-resurrection state, and they marched in triumphant procession into glory. When Christ re-entered the portals of Glory, He sat down on the right hand of God the Father as mediator between God and man (see Heb. 7:25).

Humanity longs for forgiveness. An accused man stood before a judge in court. The judge asked, "Mister, do you want justice?" to which the accused replied, "No Sir, Judge, I want mercy!" Surely all of us desire forgiveness. Man's history is filled with examples of attempts to perform acts, hoping to usher in forgiveness from God. This is the result of conscience God has granted us. Multitudes spend their lives desperately trying to merit it through all kinds of religious (or so-called spiritual) activities or "good works." But God's Word teaches:

> *For by grace you have been saved through faith; and that not of yourselves, it is the gift of God; not as a result of works, so that no one may boast* (Eph 2:8-9).

> *He saved us, not on the basis of deeds which we have done in righteousness, but according to His mercy, by the washing of regeneration and renewing by the Holy Spirit* (Titus 3:5).

Others try to bury the feeling of needing forgiveness through all sorts of diversions and preoccupations. Many unfortunately finally relegate themselves to hopelessness and trudge through a sad, tormented existence. Tragically, they have bypassed the only hope human beings have ever had for forgiveness, inner security, and joy. It resides in the truth of the resurrection.

God revealed through the resurrection that He was totally satisfied with the sacrifice of His Son, Jesus Christ, for our sins. So, when we have faith in Christ, we have complete and eternal forgiveness, assurance of salvation, and peace with God— because we are forgiven. God displayed through the resurrection that Jesus Christ was and is His son—that what had been presaged in the Old Testament prophecies was consummated in Christ, and that what Jesus had predicted did happen. Jesus predicted that after three days, God the Father would raise Him up from the dead. He did!

> *But He answered and said to them, "An evil and adulterous generation craves for a sign; and yet no sign will be given to it but the sign of Jonah the prophet; for just as Jonah was three days and three nights in the belly of the sea monster, so will the Son of Man be three days and three nights in the heart of the earth"* (Matt. 12:39-40).

> *And the angel answered and said unto the women, Fear not ye: for I know that ye seek Jesus, which was crucified. He is not here: for he is risen, as he said. Come, see the place where the Lord lay* (Matt. 28:5-6).

Through the resurrection, Christians have the certainty that they can live triumphant lives in Christ. Jesus conquered sin and death. Through the indwelling presence of the Holy Spirit, we can live our lives to please God and to benefit ourselves. The resurrection instituted a new creation; with the addition of every new believer, one more entity of this new creation is added. One day this present world and the present heavens will be destroyed and replaced with a new heaven and new earth. The completion of the new creation will be accomplished.

> *But the day of the Lord will come like a thief, in which the heavens will pass away with a roar and the elements will be destroyed with intense heat, and the earth and its works will be burned up. Since all these things are to be destroyed in this way, what sort of people ought you to be in holy conduct and godliness, looking for and hastening the coming of the day of God, because of which the heavens will be destroyed by burning, and the elements will melt with intense heat! But according to His promise we are looking for new heavens and a new earth, in which righteousness dwells. Therefore, beloved, since you look for these things, be diligent to be found by Him in peace, spotless and blameless* (2 Pet. 3:10-14).

This world longs for peace, love, joy, and forgiveness. It is discovered in only one place—in the birth, the death, and the resurrection of Jesus Christ.

8. His Ascension into Heaven. After rising from the dead, Jesus remained on earth 40 days to help His disciples. Then He ascended into heaven, later sending the Holy Spirit to indwell all Christians, beginning on the Day of Pentecost (see Acts the second chapter; also survey John chapters 14-16).

Before ascending, Jesus promised His followers: "But you will receive power when the Holy Spirit has come upon you; and you shall be My witnesses both in Jerusalem, and in all Judea and Samaria, and even to the remotest part of the earth" (Acts 1:8). The account further reported, "And after He had said these things, He was lifted up while they [the disciples] were looking on, and a cloud received Him out of their sight (v. 9).

A group of disciples was looking intently up into the sky as He was going, when suddenly two men dressed in white (angels) stood beside them (v. 10). "Men of Galilee," they asked, "why do you stand here looking into the sky? This same Jesus, who has been taken from you into heaven, will come back in the same way you have seen him go into heaven " (v. 11).

9. The Coming of the Holy Spirit. The true and living God of the Bible is a Trinity: God the Father, God the Son (Jesus), and God the Holy Spirit. Before the Day of Pentecost, the Spirit would come on God's followers temporarily. At Pentecost, He would descend and remain within every Christian throughout his life.

> *But the Helper [Comforter, KJV], the Holy Spirit, whom the Father will send in My name, He will teach you all things, and bring to your remembrance all that I said to you. . . . When the Helper [Comforter] comes, whom I will send to you from the Father, that is the Spirit of truth who proceeds from the Father, He will testify about Me* (John 14:26; 15:26).

Jesus taught:

> *Nevertheless I tell you the truth; It is expedient [necessary] for you that I go away; for if I go not away, the Comforter will not come unto you; but if I depart, I will send him unto you. And when he is come, he will reprove the world of sin, and of righteousness, and of judgment: because they believe not on me; Of righteousness, because I go to my Father; of Judgment, because the prince of this world [Satan, the devil] is judged* (John 16:7-11, KJV).

> *Howbeit when he, the Spirit of truth, is come, he will guide you into all truth: for he shall not speak of himself; but whatsoever he shall hear, that shall he speak: and he will show you things to come. He will glorify me: for he shall receive of mine, and shall show it unto you* (John 15:13-14, KJV).

10. Jesus' Return to Earth (Second Coming). As He was about to ascend the angels promised that "this same Jesus" would come again. Throughout the prophecies of the Old Testament, two comings were predicted. Jesus assured His disciples: "And if I go and prepare a place for you, I will come again, and receive you unto myself; that where I am, there ye may be also" (John 14:3, KJV).

> *For the Lord himself shall descend from Heaven with a shout, with the voice of the archangel, and with the trump of God: and the dead in Christ shall rise first: Then we which are alive and remain*

shall be caught up together with them in the clouds, to meet the Lord in the air: and so shall we ever be with the Lord (1 Thess. 4:16-17, KJV).

He who testifies to these things says, Yes I am coming soon. Amen. Come, Lord Jesus (Rev. 22:20, KJV).

Amen! Hallelujah!

CHAPTER 14

Putting on the Armor of God

(For the weapons of our warfare are not carnal, but mighty through God to the pulling down of strongholds.) Casting down imaginations, and every high thing that exalteth itself against the knowledge of God, and bringing into captivity every thought to the obedience of Christ (2 Corinthians 10: 4-5, KJV).

Can you imagine a soldier going to battle without a weapon? Or a pilot trying to fly without an airplane? Or a carpenter without a hammer, plane, or nails? Yet, too many Christians are in the middle of warfare and don't even seem to realize it. That's what Satan longs for—the blasé, unconcerned believer who is merely going through the motions, oblivious to the prince of darkness' sneaky strategies.

"Feel-good" religion wants to ignore the cold, harsh realities—that the devil and his evil minions are at work, that every believer is embroiled in a war with hell itself, and that everything is not sweetness and light. Hard-hitting Bible truth is not popular with a large segment of society, and that's why our nation is going downhill. The victorious Christian is alert and vigilant. "Be Prepared" is the motto of the Boy Scouts. That's not a far cry from "Always be prepared to give an answer to everyone who asks you to give the reason for the hope that you have" (see 1 Pet. 3:15).

How to Prepare for Spiritual Warfare

We will cover five subjects: prayer, Bible study, love, faith, and Christ's church, known as His body.

Prayer:

We need to pray daily for God's guidance. We need to establish a daily quiet time of anywhere from 15 minutes to an hour so God can listen to us and respond. List on a sheet of paper things you are concerned about and name them one by one. The quiet time can also be used for reading the Word. Review Christ's "Model Prayer" (see also Chapter 12). He taught His disciples.

Model Prayer (Matthew 6: 9-13)
Taught by Christ to His Disciples

I pray this prayer more than any other. Over time we have tried to interpret its meaning and would like to share with you my thoughts.

Our Father, who art in heaven,

- Addressing God properly
- God—You are good.
- You are my Holy God.

Hallowed be Thy name,

- Showing respect for God's name.
- Our Father, we praise You and honor Your Holy name, The name above all names

Thy Kingdom come, Thy will be done on earth as it is in heaven.

- Committing ourselves to God's plan and doing God's will
- The kingdom of God is within you (Luke 17:20-21). We are pledging our willingness to allow God's kingdom in and through us.

Give us this day our daily bread.

- Asking God to provide for our needs, not our wants.
- God wants us to feed the hungry, give water to the thirsty, clothe the naked, care for the sick and visit prisoners.

Forgive us our sins (trespasses) as we forgive those who sin (trespass) against us.

- Asking God for forgiveness of our sins as well as forgiving others for wrongs done to us. God longs to restore proper relationship with us and us with everyone else.

Lead us not into temptation but deliver us from evil.

- Asking God for protection and to shield us from temptation.
- Asking God to protect us from Satan and his angels (demons).
- Asking God to deliver us from pride and greed.
  You cannot serve both God and mammon (money, material possessions, Matt. 6:24).
- Jesus commands us to build better relationships rather than bigger personal Kingdoms.

For Thine is the Kingdom, the power, and the glory forever and ever. Amen.

- Giving God the Glory.
- Depending on the Holy Spirit for Power
- Honoring Christ for His love

Prayer for the believer is an awesome resource that, sadly, is not being used to its fullest potential and impact. It is clear, if you listen to people talk to God, how many of their conversations are misdirected. After you have made certain you have the right relationship with the God of the Bible, it is important for you to be able to speak properly with Him. The Bible gives us a perfect example and an outline of how we are to commune with God, The Lord's Prayer (often called The Model Prayer), found in Matthew 6:9-13.

This prayer shows most clearly that our fellowship with God should be God-centered, not me-centered. Above all else, our prayers must bring praise and worship to our God. Next, we present thanksgiving and confession of our sins. Then we can pray for our requests and intercede for others. We must realize that ultimately everything related to talking with God (praying) is to glorify God. Even as God answers our prayers, He is glorified.

Basics for Believers

For believers, one of the most difficult areas of consistency in our faithfulness is in the area of private prayer. Yet, in the final analysis, this, along with Bible study, is one of the most critical disciplines we must cultivate. Without prayer, believers will lack one of the true indications of their assurance of salvation. They will miss the fantastic encouragement that prayer affords, and they will miss the abundance of God's love that He desires to shower on them.

> *Therefore, confess your sins to one another, and pray for one another so that you may be healed. The effective prayer of a righteous man can accomplish much* (Jas. 5:16).

Prayer is a key that God has placed in your hand. God loves you with a passion that you cannot begin to comprehend. He desires to live in intimacy with you. Prayer is far more than the words you utter. Prayer is the continual interchange of love between you and the Father. Prayer is an openness to and an awareness of His presence and power in your life.

Prayer is a Relationship

The foundation of a prayerful life is knowing God. God has made many promises in His Word, and when you know the promises, you can trust them. When you focus on knowing God, you will come to trust His promises, and the power of prayer will become your reality.

Jesus' Story on Consistent Prayer

> *Then Jesus told his disciples a parable to show them that they should always pray and not give up. He said: "In a certain town there was a judge who neither feared God nor cared about men.*
> *"And there was a widow in that town who kept coming to him with the plea, 'Grant me justice against my adversary.'*
> *"For some time he refused. But finally he said to himself, 'Even though I don't fear God or care about men, yet because this widow keeps bothering me, I will see that she gets justice, so that she won" eventually wear me out with her coming!'"*
> *And the Lord said, "Listen to what the unjust judge says. And will not God bring about justice for his chosen ones, who cry out to him day and night? Will he keep putting them off? I tell you, he will see that they get justice, and quickly. However, when the Son of Man comes, will he find faith on the earth?"* (Luke 18:1-8).

If we are to know the Triune God and enjoy a relationship with Him, it must be done in the spirit as God is Spirit.

Prayer is a Priority

Growing in Christ is setting priorities. Old habits will trap you. You may need to restructure your time deliberately; make time for prayer. Do not underestimate the power of your prayers. When you ask the Lord to enter a life, never doubt His ability to put His power to work in their lives. Nothing you do could be more important than that. Always have a minimum of five or more people on your prayer list.

The power of prayer is even more important than the act of witnessing because prayer power works with both those who will and those who will not let you share Christ with them. Prayer opens doors for witnessing.

A Christian can talk to God in prayer about anything and everything.

Quiet Time with God

Many people all over the world try to talk with their god regularly. Some call out to their god in times of crisis or intense sorrow. But only Christians can communicate with the true God, the Almighty God, the God of the Bible. Only believers, as sinners, are able to approach a thrice-holy God as sinners, because we come under the blood of the Lamb of God, Jesus Christ our Savior. Only believers have the incredible privilege to talk (or to pray, as it is more traditionally labeled) to the God who made the heavens and the earth and maintains everything by His will and His Word. It is imperative that you are certain you have a personal relationship with the true God. You must be sure the object of your talk or prayer is the God as revealed in the Bible.

As I have mentioned, the best time for me is between 7 to 8 a.m. and 9:30 to 10:30 p.m. My wife, Jan, goes to bed at 9:30, so I cut off the TV and spend time with God in scripture and prayer. Many times the Holy Spirit speaks to me in a slight whisper, which answers problems for me. I sometimes am amazed. The real secret is to have a quiet time with God and give Him glory for everything that has happened to you that day.

Sometimes while you are praying, Satan will suggest an evil thought merely to distract and shame you. Each person has weaknesses. Satan will play on your weaknesses. Stay alert. Ask God to help you.

I have often had to say, "Satan, in the name of Jesus, get away from me." And he does.

Time for Humor

So far today, God, I've done all right.
I haven't gossiped, haven't lost my temper,
Haven't been greedy, grumpy, nasty,
Selfish, or over-indulgent. I'm really
Glad about that.
But in a few minutes, God,
I'm going to get out of bed,
And from then on I'm
Probably going to need a lot of help!

Story by Mrs. Ruth Bell Graham

One day many years ago, as I was driving home from town with one of our sons, he kept urging me to hurry. "Go faster, Mother!" he insisted. But he was too young to read the road sign that said 45 mph.

And again, "Pass him, Mother." But he was too small to see that there was a double yellow line.

Then I began applying the brake. "Why are you stopping?" he demanded.

"There's a school bus ahead that has stopped," I replied.

I thought to myself, *When God is at the wheel, we may request—but never insist. We are too young to read certain signs, too small to see what lies ahead.*

Bible:

The grass withers, the flower fades, but the word of our God stands forever (Isaiah 40:8).

The Bible is the book to live by and die by and shows the way to eternal life, which begins here and goes on in heaven. The Bible reveals most of God's will for believers and is spelled in its pages. God does not fail to provide every one of His children with everything needed in their lives of faith. Bible study is essential for every believer for their growth as a Christian. The Bible is God's instruction book.

The Universality of the Biblical Message

God made of one man every nation to dwell upon the face of the earth. We are all therefore His offspring, as the Apostle Paul declared (see Acts 17:22-31). The scriptural message is addressed to all people. When God called Abraham out of Ur of the Chaldees, He made it known that he and his descendants were to be the repository of His truth, and He assured Abraham that in him and his seed would all the families of earth be blessed. The truth of God's message was, as is seen by a careful study of both the Old and the New Testaments, committed to Israel, as the chosen nation, to deliver it to the entire world.

That the message of the Scriptures is universal is evident from the fact that the moral law of God is written in the very fiber of the souls of all men. This is seen in Paul's statement in Romans 2:13-15:

> *For it is not the hearers of the Law who are just before God, but the doers of the Law will be justified. For when Gentiles who do not have the Law do instinctively the things of the Law, these, not having the Law, are a law to themselves, in that they show the work of the Law written in their hearts, their conscience bearing witness and their thoughts alternately accusing or else defending them,*

Put on the Full Armor of God and Stand Firm

> *10 Finally, my brethren, be strong in the Lord, and in the power of his might. 11 Put on the whole armour of God, that ye may be able to stand against the wiles of the devil. 12 For we wrestle not against flesh and blood, but against principalities, against powers, against the rulers of the darkness of this world, against spiritual wickedness in high places. 13 Wherefore take unto you the whole armour of God, that ye may be able to withstand in the evil day, and having done all, to stand. 14 Stand therefore, having your loins girt about with truth, and having on the breastplate of righteousness; 15 And your feet shod with the preparation of the gospel of peace; 16 Above all, taking the shield of faith, wherewith ye shall be able to quench all the fiery darts of the wicked. 17 And take the helmet of salvation, and the sword of the Spirit, which is*

the word of God: 18 Praying always with all prayer and supplication in the Spirit, and watching thereunto with all perseverance and supplication for all saints (Eph. 6:10-18, LKV).

The belt of truth *is used to defeat* ***deception.***
The breastplate of righteousness *is used to defeat* ***guilt.***
The feet fitted with readiness *are used to defeat* ***hopelessness.***
The shield of faith *is used to defeat* ***temptation.***
The helmet of salvation *is used to defeat* ***doubt.***
The sword of the Spirit *is the* ***Word of God.***
Prayers in the Spirit *are our* ***words to God.***

The Bible is the very Word of God, supernatural in its origin, inspired (breathed upon) by God, and without error. All issues and discussions concerning doctrine should start with the Bible. The Bible is God's instruction Book on life and on how to have a personal and everlasting relationship with the Creator God.

There is no way finite creatures can know anything of an infinite God unless He chooses to reveal Himself. The Bible discloses God to man and explains man to himself.

Some might ask: How can I be certain that the Bible is God's revelation to mankind? Let's briefly examine this question.

The Bible has endured for thousands of years, yet it is as fresh and applicable today as it was when it was first written. It is timeless because it is the Word of God. It is also limitless in its applications to life, and its source of truth cannot be exhausted. As more archeological discoveries are made, more and more the accuracy of the Bible is reinforced. Many facts that were once questioned have now been proven correct by new discoveries. How the Bible reveals God could only come from God, and the way man is understood and presented could only come from the One who knows all things. The prophecies of the Bible clearly demonstrate the omniscience of its author. And, finally, the complete unity of the Bible declares its author to be divine.

The impact and influence of the Bible on individuals continue to demonstrate its supernatural power. It convicts people of sin and shows the way of pardon from sin. It is the story of God's love for fallen humanity. Its truth leads the way to salvation. It directs us in the path of sanctification, and its revelation of heaven and hell is the reality of our final destination.

God's infallible, inerrant Word is far more than a doctrinal guidebook. It generates life, creates faith, produces change, frightens the devil, causes miracles, heals hurts, builds character, transforms circumstances, imparts joy, overcomes adversity, infuses hope, cleanses our minds, and guarantees our future forever. You should consider it as essential to your spiritual life as food is to your physical life.

> *The grass withers, the flower fades,*
> *But the word of our God stands forever.* (Isa. 40:8)

The Bible is the written revelation of God and His works in the world. He inspired it, and it is without error. The Bible is God's instruction Book on life and on how to have a personal and everlasting relationship with the Creator God. It is timeless because it is the Word of God.

We learn from the Bible that Jesus is the embodiment of truth: "I am the way, the truth, and the life: no man cometh unto the Father, but by me" (John 14:6, KJV). "Whoever will call on the name of the Lord will be saved" (Rom. 10:13). "For by grace you have been saved through faith; and that not of yourselves, it *is* the gift of God; not as a result of works, so that no one may boast (Eph. 2:8-9). "That if you confess with your mouth Jesus *as* Lord, and believe in your heart that God raised Him from the dead, you will be saved; for with the heart a person believes, resulting in righteousness, and with the mouth he confesses, resulting in salvation" (Rom. 10:9-10). "And hope does not disappoint, because the love of God has been poured out within our hearts through the Holy Spirit who was given to us (Rom. 5:5). This means that this bestowal of love causes us to glorify God and seek His will for our lives. "So faith comes from hearing, and hearing by the word of Christ" (Rom. 10:17).

As we approach the end times, Satan, his fallen angels, and false teachers will try to discredit the Bible. If you listen, you will make a gigantic mistake. Walk with and be in conversation with God daily. Study the Bible so you will know God's Truths.

Review:

The Bible declares, "All scripture is inspired by God and profitable for teaching, for reproof, for correction, for training in righteousness" (2 Tim. 3:16). Further, it teaches: "For no prophecy was ever made by an act of human will, but men moved by the Holy Spirit spoke from God (2 Pet. 1:21).

God has a message He wants people to hear, so He stated it over and over through different Biblical writers down through the centuries. That message has never changed: God loves His people and wants a personal relationship with them.

Biblical Fact Sheet:

God Was Before Everything Everywhere.

"He is before all things" (Colossians 1:17 NIV).

"Before the mountains were created, before you made the earth and the world, you are God, without beginning or end." (Psalm 90:2).

God Is the Creator of All Things.

"By the word of the Lord were the heavens made, their starry host by the breath of his mouth" (Ps. 33:6, NIV).

"It is I who made the earth and created mankind upon it" (Isa. 45:23, NIV).

"We are the clay, and you are the potter. We are all formed by your hand" (Isa. 64:8, NIV).

"In his hand is the life of every creature and the breath of all mankind" (Job 12:10, NIV).

God's Nature Is Love.

"The Lord is faithful to all his promises and loving toward all he has made" (Ps. 145:13, NIV).

"For the Lord is good and his love endures forever; his faithfulness continues through all generations" (Ps. 100:5, NIV).

"For great is your love, reaching to the heavens; your faithfulness reaches to the skies" (Psalm 57:10, NIV).

If we choose to believe that God has always been, that He is the creator of all that is, and that His nature is love, we can stop making up our own versions of God.

Love:

Preparing to Use the Armor of God:

The **purpose** of my obedience is to ***glorify God***.

The **model** for my obedience is ***Jesus Christ***.
The **power** for my obedience is the ***Holy Spirit***.
The **foundation** of my obedience is ***character***.
The **tools** of obedience are the ***Scriptures*** and ***prayer***.
The **motive** for my obedience is ***love***.
The **authority** of my obedience is ***submission***.
The **measure** of my obedience is ***sacrifice***.
The **nature** of my obedience is ***service***.
The **privilege** of my obedience is ***growth***.

Love Is Supreme 1 Corinthians 13

1If I speak with the tongues of men and of angels, but do not have love, I have become a noisy gong or a clanging cymbal.
2If I have the gift of prophecy, and know all mysteries and all knowledge; and if I have all faith, so as to remove mountains, but do not have love, I am nothing.
3And if I give all my possessions to feed the poor, and if I surrender my body to be burned, but do not have love, it profits me nothing.
4Love is patient, love is kind and is not jealous; love does not brag and is not arrogant,
5does not act unbecomingly; it does not seek its own, is not provoked, does not take into account a wrong suffered,
6does not rejoice in unrighteousness, but rejoices with the truth;
7bears all things, believes all things, hopes all things, endures all things.
8Love never fails; but if there are gifts of prophecy, they will be done away; if there are tongues, they will cease; if there is knowledge, it will be done away.
9For we know in part and we prophesy in part;
10but when the perfect comes, the partial will be done away.
11When I was a child, I used to speak like a child, think like a child, reason like a child; when I became a man, I did away with childish things.
12For now we see in a mirror dimly, but then face to face; now I know in part, but then I will know fully just as I also have been fully known.
13But now faith, hope, love, abide these three; ***but the greatest of these is love.***

Defeat the Enemy

If we are to overcome Satan, we must experience a growing knowledge of Christ. And as we learn more about Christ, we discover that the devil is no match for our sovereign Lord Jesus Christ. "But thanks be to God, who gives us the victory through our Lord Jesus Christ" (1 Cor. 15:57). We are winners through His power. We should be filled with the Holy Spirit to defeat Satan's attack on us. Satan is a deceiver, a serpent, a roaring lion that comes after us to devour us. He is powerful, and in our own strength we are no match for him. Only as we are filled with the Spirit of God can we have victory in our Christian lives.

I've tried to live the Christian life in my own strength. Through tough experience, I am all too aware. That is not only difficult; it really is impossible. But there is good news! God has given us a power that is resident within us, and that power can give us the strength to live the life we could never live on our own. It is not about trying harder; it is about coming to the place where we accept by faith the truth of the Word of God.

While he was in exile on the Isle of Patmos, John, the beloved apostle, exclaimed, "You are from God, little children, and have overcome them; because greater is He who is in you than he who is in the world" (1 John 4:4). The devil and all of his demons cannot stand against one born-again, Spirit-filled believer!

God's Amazing Love

The love of a parent for a child is a mighty force. A child is born into a home and naturally offers no support to the parents. He/she has no skill, but hopefully love overrides all else. Good parents love their child with intense ardor. Now think about how much God loves us when He made a decision to sacrifice His Son to pay the penalty for our sins and re-establish our relationship with God.

God Loves His Enemies

Our God is perfect and untainted by sin, unfettered by mistakes. Where we view something as murky waters, He beholds nothing but purity. Where we may dwell in darkness, He dwells in light. We as humans have a problem: we are sinners. And God pronounces that , "The wages of sin is death" (Rom. 6:23).. As a result of the cross, believers are saved. When God the Father God looks at us, He sees Christ, and Christ says to His Father, "He belongs to me."

The Cross on the Hill

The Cross is the universal symbol of Christianity. The Cross became a symbol of hope and faith. Christ and two thieves were on crosses with Christ in the middle. One thief chose to mock Jesus. The other chose to pray to Him. The two criminals each made a decision. One chose Christ—one mocked Him. One prayed to Jesus, "Remember me when you come into your kingdom." Jesus answered, "I tell you the truth, today you will be with me in paradise." (see Luke 23:39-43). The other thief rejected Christ, and his reward was hell.

Christ is our mediator and intercessor. "For there is one God, and one mediator also between God and men, the man Christ Jesus" (1 Tim. 2:5). " Little children, I am writing these things to you so that you may not sin. And if anyone sins, we have an Advocate [a defense attorney] with the Father, Jesus Christ the righteous" (1 John 2:1). When Satan goes before God's throne to accuse believers, God turns to Jesus, and Jesus announces, "He belongs to me" (see Job chapters 1 and 2).

My heart also goes out to those who haven't accepted Christ. I urge them to receive Him now. According to the Bible, Jesus is the only one who can save you. "And there is salvation in no one else; for there is no other name under heaven that has been given among men by which we must be saved" (Acts 4:12). His name is the only power in the world given to save people. We *must* be saved through Him. Christianity is a personal relationship with Christ.

Give your heart to Christ right now:
Confess your sins.
Believe and have faith in Christ's sacrifice on the cross to pay the penalty for your sins.

The Devil Is at Work

The great enemies of Christ and the believer are Satan, his angels, and ardent unbelievers. The devil is out to defeat the Christian. He is well aware that the child of God is a dangerous enemy to his cause. He made every effort to tempt and defeat Christ, and today the devil concentrates on Christ's' followers. He is the commander-in-chief of the powers of evil, and his main attack is launched against those who have taken sides with Christ and righteousness.

The devil harasses, accuses, tempts, deceives, and lies in his dealings with Christians. He works through his allies, the world and the flesh. The devil uses the world and the flesh to wreak havoc among God's people, to hinder the progress of righteousness, to discourage and distress Christians, to stop the Gospel from being proclaimed, and to weaken the Christian offensive in advancing the kingdom of God.

Paul warned, "For we do not wrestle against flesh and blood, but against principalities, against powers, against the rulers of the darkness of this age, against spiritual hosts of wickedness in the heavenly places" (Eph. 6:12, NKJV). The devil is a powerful foe who is called "the god of this age" (2 Cor. 4:4, NKJV), "the ruler of this world" (John 14:30, NKJV), and "the prince of the power of the air" (Eph. 2:2, NKJV). Never underestimate the power of the devil.

Saving Faith:

> *For by grace you have been saved through faith; and that not of yourselves, it is the gift of God; not as a result of works, so that no one may boast* (Eph. 2:8-9).

Faith is essential for salvation. There are various kinds of belief or faith, and not all are linked to salvation. Faith in the New Testament means more than intellectual belief; it involves trust and commitment. We may claim to believe that a bridge will hold our weight, but we truly believe it only when we commit ourselves to it and walk across the bridge. It is possible to believe in the life and death of Jesus in history, but faith in the historical record of Jesus is not saving faith. Even Satan believes that biblical history concerning Jesus is true, but Satan is still condemned. His demons also believe: "You believe that God is one. You do well; the demons also believe, and shudder" (Jas. 2:19).

Then there is a theological faith that believes Jesus died for sinners. This is a statement of truth about God that makes even the demons in hell shudder yet doesn't lead sinners to saving faith. Saving faith involves an act of commitment and trust, in which we commit our lives to Jesus Christ and trust Him alone as our personal Savior and Lord. Saving faith is a personal and individual decision.

Faith is more than assent to historical or theological truth given to us in God's Word. It is faith in the promises of God as the believer's only hope for eternal life. The essential truths of the Gospel do not change. All things were created by God and He sustains all creation, so the message of His saving grace is applicable to all. The facts concerning Jesus' virgin birth, His sinless life, His sacrificial and substitutionary death, His resurrection and ascension to the right hand of the Father, and the glorious hope of His return must not in any manner be diluted or distorted.

Our faith is built on . . . Christ's resurrection—That is our foundation

Jesus is not only "Christ," He also is "God, our Savior and Lord." This is a staggering, almost incomprehensible, truth: God Himself has come in the Person of His only Son. The incarnation and the full Deity of Jesus are the foundation of the Christian faith. Jesus Christ is who He said He is: God Himself in human form. And that is a crucial truth that undergirds the reality of our salvation.

How Can We Know the Truth About God?

Must we grope around in the dark, only guessing and never knowing the truth? Is religion merely a matter of personal opinion or viewpoint? The Bible makes it plain that we *can* know the truth, because God revealed Himself in the Garden of Eden, and He has continued to reveal Himself in history. God gave Israel the Ten Commandments and also prophets whose divinely inspired predictions were absolutely trustworthy.

But most of all, God revealed Himself in the Person of His Son, Jesus Christ: "No one has seen God at any time; the only begotten God who is in the bosom of the Father, He has explained Him" (John 1:18). He confirmed that Jesus is truly God the Son by His miracles and by raising Him from the dead. Our faith is not anchored in a church, in religious traditions, or in personal feelings. Our faith is rooted and grounded in the assurance of what God has done in history and revealed in the Bible.

We must be thoroughly convinced of the infallibility of Scripture. Our authority comes from the pages of the totally trustworthy Word of God, the Bible. In it Jesus is revealed. We believe in and trust Him; we proclaim Him as Savior, and we confess Him before others as our Lord. Because Jesus is one with God and was sent by the Father into human history, the cross is an objective demonstration of divine love. Our faith is built on the fact of Christ's resurrection. Well did Edward Mote write:

My hope is built on nothing less
Than Jesus' blood and righteousness
I dare not trust the sweetest frame
But wholly lean on Jesus' name.
On Christ the solid rock I stand
All other ground is sinking sand
All other ground is sinking sand.

Faith is the noun for believe. Belief suggests trust, commitment, and confidence. Trust carries the idea of taking refuge in or learning upon. Faith is the body of revealed truth on Christianity or the Christian faith. The chief elements of this education are the death, burial, and resurrection of Jesus; that in dying He atoned for human sin and in rising from the grave He abolished death. Paul exclaimed:

1Now I make known to you, brethren, the gospel which I preached to you, which also you received, in which also you stand,
2by which also you are saved, if you hold fast the word which I preached to you, unless you believed in vain.
3For I delivered to you as of first importance what I also received, that Christ died for our sins according to the Scriptures,
4and that He was buried, and that He was raised on the third day according to the Scriptures,
5and that He appeared to Cephas, then to the twelve.
6After that He appeared to more than five hundred brethren at one time, most of whom remain until now, but some have fallen asleep;
7then He appeared to James, then to all the apostles;
8and last of all, as to one untimely born, He appeared to me also.

The Nature of Faith

What is faith? Faith is believing; and in believing we trust and obey. Faith in God is believing all He has declared in the Scriptures and His personal teaching while on earth, accepting His Word as truth and trusting Him to fulfill all He has promised.

Easton wrote:

"Faith is in general the persuasion of the mind that a certain statement is true (Phil. 1:27; 2 Thess. 2:13). Its primary idea is trust. A thing is true, and therefore worthy of trust. It admits of many degrees up to full assurance of faith, in accordance with the evidence on which it rests.

"Faith is the result of teaching (Rom. 10:14–17). Knowledge is an essential element in all faith, and is sometimes spoken of as an equivalent to faith (John 10:38; 1 John 2:3). Yet the two are distinguished in this respect, that faith includes in it assent, which is an act of the will in addition to the act of the understanding. Assent to the truth is of the essence of faith, and the ultimate ground on which our assent to any revealed truth rests is the veracity of God. To believe in God is to rely upon or have understanding assurance of the truth of God's testimony, even though it is unsupported by any other evidence, and to rely upon an unfaltering assurance of the fulfillment of His promises, even though everything seems against fulfillment."

Trust is the result of faith. According to the faith, be it unto you (Matt 9:29). The greater the faith, the greater the experience of God's power. Christ should be the object of our faith. We are saved by God's grace through faith. God provides grace and the faith as well, but it is up to us to exercise faith.

An essential concomitant of faith is repentance. Without genuine repentance involving a deep consciousness of sin, and the confession of it, there cannot be saving faith. "Solemnly testifying to both Jews and Greeks of repentance toward God and faith in our Lord Jesus Christ" (Acts 20:21). Repentance is directed toward God, while faith is directed toward our Lord Jesus Christ. This precious faith is obtained exclusively "by the righteousness of our God and Savior, Jesus Christ " (2 Pet. 1:1).

The righteousness that opens every successful door is the righteousness of Jesus Christ Himself, imputed to the believer as we trust Him and His finished work for us on Calvary. We are made wholly righteous in the eyes of God.

Like Precious Faith

> *Simon Peter, a bond-servant and apostle of Jesus Christ, To those who have received a faith of the same kind as ours, by the righteousness of our God and Savior, Jesus Christ: Grace and peace be multiplied to you in the knowledge of God and of Jesus our Lord; seeing that His divine power has granted to us everything pertain-*

> *ing to life and godliness, through the true knowledge of Him who called us by His own glory and excellence* (2 Pet. 1:1-3).

The faith we possess because of our relationship with Jesus Christ is equal in measure and quality to that of the apostles themselves. The identical faith, in measure and quality, that energized the lives of Paul, Peter, James, and John, as well as other stalwart Christians throughout history, belongs to you and me. Amazing but absolutely true!

The Body of Christ, The Church:

He [Christ] is also head of the body, the church; and He is the beginning, the firstborn from the dead, so that He Himself will come to have first place in everything. For it was the Father's good pleasure for all the fullness to dwell in Him (Col. 1:18-19)

The Church—God's Appointed Agency for the Salvation of Mankind

It was organized for service, and its mission is to carry the Gospel to the world. From the beginning God planned that His Church would reflect His fullness and sufficiency. The members of the church—those He has called "out of darkness into His marvelous light" (2 Pet. 2:9, KJV) —are to reflect His glory.

The Church: The Vehicle of God's Grace

The Church is the repository of Christ's riches of grace. Through the church the final full display of God's love will eventually be shown, even to "the principalities and powers in heavenly places" (Eph. 3:10, KJV). The church alone can provide a moral vision to a wandering people. Only the church can step into the vacuum and demonstrate that there is a sovereign, living God who is the Source of truth. According to the New Testament every saved person is a member of God's family, the church.

A church is on mission with Christ carrying out His "Great Commission."

> *And Jesus came up and spoke to them, saying, "All authority has been given to Me in heaven and on earth. Go therefore and make disciples of all the nations, baptizing them in the name of the Fa-*

ther and the Son and the Holy Spirit, teaching them to observe all that I commanded you; and lo, I am with you always, even to the end of the age" (Matt. 28:18-20).

Now all these things are from God, who reconciled us to Himself through Christ and gave us the ministry of reconciliation, namely, that God was in Christ reconciling the world to Himself, not counting their trespasses against them, and He has committed to us the word of reconciliation. Therefore, we are ambassadors for Christ, as though God were making an appeal through us; we beg you on behalf of Christ, be reconciled to God (2 Cor. 5:18-20).

For we are God's fellow workers; you are God's field, God's building (1 Cor. 3:9).

The Beginning of the Body of Christ, the Church

Shortly after Christ ascended to the Father, God moved through the Jerusalem believers to officially establish the church, even though that organism, in essence, already existed. The full-blown church was inaugurated on the Day of Pentecost, when on that Jewish holy day the apostle Peter, filled with the Spirit, delivered the first Gospel sermon in the name of the risen Christ. Three thousand people responded and were drawn together into an organic, spiritual union (see Acts 2). That day the Holy Spirit was sent to indwell permanently the hearts of all believers, whereas previously He would enter a person on occasion and then depart. Jesus Christ founded the church, died for the church, sent His Spirit to the church, and will one day return for it (1 Thessalonians 4:13-18).

Five Elements of the Christian Lifestyle

The purpose of the Church is to facilitate these elements:

Every believer is a **missionary**. "Go make disciples of all nations," Jesus commanded. Our purpose: To evangelize the world.

Every believer is a **member** of Christ's Family. "Baptize them in the name of the Father, Son, and Holy Spirit." Our purpose: To *encourage* one another.

Every believer needs **maturity**. "Teach them to obey everything I have commanded you." Our purpose: To *edify* (build up) one another.

Every believer is to **magnify** the Lord. "Love the Lord your God with all your heart." Our purpose: To *exalt* Christ in worship.

Every believer is a **minister**. "Love your neighbor as yourself." Our purpose: To *equip* for service. Loving your neighbor is what ministry is all about.

There are numerous analogies for a Christian disconnected from a church: a football player without a team, soldiers without a platoon, a sheep without a flock, a child without a family.

The Two Ordinances of the Church

Baptism

The ordinance of baptism in the name of God the Father, God the Son, and God the Holy Spirit symbolizes the believer's faith in a crucified, buried, and resurrected Savior. It also stands for the believer's death to sin, the burial of his old life, and, through Christ's resurrection, his new life. Paul explained, "Therefore we have been buried with Him through baptism into death, so that as Christ was raised from the dead through the glory of the Father, so we too might walk in newness of life" (Rom. 6:4). When the Christian minister baptizes the believer in water to typify the work of the Spirit, the rudiments of the Gospel message are pictured (see 1 Cor. 15:3-4).

The Lord's Supper—Communion

The Lord's Supper represents the atonement of Christ as the only means of our justification (God's receiving us as righteous) and the only support for the new life we have in Christ. There is no magic in it. The supper is memorial in nature (see 1 Cor. 11:23-26). It "shows forth" and dramatizes the agonizing death of our Lord on the Cross. When we partake of the Lord's Supper, it means that we believe Christ has made an all-sufficient substitutionary sacrifice for our sins.

The Purpose of the Lord's Table

The gathering of the Lord's people to observe the Supper has a sacred meaning that is essential to the spiritual well-being of the church's members. For that reason Communion is a special object of Satan's attack. Christ taught:

The purpose of this gathering is to "remember" Him and His death until He comes again.

The symbols—the bread and the cup—speak not only of His complete gift of Himself but also of our own total identification in it. He lives within us (see also Matt. 26:26-29; Mark 14:22-25; Luke 22:17-20).

During the interval between His Ascension and His second coming, we are to keep His atoning death central in the practice and preaching of the Church, His Body. Most evangelicals believe this ordinance is essential because it honors the Lord's request but do not feel it bestows saving grace.

Churches Grow When They Are:

***Warmer** through fellowship*
***Deeper** through discipleship*
***Stronger** through worship*
***Broader** through ministry and*
***Larger** through evangelism.*

Relationships

Each Sunday or other designated worship time presents a wonderful opportunity for every believer to celebrate and deepen his relationship with God and other believers through the act of worship in a church body setting. In participating in this important act we learn to fulfill the two greatest commandments as spoken by our Lord in the twelfth chapter of Mark's Gospel: "Love the Lord your God with all your heart, soul, mind, and strength, and your neighbor as yourself." Through the act of worship, the believer has the opportunity to focus on strengthening this relationship through songs, prayer, and learning the Word of God. It should be our platform to begin each new week, impacting our conduct toward God and toward our neighbors.

Proper worship should usher the believer into a special time in the presence of God and guide him in the direction of thanksgiving, repentance, and holy living. It is a time to listen to God and to what He has said to us through His Word.

Another blessing of strengthening our intimacy with God is the effect it has on the entire family. As husband and wife come closer to the Lord, they become closer to each other. As families worship together, they are nourished by the experience and their foundation as a unit is made firm. Their relationship to one another is fortified, and they learn how to live godly lives together in acceptance and love. They hear God's commandments and seek to relate these truths with one another.

As we grow in the Lord and mature in our understanding of His Word, we become better neighbors; people God has placed in our lives are drawn to Christ. This is one of the main channels God has used to expand His kingdom.

The Church Family

God's family is the church of the Living God, "the pillar and ground of truth" (1 Tim. 3:15, KJV). We were created for community, fashioned for fellowship, and formed for family. None of us can fulfill God's purposes by ourselves. The Bible calls the church the Bride of Christ and the Body of Christ. A church family identifies you as a genuine believer. Your love for one another will prove to the world that you are His disciples.

Biblical fellowship is being as committed to one another as we are to Jesus. It requires both God's power and our effort to produce a loving Christian community. You were formed to be a part of God's family. You need to learn how to love and relate to others. Peacemaking is one of the most important skills you can develop. Do everything possible to live in peace with everybody.

Relationships are always worth restoring. Forgive others for wrongs done to you. Forgiveness is letting go of the past. Trust has to do with future behavior. The church (Body of Christ) is God's instrument on earth.

Jesus Christ Is Its Head

The New Testament teaches that there is only one universal church, but there can be any number of local churches formed into various denominations, societies, or councils. The New Testament also teaches that, even though there may be many cleavages and divisions within the structure of the church, yet we have only one Lord Jesus Christ is the Head of this great universal Church.

> *And he is the head of the body, the church: who is the beginning, the firstborn from the dead; that in all things he might have the*

preeminence. For it pleased the Father that in him should all fulness dwell (Col. 1:18-19).

From Him should spring all the activities and missions of the church. The commandments and commission given us by Christ makes it easy to select our life's work. God is at work in the world, and He wants us to join Him:

1. **"Love God with all your heart"**: You were planned for God's pleasure, so your purpose is to love God through *worship.*
2. **"Love your neighbor as yourself"**: You were shaped for serving, so your purpose is to show love for others through *ministry.*
3. **"Go and make disciples"**: You were made for a mission, so your purpose is to share God's message through *evangelism.*
4. **"Baptize them into . . ."**: You were formed for God's family, so your purpose is to identify with his church through *fellowship.*
5. **"Teach them to do all things . . ."**: You were created to become like Christ, so your purpose is to grow to maturity through *discipleship.*

A GREAT COMMITMENT TO THE GREAT COMMANDMENT AND THE GREAT COMMISSION WILL MAKE YOU A GREAT CHRISTIAN!

CHAPTER 15

Where Will You Spend Eternity—Heaven or Hell?

If we confess our sins, He is faithful and righteous to forgive us our sins and to cleanse us from all unrighteousness (1 John 1:9).

For what does it profit a man (or woman) to gain the whole world, and forfeit his (her) soul? (Mark 8:36).

That last question is inescapable. And all of us have no choice but to choose. Each and every person chooses heaven or hell by the choices they make and their style of life. God gives us a choice. We can choose to serve Christ or Satan. When one rejects Christ and goes his (her) own way, one automatically chooses Satan. There are only two highways to eternity.

The Bible is our road map to eternity as well as life on earth. The Bible not only teaches us how to live a full and meaningful life but how to reach heaven.

VISIONS OF GLORY OR TORMENT

The Lord Jesus in the New Testament said more about hell than heaven and employed the most descriptive pictures. He instructed us not to fear those who can merely kill the body but to fear "the One who, after He has killed, has authority to cast into hell; yes, I tell you, fear Him!" (Luke 12:5).

Jesus taught that there are two roads in life: a broad road that leads to judgment, destruction, and hell. On that road the devil deceives people into thinking they are having a party, Dude! And a narrow road that is entered by a narrow gate. That leads to heaven. Traveling on that road seems difficult for a season because we are going against the tide of all the pleasures and sins of this world. Yet, only those who are prepared to die are really prepared to live! Are you prepared to die?

Death Is a Reality

Every second of the day we are faced with the reality of dying. Heart attacks, snipers, car wrecks, you name it. Death, though, is not our final destination. Death is only the doorway to our destination. Death is the point beyond which we do not return to life on earth. The Bible declares: "It is appointed unto men once to die, but after this the judgment" (Heb. 9:27, KJV). When you die physically, either you die with Christ in your heart, or you die with Him outside your heart. The poet wrote: "Only one life, 'Twill soon be past, Only what's done for Christ will last." You are either on the narrow road or on the broad road. And you need to decide now, today, where you want to spend eternity.

Jesus Is The Way!

Life is often compared to a journey. The entire meaning of the Christian faith is compacted into only four of Jesus' words: "I am the way." Jesus is the Way, the only Way.

There are three ideas in Isaiah 35:8 that refer to the way. "A highway will be there, a roadway, And it will be called the Highway of Holiness. The unclean will not travel on it, But it will be for him who walks that way, And fools will not wander on it" (Isa. 35:8). First, it is a highway. When highways of God are built, it means many old entities are done away with. Matters change (see 2 Cor. 5:17). A person in Christ is a new creature or creation. The past is gone, and life has become fresh and new.

Has Your Life Changed?

Has there been that kind of change in your life? Oh, maybe you have been baptized. Perhaps you may belong to a church or another religious organization. You might have gone through all kinds of rituals, but deep in your heart you may have doubts about whether you have really accepted Christ and know Him personally. Are you on that narrow road that leads to heaven? Will you go to your grave with those gnawing doubts? Or you can settle it today and make absolutely certain that you're on the right road.

What Is Expected?

You may ask, "Do I have to give up anything when I come to Christ?" Yes sir and ma'am, you do. You'll have to give up the life controlled by sin. But then you also give up emptiness, loneliness, guilt, and fear of death.

And what will God give you in return? A life that is full. You now have a Friend that sticks closer than a brother (Prov. 18:24, KJV). You'll never be alone again. Your sin and your guilt will be removed. You can have the consummate assurance that you are going to heaven.

Why? Because Christ has guaranteed all of these blessings through His death and resurrection. In the cross and the empty tomb we discover the we find the very heart of the Gospel, the Good News, that God wants to share with you—that He loves you.

Second, it is a plain way. Fortunately, on most of our highways are signs to mark the routes of travel. Those signs often warn us of dangerous conditions and point us toward the correct route to our destination. The Bible is our map, and God's Spirit is our Guide. This Bible was supernaturally written, inspired by the Holy Spirit. It's God's message to you and to me, and it teaches us how to live. God tells us specifically how we can go to heaven, and He candidly warns us about the hazards en route.

Why Are You Living?

Every person ought to have a purpose, a reason for existence, for being here. What is your purpose? Why are you living? The Apostle Paul was well aware of his purpose. He testified, "For to me to live is Christ, and to die is gain" (Phil. 1:21, KJV). If you were to explain your life's purpose, what would it be? Is it to have possessions, sex, fun, success? What do you live for?

Third, it is a safe way. Do you feel the highways of the United States are safe? We read about people being shot or hit with rocks on highways for no apparent reason. But in Christ there is spiritual safety.

You are assured of salvation when you have faith in Christ's crucifixion and resurrection. On God's highway we are safe. No one can or will destroy your soul if you have Him as your Lord and Savior.

The Psalmist sang, "He that dwelleth in the secret place of the most High shall abide under the shadow of the Almighty" (Ps. 91:1, KJV). I am not indicating that, if you travel on God's highway, nothing bad will ever happen to you. Many godly people suffer and die, but they are spiritually safe and headed for heaven. But nothing will ever separate you from God. Nothing!

> *Who will separate us from the love of Christ? Will tribulation, or distress, or persecution, or famine, or nakedness, or peril, or sword? Just as it is written, "For Your sake we are being put to death all day long; We were considered as sheep to be slaughtered." But in all these things we overwhelmingly conquer through Him who loved us. For I am convinced that neither death, nor life, nor angels, nor principalities, nor things present, nor things to come, nor powers, nor height, nor depth, nor any other created thing, will be able to separate us from the love of God, which is in Christ Jesus our Lord* (Rom. 8:35-39).

Nor "any other created thing" also includes the devil and all his demons! Once you are in Christ Jesus, nothing can snatch you out of His loving care.

The Highway Through: Our Prayers, God's Word, and the Holy Spirit

God guides us on the highway through our prayers. As followers of Christ, we have a direct connection with God. Today we are subjected to all kinds of voice-mail messages on the phone. We are given a number of options before we even can speak to a real person—and sometimes never hear a genuine voice. But when we call out to God in heaven, we don't hear, "Hello, you've reached heaven. Unfortunately, God is not available to hear you at this time. Please press 1 if you need direction; press 2 if you need forgiveness . . ." God is always open to our call.

How does God lead us? He moves within our hearts and minds, spiritually gripping our hands. Will you allow Him to lead you from this moment on? The Scripture says about itself, "Thy word is a lamp unto my feet, and a light unto my path" (Ps. 119:105, KJV). The Holy Spirit touches our lives as our Teacher and our Guide. He is our Counselor to lead us in the way of truth.

Sadly, many people read horoscopes every day, trying to locate guidance. That is unnecessary, for we have the Word of God and the guidance of the Holy Spirit. Read the Bible and allow the Holy Spirit to illumine you.

The Bible makes it plain that those who call upon the Lord shall be saved: "But as many as received Him, to them He gave the right to become children of God, even to those who believe in His name" (John 1:12).

Salvation is not limited to one ethnic group—to Africans or Asians or Latin Americans or Caucasians in Europe. Jesus opens His arms wide, and He invites:

> *Come to Me, all who are weary and heavy-laden, and I will give you rest. Take My yoke upon you and learn from Me, for I am gentle and humble in heart, and you will find rest for your souls. For My yoke is easy and My burden is light*" (Matt. 11:28-30).

What's Needed?

You may ask, "What must I do?" A jailer in Philippi asked that almost 2000 years ago. You need to say, "I open my heart to Christ. I want Him to take over my life. I want to be sure that I'm on that narrow road. I want to change my way of living. I confess that I have sinned. I want Jesus as my Savior and Lord and Master, and I want to be sure of it."

GOD'S WRATH

People still believe in God—or at least they claim to—but they refuse to believe that wrath is one of His divine attributes. They adore the kind of Christianity in which "a God without wrath brought men without sin into a kingdom without judgment through the ministrations of a Christ without a cross," to quote an unknown author.

GOD'S WRATH REVEALED

"A God without wrath" is not the God of the Bible, whom the Scriptures portray as displaying "the wrath of the Lord Almighty" (Isa.

13:13, KJV). The impact of His anger will be seen on what the Bible terms "the day of wrath." Sinners who refuse to repent are accumulating wrath against themselves "for the day of God's wrath" (Rom. 2:5, KJV).

Yes, the full extent of God's wrath is kept for the day of judgment, it is even now "being revealed from heaven against all the godlessness and wickedness of men" (Rom. 1:18, KJV). In fact, God "expresses his wrath every day" (Ps. 7:11, KJV) against sinners who are "by nature children of wrath" (Eph. 2:3, KJV).

Many seem to think God's wrath is limited to the Old Testament, or that it is characteristic only of the Father but never to the Son. Yet, the New Testament definitely mentions "the wrath of the Lamb" (Rev. 6:16), who judges sin with "the fury of the wrath of God Almighty" (19:15). Those references plainly refer to our loving, kind Savior, who is a Lamb of meekness and mildness to those who love Him but a Lion of judgment and righteousness to those who have rejected Him.

The same Jesus who is so sweet to His friends is completely fierce toward His enemies. He will remain like that forever, for "those who do not know God and to those who do not obey the gospel of our Lord Jesus . . . These will pay the penalty of eternal destruction, away from the presence of the Lord and from the glory of His power (1 Thess. 1:8-9).

Wrath is one of God's perfections, a necessary side of His character, and an essential part of Christian teaching about God.

WHAT GOD'S WRATH MEANS

What does God's Word mean when it refers to God's wrath? His wrath is different from human anger. John Stott explains the difference: "Human anger is usually arbitrary and uninhibited; divine anger is always principled and controlled. Our anger tends to be a spasmodic outburst, aroused by pique and seeking revenge; God's is a continuous, settled antagonism, aroused only by evil, and expressed in its condemnation."

When the Bible depicts God in language that men can understand, it does not reduce God to human terms. For instance, although the Bible speaks of "the arm of God," it does not mean that He literally has a bicep. Also, while the Bible often shows God as having human emotions, He does not experience them as we do. Thus, when the Bible states that God is angry, we should not conclude that God is fussy or cruel as we are. Our anger is poisoned by sin.

The Continuing Struggle

We should always remember that in this life there will always be a struggle, spiritual warfare, both within and without. As explained in previous chapters, the devil is an unrelenting enemy, always busy. Through the world and the flesh, he appeals to the old nature within Christians to reassert itself. He appeals to our lusts, our covetousness, and our pride. We always will sense the inclinations to sin.

But we have the Holy Spirit within us: "You are from God, little children, and have overcome them; because greater is He who is in you than he who is in the world (1 John 4:4). If we rely on Christ for help, He will provide us the power to resist temptation.

In Romans 7, Paul didn't teach that he cannot help but sin because he can't control his old sin nature. Rather, he described the warfare all of us will face, explaining that we can have victory in Christ by the power of His Holy Spirit who lives within us.

Jesus Christ was perfect, and we are to seek perfection as we grow in God's grace and His attributes. Whether or not we realize it, we grow spiritually through the turbulence, troubles, temptations and testings that afflict all Christians.

One day all of this will be past. In the meantime, day by day, week by week, and month by month, we are counseled to walk in the Spirit. Walking in the Spirit means being directed by the Holy Spirit. "But if we walk in the Light as He Himself is in the Light, we have fellowship with one another, and the blood of Jesus His Son cleanses us from all sin" (1 John 1:7).

The Apostle Paul wrote, "But I say, walk by the Spirit, and you will not carry out the desire of the flesh" (Gal. 5:16). The flesh is the self-life: what we are when we are left to our own devices. At times we behave ourselves, doing good. We are moral and have high ethical standards.

Sooner or later, though, we reveal our carnal (fleshly) side. Paul wrote that the flesh has a mind of its own and that "the natural mind" is not subject to the Law of God: "I know that nothing good dwells in me, that is, in my flesh [the sinful nature]" When we realize this and yield to the Holy Spirit, deeper spiritual maturity and greater love, joy, and peace will reveal themselves.

If we as Christians struggle to make ourselves better or good or even acceptable to God by our human effort, we will fail. The Holy Spirit dwells in believers, and God does His work in us by the Holy Spirit. We must yield ourselves to the Spirit of God so He may give us power to put off the old and put on the new.

Paul pointed out that the flesh sets its desires against the Spirit, and the Spirit against the flesh, and that those are antagonistic to each other. This makes it plain what the real conflict is in the hearts of true believers. As long as there is not the surrender of mind and body every moment of every day, the old nature asserts itself. Only as we yield to Christ and obey Him do we win the victory. Yielding is the secret: "Therefore I urge you, brethren, by the mercies of God, to present your bodies a living and holy sacrifice, acceptable to God, which is your spiritual service of worship. And do not be conformed to this world, but be transformed by the renewing of your mind, so that you may prove what the will of God is, that which is good and acceptable and perfect" (Rom. 12:1-2).

All over the place human nature calls the signals and produces the works of the flesh. Many people feel that since they have become believers that they should have immediate transformation, a "quick fix," miraculous deliverance and pain free. Experience shows we have to desire spiritual change, and change is a process. "For whatsoever is born of God overcometh the world: and this is the victory that overcometh the world, even our faith. Who is he that overcometh the world, but he that believeth that Jesus is the Son of God?" (1 John 5:4, KJV).

THE CONFLICT OF THE AGES

Satan's hatred for mankind becomes clear as we examine the conflict of the ages as it is revealed in the Bible. In early ages, Satan attempted to destroy mankind, whereas God has sought to save people through Jesus in the death on the cross for the sins of the whole world. When Jesus cried on the cross, "It is finished," He did not indicate that the conflict of the ages was over. He meant that the temporary sacrificial system of the Old Testament was no longer required, and that then a permanent means of escaping the deception of Satan and the consequences of sin had opened up—the plan of salvation by grace through faith in Christ. In addition, Christ sent His Holy Spirit to indwell believers.

This not only protected them against the deceptions of Satan and the world, but it did mean Christians would have supernatural power that would combat and overcome Satan.

Chapter 16
Highway to Heaven

You Were Created to Become Like Christ

Let your roots grow down into Christ
and draw up nourishment from Him.
See that you go on growing in the Lord,
and become strong and vigorous in the truth (Col. 2:7, TLB).

Thoughts of Heaven

I ofttimes think of Heaven
With all its joy and peace,
When from this world of sadness
My soul shall find release.
I wonder how 'twill seem, when
I've reached the golden shore;
With loved ones waiting for me;
Where we shall part no more.
I think of many mansions
Prepared by Christ's dear hand;
And of His shining glory
In that far distant land.
How blessed it will be when
I'm caught up in the air;
From earth or grave He'll call me,
Heaven's joy with Him to share.
'Twill only take a moment;
The twinkling of an eye;
I'll be changed and travel
Beyond the starry sky.
These thoughts of Heaven lure me
As nothing else can do.

Some day my Lord will tell me
My work on earth is through;
That day the trump shall signal;
And I shall hear the sound;
Time and earth I'll leave far behind
When I am heaven bound.
The time shall not be long now
As prophecies unfold;
Till I see my Savior
And walk those streets of gold.
—Author Unknown

HEAVEN—A PREPARED PLACE FOR PREPARED PEOPLE

> *"Blessed are those who wash their robes, that they may have the right to the tree of life and may go through the gates into the city"* (Rev. 22:14).

So, if we are to reach the "sweet bye and bye," we must prepare for it in the "nasty here and now." Heaven is the destination of a life that is turned toward God, seeking His will now. Now! I can only feel sorry for the billionaire who more than once has publicly chortled, in essence, "I wouldn't want to go to heaven. For me that would be boring. All they do up there is pray and sing and all that stuff." At least he's honest. Now, he may not believe in hell, but that's the place he's preparing for.

Preparation for heaven—and hell—begins *right now*. Here is Christ's will concerning you: "Now this is eternal life: that they [Jesus' disciples] may know you, the only true God, and Jesus Christ, whom you have sent" (John 17:3, KJV).

You can know if you're going to heaven by yielding your heart and life to Christ right now. Many people are worried about the doctrine of calling and election, fearful that maybe God will not save them. Not to worry. What should you do if you don't have the assurance of salvation? Simply follow the apostle Peter's counsel: "Wherefore the rather, brethren, give diligence to *make your calling and election sure*: for if ye do these things, ye shall never fall" (2 Peter 1:10, KJV, my italics). Call on the Lord this moment and ask Him to give you inner assurance.

What Happens When We Die?

Most probably, you will behold angels who have been assigned to escort you to your destination, even as the angels carried Lazarus to "Abraham's bosom" (Luke 16:22, NASB).

When my mother-in-law died, the nurse stepped in to check on her and was holding her hand. Suddenly Nannie turned and exclaimed, "Aren't those angels beautiful?" She laid her head down and was carried to heaven.

You will be keenly aware that you have arrived in heaven, and as you enter its gates, you will gaze upon Christ who welcomes you home. Since He stood to welcome Stephen into the glories of heaven (Acts 7:56), it is reasonable to believe He will be on hand to bid your entry.

You will know who He is, and He will obviously know who you are. Because you are one of His sheep, He will call you by name. You will look into His eyes and see compassion, love, and understanding. You will know His welcome is genuine. You will view His nailprints, triggering memories that make you fall on your face and worship. Were it not for His tender hand helping you to your feet, you would not be able to arise.

So much is different, yet you are quite the same. You have entered heaven without a break in consciousness. Back on earth your friends will bury your body, but they cannot bury you. Just before Stephen died, he said, "Lord Jesus, receive my spirit"; he did not cry, "receive my body" (Acts 7:59).

YOUR PERSONALITY CONTINUES

The moment after we die physically, our minds, our memories, will be clearer than ever before. Consider Jesus' account in Luke 16 of the rich man who descended into hades with his memory intact. He thought about his family on earth and pled, "I have five brothers" (v. 28). Death does not change what we know. Our personalities will go on with the same information we have stored in our mind today.

Reflect on your background, your family, and friends. You will remember all of this and more in heaven. As soon as we reach heaven, we will meet a host of others—some we have known in this life or through the pages of the Bible or church history. On the Mount of Transfiguration, three of the disciples—Peter, James, and John—met Moses and Elijah (Matt. 17:1-8). They recognized yet Moses had been gone for around 1,400 years and Elijah, for at least 950. There was no need for introductions or ID tags. In heaven there will be intuitive knowledge, for our minds will be delivered from the limitations sin imposed on them in this life. Paul explained this in his famous love chapter:

> *For now we see through a glass, darkly; but then face to face: now I know in part; but then shall I know even as also I am known. And now abideth faith, hope, charity, these three; but the greatest of these is charity* (1 Cor. 13:12-13, KJV).

Christ taught that marriages will not continue in heaven (Matt. 22:30). Yet, as far as we can ascertain, we will keep our female and male genders. Your mother will be recognized as your mother in heaven; your son or daughter will be known as a member of your earthly family.

Our love for God will intensify. In heaven we can love God without distractions. We will keep loving whatever we loved on earth, apart from sin. In heaven our sentiments will be as they were on earth, except more intense and powerful. Meditate on your purest joy on earth. Then magnify and multiply that infinitely, and you might have the slightest inkling of heaven's supreme bliss. David sang to God, "In Your presence is fullness of joy; At Your right hand are pleasures forevermore" (Ps.16:11, NKJV).

There will be pain and sorrow until God wipes away every tear from our eyes "for the Lamb in the center of the throne will be their shepherd, and will guide them to springs of the water of life; and God will wipe every tear from their eyes" (Rev. 7:17). "And God shall wipe away all tears from their eyes; and there shall be no more death, neither sorrow, nor crying, neither shall there be any more pain: for the former things are passed away" (Rev. 21:4). When we ruminate on the opportunities we squandered; when we consider how imperfectly we loved Christ on earth, we will grieve. That remorse will vanish, but for now the reality of what could have been will assail us. Robert Greenleaf Whittier wrote, "The saddest words of tongue or pen are these: it might have been."

PERSONAL ACTIVITIES CONTINUE

In heaven we will rest, but it is not the rest of inactivity. We will in all likelihood continue many of the activities we experienced on earth.

Artists may well create art as never before; scientists may be invited to continue their exploration of God's magnificent creation; musicians will perform music; all of us will continue with our skills.

The Christian will discover that he has vacated this earthly body of flesh and put on a celestial body that God has prepared for him, a resurrection body tailor-made for him to live in. Of this Paul wrote:

> *For we know that if the earthly tent which is our house is torn down, we have a building from God, a house not made with hands, eternal in the heavens. For indeed in this house we groan, longing to be clothed with our dwelling from heaven, inasmuch as we, having put it on, will not be found naked* (2 Cor. 5:1-3).

The Christian will find that he is now completely surrounded and breathes an atmosphere of holiness, righteousness, and love prepared for him by the Lord Jesus.

The Christian will be reunited with his loved ones who have preceded him. The guardian angel will have informed his loved ones he is coming (Heb. 12:1).

The Christian will meet and have fellowship with the great saints and Christian leaders who have gone before, i.e., Abel, Noah, Abraham, Ruth, Moses, Joshua, Samuel, David, and other Old Testament patriarchs and prophets; and New Testament personalities like Mary the mother of Jesus, Mary Magdalene, Paul, Peter, James, John, Stephen, Barnabas, Silas, Priscilla and Aquila, Timothy, Titus, and others.

The Christian will realize that he was created for two worlds — the physical he departed from and the spiritual mansion prepared for him by the Lord: "I go to prepare a place for you" (John 14:2b, KJV).

The Christian will experience and be aware of seeing and standing in the presence of the Lord Jesus Christ: "They will see his face, and his name will be on their foreheads" (Rev.22:4).

One of Two Destinations . . . Which Will It Be?

The Bible teaches that the departed soul will spend eternity in a real heaven or a real hell. The most dreadful condition we can conceive of is to live without God and die without Jesus Christ as our Savior. Nothing can fully describe God, in all of His awesome majesty, His eternal home and that of all who have received Him through the ages. It is staggering and beyond all human understanding. Paul struck this chord when he virtually shouted, "But as it is written, Eye hath not seen, nor ear heard neither have entered into the heart of man, the things which God hath prepared for them that love him" (1 Cor. 2:9).

God's holy angels, at the death of the believer, will carry her/him to heaven. It is a place of indescribable beauty and ecstasy. The angels transport the person's spiritual being into the very presence of God. Ezekiel in a vision beheld the awesome glory and majesty of God that produces a spectacular glow like a fire and a brilliant light that surrounds Him.

Eternal rewards (Revelation 22:12; 2 Corinthians 5:10)

We are saved by grace through faith (Eph. 2:8-9), and that insures us a place in heaven, but we will be rewarded according to what we have done on earth. "But why dost thou judge thy brother? for we shall all stand before the judgment seat of Christ" (Romans 14:10, KJV). "For we must all appear before the judgment seat of Christ; that every one may receive the things done in his body, according to that he hath done, whether it be good or bad" (2 Cor. 5:10 KJV; see also 2 Cor. 5:10, TLB; Jer. 17:10; Heb. 6:10; Rev. 14:13; 1 Cor. 4:5).

Many people who have lived humble lives here on earth will receive special blessings at the judgment seat of Christ (Matt. 19:30). Christians who are soul-winners will have the highest commendation from the Judge, shining as stars (Dan. 12:3).

The Final Resurrection—at the Rapture (1 Thessalonians 4:13-18)

Death does not release us into the final resurrection body condition. This intermediate state of incompleteness will ensue because we will not yet have the final resurrection body. We will wait for it until we are given it at the rapture before we again are a complete person—body, soul and spirit back together. This was Paul's prayer for the Thessalonian Christians: "Now may the God of peace Himself sanctify you entirely; and may your spirit and soul and body be preserved complete, without blame at the coming of our Lord Jesus Christ" (1 Thess. 5:23).

Believers will have vacated this earthly body of flesh and will have been clothed with a celestial body that God has especially prepared for them (see again 2 Cor. 5:1-3). Hallelujah!

Other Delights in Heaven

No sorrow, tears, regrets, or loneliness;
No more death, pain, or diseases;
No more jealousy, anger, temper;
No mortgage, lawsuits, or hunger (or taxes!);
No more sin or evil influence;

We will glory in perfect health and luxuriate in the joy of the Lord. Throughout this book I have asked this urgent question, "Have you given your heart and life to Christ?" If you have, your reservation is confirmed for your trip to your eternal home in heaven. "Behold, now is the accepted time; behold, now is the day of salvation" (2 Cor. 6:2b, KJV). God never promised us tomorrow. *His time is now*. You may think, *Oh, I can come to Christ just anytime I want to*. According to Jesus that is not the case: "No man [meaning woman as well] can come to me, except the Father which hath sent me draw him: and I will raise him up at the last day" (John 6:44, KJV).

There are specific times when God is tugging on you through the convicting power of the Holy Spirit. If you sense the slightest inclination to accept Christ, *do it right this moment!*

SAFELY HOME

I am home in Heaven, dear ones;
Oh, so happy and so bright!
There is perfect joy and beauty
In this everlasting light.
All the pain and grief is over,
Every restless tossing passed;
I am now at peace forever,
Safely home in Heaven at last.
Did you wonder I so calmly
Trod the valley of the shade?
Oh! but Jesus' love illumined
Every dark and fearful glade.
And He came Himself to meet me
In that way so hard to tread;
And with Jesus' arm to lean on,
Could I have one doubt or dread?

Then you must not grieve so sorely,
For I love you dearly still:
Try to look beyond earth's shadows,
Pray to trust our Father's Will.
There is work still waiting for you,
So you must not idly stand;
Do it now, while life remaineth—
You shall rest in Jesus' land.
When that work is all completed,
He will gently call you Home;
Oh, the rapture of that meeting,
Oh, the joy to see you come!
--Author Unknown

Chapter 17
Is Hell Real?

If we are to overcome Satan, we must experience a growing knowledge of Christ. And as we learn more about Christ, we discover that the devil is no match for our Sovereign Lord Christ.

"Thanks be to God, who gives us the victory through our Lord Jesus Christ" (1 Corinthians 15:57).

Let us live as victors!

Satan—Sin and Hell

Satan

Satan is not merely a wicked force or principle of evil as some believe. Rather, he is a supernatural being who leads a kingdom of fallen angels and demons. His presence and power are extensive. We would benefit from understanding how he works so we can protect ourselves from him. Peter warned, "Be sober, be vigilant; because our adversary the devil, as a roaring lion, walketh about seeking who he can devour (1 Pet. 5:8, KJV).

Satan was known as Lucifer, the created and anointed angel who disobeyed God. One third of the angels who sided with Lucifer were kicked out of Heaven with him. He became Satan (the devil), the adversary of God. Satan was permitted to visit heaven to accuse believers in Jesus (see Job Chapters 1 and 2; also Chapter 5 of this book).

LUCIFER'S HISTORY

From Isaiah 14 and Ezekiel 28 emerges a rather extensive picture of Satan before his rebellion.

His Person.

He was the most exalted being of all creation (Ezek. 28:13, 15), the grandest of all God's handiwork, a radiant celestial being who most perfectly reflected the splendor of his Maker. So, he was aptly called Lucifer. The word is derived from a Hebrew root meaning "to shine" and is used only here as a title to reference the star that shines most brightly, that resists the rising sun most heartily.

SATAN'S FALL

At this point we encounter one of the most profound mysteries of the moral universe as revealed in Scripture: How come sin entered the universe? It is plain that sin entered in connection with Satan's rebellion, but how did such wicked impulses arise in the heart of one created by a perfectly Holy God? Three realities ought to be stressed:

First, Lucifer's fall was a result of his abysmal, wicked mindset to wrest God's glory. This is made specific in five "I-will" statements in Isaiah 14:13-14.

But you said in your heart,
"I will ascend to heaven;
I will raise my throne above the stars of God,
And I will sit on the mount of assembly
In the recesses of the north.
I will ascend above the heights of the clouds;
I will make myself like the Most High."

There is the substance of sin—the evil yearning to live as if the creature were more important than the Creator. Second, Satan is completely and exclusively responsible for his wicked choice. By reason of his rebellion, Satan became the entrenched enemy of God and all that is godly. His fall—and that of those angels who followed him—is permanent with no hope of redemption.

A Holy God irretrievably withdrew fellowship from Satan and his cohorts. The devil still has access to the throne room of the universe in his role as accuser of the brethren (Job 1:2; Zech. chapter 3; Luke. 22:31; Rev. 12:10). However, that is access without acceptance by God. Because of his treason, the most horrendous in the history of the cosmos, Satan and his angels can look forward to nothing but condemnation and eternal punishment. "Then He will also say to those on His left, 'Depart from Me, accursed ones, into the eternal fire which has been prepared for the devil and his angels'" (Matt. 25:41, KJV).

The Bible makes it plain that the gross evil of the visible world is driven and sustained by a realm populated by invisible, fallen spirits (Dan. 10:12-13; Eph. 6:12). In their pernicious and doomed-to-failure onslaught to frustrate the leadership of the true God, those evil spirits are directed by Satan, the "god of this age" (2 Cor. 4:4).

SIN (See also Chapters 2 and 5)

Sin is behind all of the dreadful, terrible thoughts and acts that have occurred in the history of mankind. Sin is the reason for death and disease. Sin created a divine necessity for hell. As one thinks about the subject of sin, it becomes apparent that this is a crucial issue that every person should strive to understand.

What is sin? Sin is anything that is contrary to the holy character of God, anything that corrupts holiness. It is plain: anything done that is not consistent with God's holiness is sin, and anything not done that God requires of us is sin.

> *For whatsoever is not of faith is sin* (Rom. 14:23b, KJV).

> *Therefore, to one who knows the right thing to do and does not do it, to him it is sin* (James 4:17).

An understanding of God's requirements and standards makes it plain that all have fallen so far below His expectations that degrees of sin are not the issue. A prominent word for sin in the New Testament is *hamartia*, which means to "miss the mark," as though one is aiming for a target. "For all have sinned and fall short of the glory of God" (Rom. 3:23).

ALL.

Since the fall of mankind in the Garden of Eden, every person is born a sinner. David cried, "Behold, I was shapen in iniquity; and in sin did my mother conceive me." . . . "The wicked are estranged from the womb: they go astray as soon as they be born, speaking lies" (Ps. 51:5; 58:3, KJV). We sin because we are sinners, sinners by nature. Sin ushers in God's condemnation. Everyone who sins is under God's sentence of eternal damnation (Rom. 6:23; John 3:18-19, 36). The Bible also signifies that as sinners we are slaves to sin. We will never be completely free from sinning in this life.

Sin is a disastrous condition with eternal consequences. It is clear that in ourselves we have no genuine solution. Our condition is hopeless. Apart from a miracle, the human race would be doomed. Fortunately, there was a miracle. It is called the Incarnation. That means God came in the form of a man, the man Christ Jesus, and lived among us (John 1:14).

The Bible has explained how evil (bad) originated and how it was passed on to mankind. Evil is the result of sin's introduction into the human race, what is called the fall.

When God created Adam, He made him the representative of all mankind. God placed Adam in the Garden of Eden along with his wife, Eve. God prescribed the instructions of life for Adam, and they included a warning against disobedience to His rules. Adam, however, disobeyed and fell from his right relationship with God. When Adam chose to disobey God, sin entered into Adam and all of his descendants. This was the repercussion of the fall. Fellowship with God was destroyed and a curse was placed on Adam and Eve, the earth itself, and Satan. Death entered the world. Until the end of time, God will allow Satan a limited amount of influence, sin will flourish, and all of creation will need to be rescued from final destruction.

Amazingly, God was not surprised by the fall. He had designed a plan for three miraculous events that would provide an avenue for victory over sin. What miracles are those? That Christ came, that He died, and that He rose from the grave.

How Can Mankind Be Forgiven for Sin?

1. You are convicted of your sin by the Holy Spirit, and He carries you to the point of conversion.
2. You confess you are a sinner and ask God for forgiveness.
3. You believe by faith that Jesus loves you, died on the cross to pay the penalty for your sins, and was resurrected on the third day to assure believers that they will also be resurrected to heaven in the future.

4. You invite Christ into your life, place your trust in Him, and accept Him as your Lord and Savior.

Hell—the Eternal Dwelling Of The Lost

Most of us humans have a tendency to put off everything from emptying the garbage to paying our insurance premiums to having a physical checkup. Not carrying out the garbage can eventually invite roaches and rodents. Many a "put-off" person has had a car wreck, only to find out his insurance had expired. Failure to have a health checkup could lead to physical death when it could have been avoided.

A delayed decision can result in a heart that becomes hardened to the call of God's Spirit. "He, that being often reproved hardeneth his neck, shall suddenly be destroyed, and that without remedy" (Prov. 29:1, KJV).

TODAY is the day of salvation. Elvis sang, "There's No Tomorrow." Literally, there may not be a tomorrow. Tomorrow may be too late. Situations beyond our control can constantly snatch a tomorrow from us: wrecks, heart attacks, accidents, strokes, you name 'em. Ask Christ to become your Lord and Savior now!

> *The Lord is not slow about His promise, as some count slowness, but is patient toward you, not wishing for any to perish but for all to come to repentance* (2 Pet. 3:9).

> *That if you confess with your mouth Jesus as Lord, and believe in your heart that God raised Him from the dead, you will be saved; for with the heart a person believes, resulting in righteousness, and with the mouth he confesses, resulting in salvation. . . . "Whoever will call on the name of the Lord will be saved"* (Rom. 10:9-10, 13).

You and I have no idea that there will be a tomorrow. Neither do we have any assurance of continued physical life for another second.

The Death of the Unbeliever

> *He who believes in the Son has eternal life; but he who does not obey the Son will not see life, but the wrath of God abides on him"* (John 3:36).

Once there was a Gospel tract. On the front it read, "What Must I Do to Be Lost?" Inside it simply said: "Nothing." Then it explained God's plan of salvation. You can reject Christ and be lost by merely failing to accept Him.

The unbeliever goes through life with one birth, yet the believer has a second birth when he accepts Christ as Savior and is born again. The unbeliever's life consists of ups and downs and may be successful or fail from an earthly standpoint . . . but the unsaved person has no future with God—only the certainty of divine judgment.

Further, the unbeliever has one life but two deaths. The first is physical death and the second, spiritual death (final, permanent separation from God). Revelation 2:11; 20:6, 14; and 21:8 refer to "the second death," which is not a cessation of existence but an eternity separated from God and all that is decent, lovely, and good.

When an unsaved person dies physically (they are already dead spiritually), their souls go to an awful place called *hades* in the Greek New Testament, referred to as "hell" in most English translations. This is a temporary place where the lost person suffers until a final disposition is made at God's last judgment, the great white throne judgment (see Rev. 21:11-15). The human spirit is "quickened" (made alive) at the moment of conversion when a person receives Christ (Eph. 2:1).

At the last judgment, *hades* delivers up its dead, which is the second resurrection (Rev. 20:5-6, 11-15). The first resurrection will have already occurred at the rapture of the Church when Christ comes back to receive His own (see 1 Thess. 4:16-18). Both soul and body will suffer as the unbeliever is cast into the lake of fire (*geenna* in Greek, gehenna in English) which has already been prepared for Satan and his angels (Matt. 25:41). It was not originally intended for human beings, but they go there if they choose the devil instead of Christ.

Hades

The first compartment, which Jesus Christ called "Abraham's bosom" (Luke 16:22), was also referred to as paradise (Luke 23:43). It was the area where the souls of all Old Testament saints were carried after death. The second compartment was where unbelievers go to torment. When Jesus was resurrected, He transferred all who were in paradise with Him when He ascended to heaven (Eph. 4:2, 9; 2 Cor. 2:2). Unbelievers remain in the torment section of hades until the final judgment (Rev. 20:5).

The Doctrine of Hell

I am well aware that today the doctrine of a literal hell is highly unpopular. Since the Scriptures, including Jesus' words, are literally true, it behooves us to accept all other statements of doctrine as meaning specifically what they state. Jesus spoke more about hell and judgment than He did about heaven and justification.

It is clear from these passages—and we could examine numerous others—that the Bible teaches there is such a place as hell for future punishment. All who are willing to receive the Biblical testimony are driven to accept the fact that the Scriptures teach a place of future retribution, even as they speak of a place called heaven.

The choice is yours alone

This question is frequently asked, "How could a loving God create some of His creatures for eternal punishment?" God did not create any of His creatures for that. He created all persons (celestial and human) to love, obey, and enjoy Him forever. He created beings with the capacity of choosing for themselves either good or evil. The majority seem to choose evil. But God has not abandoned them but has sacrificed His only begotten Son to save them from their hell-driven choice. If people see fit not only to choose evil but also to deliberately and persistently refuse the free offer of salvation, then their eternal punishment is their own fault. To blame God for one's lost state is not only unjust but ungrateful and unreasonable.

People Condemn Themselves

Men and women condemn themselves to everlasting punishment by rejecting Jesus Christ, thus refusing the mercy and grace of God. If people will not allow God to save them from sin and its consequences, they must necessarily continue in it. And if they continue in it, they must suffer anguish as long as they do so. The time will come, sooner or later, when repentance becomes impossible; so salvation will not be forthcoming. Whether or not they are aware of it, people choose their eternal destiny. As one forceful African-American preacher put it, "The Savior and Satan are having an election. You *have* to cast your vote."

It is not a few years of sin that cause eternal punishment. A person might continue for years in sin and still escape eternal torment *if they will only repent and accept Jesus Christ!* It is the rejection of Jesus Christ (cause) that ushers in an eternity of torment (effect).

Those who opt not to receive Christ when He is presented to them, and demonstrate no concern for God's truth and goodness, will after physical death remain without hope, eternally and consciously separated from God. Those who reject Him, after death will never be given another chance! "And as it is appointed unto men once to die, but after this the judgment" (Heb. 9:27, KJV).

How dreadful and horrifying are Jesus' statements: "Then shall he say also unto them on the left hand, Depart from me, ye cursed, into everlasting fire, prepared for the devil and his angels" (Matt. 25:41, KJV). "There shall be weeping and gnashing of teeth" (Matt. 8:12, KJV).

WHAT WILL HELL BE LIKE?

A Place of Punishment

Realize that *degrees of punishment* exist in hell (Luke 12:48). Each day of every life will be analyzed in minute detail. The hidden thoughts and motives of each hour will be replayed, along with all the actions and attitudes. The words spoken in secret will be made public, the intentions of the heart displayed for all to see. Yet, the sufferers will have no attorney to whom they may appeal, no loopholes by which they can escape—nothing but bare, indisputable facts.

I believe that the balance of justice will be so accurate that a pornographer will wish he had never published such material; a thief will wish he had earned an honest living; and an adulterer will regret that he lived an immoral life. Faithfulness to his marriage vows would not have earned him a place in heaven, to be sure, but it would have made his existence in hell slightly more bearable.

A Place Without Hope

Despite the torments of hell, we should not think unbelievers would be happier in heaven. One prominent billionaire has publicly scoffed several times, "I wouldn't enjoy heaven with all of those people singing hymns and praising God! Ugh!" At least, for once, he was telling the truth. If transported into the presence of the Lord, unbelievers would flee as far as possible from the One whom they have refused to love. Because they have a fallen nature, the holiness of God would be terrifying. Rather than repent, they would, like those experiencing the Tribulation, vent their anger and curses. "Men were scorched with fierce heat; and they blasphemed the name of God who has the power over these plagues, and they did not repent so as to give Him glory" (Rev. 16:9).

Hell—A Place of Suffering

Three different words in the New Testament describe hell. The first is *hades*, translated "hell" in the King James Version. Most newer versions leave it untranslated, because it means the same as the Old Testament *sheol*, the shadowy region of departed spirits. *Sheol*, or *hades*, appears to have two compartments, as seen in the story Jesus told about the rich man and Lazarus. After death, the rich man was in torment; the other in a state of bliss. They could speak to one another, but between them a great gulf (chasm, gap) was fixed (Luke 16:26).

Most important, the rich man was fully conscious after death. Memory, speaking, pain, and regret—all were a part of his experience. He spoke nothing about how unfair it was that he should suffer. Repentance, he realized, was what his brothers needed to avoid joining him in his misery. He begged that Lazarus be sent back to his father's house, "for I have five brothers. Let him warn them, so that they will not also come to this place of torment" (v. 28).

Since Jesus' ascension, I believe that those who have faith in Him go directly to heaven and no longer exist alongside the souls of the unbelieving dead in hades. Yet, it appears that today hades is still the abode of the unbelieving dead.

A Place of Fire

Christ spoke of it as a *place of fire*. In Revelation 19, 20, and 21 (NASB) we read of "the lake of fire and brimstone." Yes, the torments of hell could include physical fire, since the bodies of those present will have been re-created and made indestructible. Yet hell is also referred to as a place of "outer darkness" (Matt. 22:13), which would seem inconsistent with a lake of blazing fire.

Fire—"For our God is a consuming fire" (Heb. 12:29). Jesus employed this symbol several times. Certain scholars believe it means a thirst for God that is never quenched.

Darkness—The Bible teaches that God is light (John 1:4-9; 1 John 1:5). Hell will be exactly the opposite for unbelievers, for they will be thrown outside into darkness (Matthew 8:12). Hell is described as a fire, but that ceaseless fire will not give light! Those who have rejected Christ will be separated from this light and subsist in darkness.

Another kind of "fire" might be worse than literal fire. That is the fire of unfulfilled passion, the fire of desires that are never satisfied. Perpetually burning lusts never subside, and the tortured conscience burns but is never sated or appeased. Hell, then, is the raw soul joined to an indestructible body, exposed to its own sin for eternity.

Hell is the place of unquenchable, raging, unmet emotional needs, without painkillers or sedation. Hell is a place of eternal regret.

A Place of Abandonment

The most terrifying suffering of hell will be the *sense of abandonment*, the knowledge that one must live with an eternity of loneliness and regret. "They will be punished with everlasting destruction and shut out from the presence of the Lord and from the majesty of his power" (2 Thess. 1:9).

Please, Accept Christ as Your Savior!

God loves you with an everlasting love (Jer. 31:3). He yearns for you to return His love. He has reserved a place for you in His heavenly home. "Now is the accepted time; behold, now is the day of salvation" (2 Cor. 6:2, KJV).

Epilogue

Under the leadership of the Holy Spirit, as best I could I have shared through ***God's Good News*** the truths of God's Word with you, my readers. My main purpose was to reflect the grandeur and love of the true and living God, as revealed through His only begotten Son, the Lord and Savior Jesus Christ, who not only is God but the only Way to God.

Yours truly has agonized and labored over this work. From start to finish, it was clear that the prince of darkness hates this effort and has done all within his diabolic power to hinder the release of this book. It is my fervent prayer that it has blessed you and opened up God's Word to your heart and mind.

My two purposes were: to enrich the lives of believers and to reach those who have never accepted Christ and become believers. If even one person has trusted the Lord, this book has been more than worthwhile.

If ***God's Good News*** has touched you I have a parting request: make this book available to others. Feel free to contact me at 938 Downey Drive, Nashville, Tennessee 37205, or call me at (615) 352-0267.

If I don't ever see you down here, my prayer is that I will see you in heaven.

Index

Abraham's Faith 45, 54, 59, 256
Adam and Eve 35
Adoption into God's Family 192
Apostles (Disciples) 110
Armor of God 238, 256
Babes in Christ 166
Beatitudes 102
Beliefs to Know 225
Bible (Holy Scriptures) 243
Born Again 158–159
Body of Christ 255
Christ:
- Advocate for Us 53
- Ascension 86, 235
- Atonement 88
- Beatitudes 102
- Beginning from the 62
- Body and Spirit 255
- Character (Human) 115
- Christ in Us 120
- Cross 109
- Crucifiction 80, 235
- Death of Christ 75
- Deity 226
- Eternal Life Assured 58
- Life and Ministry 104
- Living in Christ 217
- Mediator 53, 87
- Nativity Story 56
- Redeemer 53
- Resurrection 61
- Return of Jesus 236
- Services on Earth 114
- Sinlessness 113
- Teacher 115, 121
- Tempted by Satan 108
- Virgin Birth 106

Christian, How to Live 223–227
Christian Life, Five Elements 256
Church, Christ's Body 255
Commandments:
- Ten 101
- Two Great 201

Commission, Great 199
Commitment 189
Conscience 184
Cross 250
Death (What Happens) 262–273
Deity of Christ 226
Elect (Who) 198
Eternity, Heaven or Hell 261
Faith (Savings) 251
Fellowship 174–182
Forgiveness 175
Freedom, Penalty of Sin 144
Free Will of Man 157
Fruits of Spirit 203
Gifts of Spirit 206
Glory of God 194
God: Godhead
- Abundant Life in 213
- Angel Rebellion 18
- As Father 12
- As Son 12
- As Holy Spirit 12
- Attributes 3
- Armor of 241
- Creation by 31–32
- Discipline 17
- Distance of 223
- Free Will 162
- Grace of 51
- Holiness of Life 213
- Is All-Knowing 4
- Is Everywhere 5
- Is Powerful 5
- Kingdom of 99
- Love 7
- Lucifer (Satan) 20
- Man/Woman of 30
- Master Plan 196
- Names 14
- Sovereignty 17
- Wrath of 265

Golden Rule of Living 189
Golden Rules 193
Grace 256
Grow Up (Maturity) 196

Hades 60, 283
Heaven 271–276
Hell 278, 282, 285
Highway to Heaven 270
Holy Spirit: 119
  Baptism (Definition) 121
  Convicts 149
  Characteristics 212
  Fruits of 209
  Fullness of Spirit 133–134
  Gifts of 206–211
  Manifestation 137–138
  Outworkings of 123
  Sanctification 130, 154
  Walking in Faith 122
  Free Will of Man 157
Humility 198
Incarnation (God/Man) 227–228
Israel Nationally 94
John the Baptist Baptizes Jesus 107
Journey Through Life 195
Living a Christian Life 169, 211
Loneliness and Hurting 173
Love 247
Man's Natures 176–177
Mature Christian, Steps to 196
Mediator of Messiah 87
Miracles, First 110
Miracles Performed 111
Noah and Ark 45
Ordinances:
  Baptism 257
  Communion 258
Parables of Jesus 115–116
Paul the Apostle 85
Peter the Apostle 75–77
Plan of Salvation 142
Point of Reference to Christ 167
Potter, God is 197
Prayer:
  Model 224
  Consistent 214
  Quiet Time 219
Prodigal Son 112
Pride (Stubborn) 181
Purposes 195–199, 216–229
  Purposes for Living 263
Rapture 275
Redeemer 53
Relationships 258
Religious Leaders 109
Repentance 148–161
Resurrection 232–233
Rewards 275
Salvation:
  Confession 156
  Forgiveness 281
  Gift of God's Grace 147
  God's Plan for All People 148
  Receiving Christ 154
  Salvation Plan 172
  Sealed in Christ 157
  Steps to Salvation 151–152
Sanctification 165
Satan 192
Satan's Fall 279
Self or Christ 184
Sermon on Mount 166
Servicing Others 202
Sin:
  Forgiveness 280
  Role of Sin 97
  Unpardonable Sin 123
Sovereignty of God 164
Spiritual Warfare 239
Struggles 267
Temptation 187
  Satan's Steps to 188
Troubles 183
Truths 163, 252
Value (Our) 182
Virgin Birth 55, 231
Virgin Mary 105
Walking in Daily Faith 122
Woman at Well 111
Working Together 189
Wrath of God 265
What it Means 268